Career Burnout

Career Burnout

Causes and Cures

———•———

Ayala Pines
Elliot Aronson

THE FREE PRESS
A Division of Macmillan, Inc.
NEW YORK

Collier Macmillan Publishers
LONDON

The Free Press
A Division of Macmillan, Inc.
866 Third Avenue, New York, N.Y. 10022

Collier Macmillan Canada, Inc.

Printed in the United States of America

printing number
1   2   3   4   5   6   7   8   9   10

Library of Congress Cataloging-in-Publication Data

Pines, Ayala M.
   Career burnout.

   Rev. ed. of: Burnout.   c1981.
   Bibliography: p.
   Includes index.
   1. Work—Psychological aspects.   2. Burnout
(Psychology)   I. Aronson, Elliot.   II. Pines, Ayala M.
Burnout.   III. Title.
BF481.P63   1988   158.7   88-2813
ISBN 0-02-925351-9

If I am not for myself, who will be for me, if I am only for myself, what am I, and if not now, when.

—Hillel, *Wisdom of Our Fathers*

Contents

Preface

THE two of us have been working on the problem of burnout for well over a decade. Through formal research involving more than 5,000 participants, and through hundreds of cognitive and experiential workshops, we have discovered what causes burnout, how it affects people, and how best to cope with it.

Participants in our research and workshops represented a wide range of professionals including, among others, physicians, nurses, medical and dental personnel, psychologists, psychiatrists, social workers, counselors, teachers in all levels of the educational system from kindergarten to college, probation and police officers, journalists, lawyers, politicians, people of the clergy, organizational consultants, and administrators and managers in all levels of corporate management. They came from different cultural backgrounds and included, in addition to Americans, Israelis, Australians, Germans, Canadians, and Japanese.

In our research we used a variety of research strategies: we observed professionals at work, we analyzed their responses to extensive questionnaires describing themselves and their work environments, we interviewed them in depth, we worked with them in groups during short-term and long-term workshops, and we saw them in individual therapy.

When we began our work, the concept of burnout was scarcely known. During workshops, when we first introduced the concept, we discovered that the use of the term, in and of itself, had a healing effect: people who had been experiencing the debilitating symptoms of burnout, but who felt that there was something uniquely wrong with *them*, realized for the first time that what they were experiencing had a name! The mere fact that it had a name implied that it was a set of symptoms that they shared with others and that was produced by a particular set of environmental stresses. This insight gave these individuals the hope that something could be done about their problem. And something *could* be done. Through our experience with thousands of burnout victims, we were able to discover ways of coping that proved to be useful.

In our society, it is usually undesirable to admit our own limitations, vulnerabilities, ignorance, and problems, especially in our work. A professional is expected to be impeccable and in control. When problems do arise most people feel at fault and hide the problems from others, thinking that "everybody else" is coping effectively and they alone are failing. The result is what social psychologists call "the fallacy of uniqueness" or "pluralistic ignorance": the individual's false assumption that he or she is the only one responding in this undesirable way.

When people are brought together in a burnout workshop, they are encouraged to share their experiences. While most people, understandably, are reluctant to share the symptoms of burnout, a supportive atmosphere and climate of safety can reduce resistance. Once people begin to share, the fallacy of uniqueness vanishes. They discover that they are not alone, that many people in their field, and nearly everyone in their department, is having some of the same symptoms of burnout. They shift from searching for causes by finding deficiencies inside themselves to looking for causes and solutions in their work situation.

When participants realize that the most committed workers burn out most severely, it frees them to admit burnout without shame or embarrassment. You will probably not be surprised to learn that people admit to higher levels of burnout after being informed about the relationships between burnout and initial idealism.

In one study, corporate managers who simply filled out the burnout measure (which appears at the end of the book) were compared to corporate managers who were first told that "the most idealistic burn out most" and then asked to fill out the measure. Results indicated that the second group reported a significantly higher degree of burnout. The realization that the severity of their symptoms is somehow a reflection of their initial idealism and caring imbued those symptoms with a degree of positiveness. The energy that had been used for hiding the symptoms of burnout could now be used for better coping.[1]

Our work had a dual focus: research on the causes and consequences of burnout, and application of our findings to the real-life problems of people. This book combines both these features—insight and action. In it we tried to convey both the feel and the psychological dynamics underlying the experience of burnout. The first part of the book provides a description of the experience and the process of burnout. Chapter 1 is devoted to a formal definition of burnout and a description of its symptoms. Chapter 2 explains the development of burnout, presenting burnout and peak performance as the two opposite paths for highly motivated individuals who are looking to find in their work a sense of meaning for their lives. The second part of the book addresses its second purpose—to describe common causes of burnout in business, in social service work, in bureaucratic organizations, and in women. The third part is devoted to "what to do about it," because we strongly believe that it is not enough to be aware of a problem and its causes. The crucial step is to find and apply solutions. Some of the solutions we offer are for the individual, some are for support groups at work places, and some are for the organization. All three perspectives are combined in the description of our burnout workshops.

In 1981, after seven years of doing research and leading workshops we published our first book on the subject: *Burnout: From Tedium to Personal Growth*, which succeeded in opening new doors for study. But it also left many areas uncovered.

Alas, since the publication of that book, the term "burnout" has become extremely popular—perhaps too popular; it has been so loosely used that it has become almost meaningless. While burnout applies to a wide variety of occupations, it is not synonymous with job stress, fatigue, alienation, or depression. To use the term loosely is to diminish its usefulness. This does not mean that the *area* of its applicability is limited; indeed we have found that if the term is used precisely and grounded in empirical research, the applicability of "burnout" can be effectively extended beyond its original meaning.

Accordingly, the time seems ripe for a new look at burnout. During the past seven years, we have expanded our work beyond the human service professions to include individuals in all levels of corporate management. We also looked beyond the work sphere to examine the effects of burnout on other aspects of a person's life—especially marriage and other intimate relationships.

In recent years, we have also come to realize that a major part of the cause of burnout is existential—that it rests in the human need to ascribe meaning to life. When work makes this possible, highly motivated individuals are able to achieve peak performance; when specific aspects of the work environment make this impossible, burnout is inevitable. The implications of this discovery for understanding the process of burnout, how to prevent it, and how to cure it are explored throughout this book.

Thus, *Career Burnout: Causes and Cures* is more than a simple revision of our previous work; it is a fresh look at burnout—complete with new insights into the depth and breadth of its impact as well as new ideas for prevention and cure.

Our purpose in writing this book is to be able to take what we've learned from our research and our workshops and share it with you. It is our hope that this book will not only help you increase your awareness of burnout in general and your own potential for burnout in particular but in addition will help provide you with the orientation and tools to cope successfully with the problem.

Acknowledgments

A GREAT many people contributed directly and indirectly to this volume. First we would like to express our gratitude to Ditsa Kafry who helped in the collection and analysis of the data that provided the basis for the book. Our friend and colleague Christina Maslach helped spark our own interest in burnout, and one of us (A.P.) collaborated with her in some of that early work. This volume has benefited from the contributions of our colleague in Israel, Dr. Dalia Etzion, who collaborated with us in the cross-cultural studies and provided many helpful comments on an earlier version of the manuscript. We are also indebted to Isamu Saito of Rissho University in Tokyo, Japan, Matthias Burisch of West Berlin, Germany, and Dale Stanley of the Community Health Clinic in Saskatoon, Canada, who worked with us on the cross-cultural research. Jacob Golan and Edna Eldar studied burnout in Israel and Dov Edden of Tel Aviv University supplied some valuable insights on the conceptualization of the coping process.

Several students at the University of California at Berkeley took an active part in the research: Alan Kanner, who generated and coauthored two different studies, Liz Lopez, Teresa Ramirez, and Susan Rauss. We are indebted to them all. Steve Weinberg and the Management Training Program staff at the University of Alabama collaborated with us on the studies of institutional factors affecting burnout.

We are grateful to all those who provided us with observations, interviews, and personal insights about the burnout process, most notably Sue Gershenson, David Woods, Harriet Herman, Diane Crawford, Sylvia Guendelman, Irene Melnick, Moshe Kafry, and the teachers at Smyth Fernwald Child Care Center.

We thank our agent Judith Weber for her help and support.

Finally, and perhaps most important, we are pleased to express our gratitude to the thousands of former burnt-out individuals who took part in our research and workshops and on whose experiences this volume is based.

PART ONE

What Is Burnout?

ONE

The Burnout Experience

Perhaps the best way for us to communicate how burnout operates is to provide a few examples.

The most striking cases of burnout that we have ever encountered involved hospital nurses working with terminal cancer patients. We think it can be quickly understood why burnout would be such a severe problem in this setting. First of all, most of the nurses who volunteer for this assignment are incredibly idealistic. They really want to help people, and they care deeply about their patients. Yet they burn out after a relatively brief period of time. This is partly because they care so much about their patients, coupled with the fact that their patients keep dying. The nurses are attentive, become involved—and then their patients die. The stress is enormous. Moreover, people dying of cancer are frequently in great pain and, of course, are under a great deal of psychological stress. It goes without saying that most are not in a frame of mind to be considerate, grateful, responsive patients. While this is certainly understandable, it can nonetheless add to the stress of nurses who are giving a great deal and getting little concrete gratification in return.

Without realizing it, most nurses begin to do things to protect themselves from being overwhelmed by their situation. Many begin detaching themselves emotionally from their patients. Others will occasionally engage in a kind of gallows humor in which they might put down or mock their patients whether in their own mind or when talking to their closest friends. The fact that they are experiencing less attachment (for their own protection) to patients who are quite demanding (and relatively lacking in expressions of gratitude) leads many nurses to begin resenting the very people whom they are supposed to be helping. As this resentment becomes increasingly manifest, the typical nurse will begin to feel guilt and shame about her behavior, attitudes, and general mental state. The hard work, the feelings of resentment, helplessness, hopelessness, being trapped, as well as the guilt and shame, are continually recycled and lead to feelings of exhaustion and malaise, which in turn increase the feelings of resentment—and the cycle continues.

Moreover, because, for the most part, these particular nurses were once idealistic, the guilt and shame are enormous. "I, of all people, am not supposed to be feeling this way" is a statement we have heard from a great many nurses. This tends to lead many of them to attempt to hide their feelings from one another. Several nurses in such a situation informed us that, while they felt miserable on the inside, they tried to look crisp, efficient, sometimes even ebullient on the outside. And here is the supreme irony: imagine nurses in this situation. They are feeling all the symptoms of burnout, but as they look around, what do they see? What they *don't* see are other nurses hurting and feeling anguished and guilty. A few nurses are expressing gallows humor and resentment, but most nurses are looking crisp, efficient, and cheerful. Virtually all of them are experiencing inner turmoil and are desperately trying to mask it—either with sarcasm or with a show of false valor. Indeed, several of the nurses who look so valiant, crisp, and efficient are secretly envying others because they look so valiant, crisp, and efficient.

What can we conclude from such a situation? A great many of our nurses told us *they* concluded: "Most people around here seem to be doing O.K., therefore there must be something wrong with me. Perhaps I'm too delicate or hypersensitive; maybe I'm going crazy; I must not be cut out to be a nurse." In short, because the nurses were ashamed to share their innermost feelings, they didn't realize that they were not alone. This increased their stress by making them feel (incorrectly) particularly inadequate. They blamed their burnout on themselves rather than seeing it for what is: a response to a highly stress-producing situation that is so powerful it affects almost everyone in a similar manner.

How individuals perceive the cause of their burnout and attribute the "blame" has enormous consequences for action. If they attribute the cause to a characterological weakness or inadequacy in themselves, they will take a certain set of actions: quit the profession, seek psychotherapy, and so forth. However, if they see the cause as largely a function of the situation, they will strive to change the situation to make it more tolerable, a totally different set of remedial actions. In some cases, the primary cause does lie in the individual or in the fit between the individual and a particular job situation. In these cases, changing jobs or seeking individual therapy may be the best solution. On the other hand, our work has made it clear that, in the vast majority of cases of burnout, the major cause lies in the situation. Clearly, in the example involving nurses in a terminal cancer ward, we cannot do much to change the source of stress in the situation: all of the nurses will experience the death of most of their patients. But there are countless ways to reduce the resulting burnout by changing the situation surrounding it. These coping strategies have proven to be very helpful and will be discussed in subsequent chapters.

For now, let is suffice to say that the first and most important step would be to change the focus from "What's wrong with me?" to "What can I do about the situation?" Indeed one of the most exciting events in our burnout workshops occurs near the beginning when we simply ask the participants to write down the major sources of stress that they experience on their jobs. We then ask them to meet in groups of four and share what they've written. When we did this during a workshop with the cancer nurses, there were many expressions of excitement and delight as each of the individuals discovered for the first time that she or he was not alone—after years of experiencing the lonely and agonizing feelings of guilt and inadequacy they suddenly became aware that behind the smiling masks of their colleagues were similar feelings of inadequacy. From that point in time they could begin focusing on the problem as a situational problem, not as a problem of their own individual failure.

Nurses are, admittedly, an extreme example. At the same time, it would be unfortunate if the reader were to conclude that burnout occurs only among people who are dealing with death while working in tight bureaucratic organizations such as hospitals. Burnout can occur in occupations where, from all outward appearances, the individual seems to have it made. Let us look at just such a group of people—dentists. Dentists are professionals with whom almost all of us have had experience; most people are surprised to learn that dentists suffer from burnout, because on the surface dentistry seems like a relatively easy, lucrative, nonstressful profession. No one dies on the dental chair; the dentist is captain of his or her own ship—not part of a bureaucracy—he or she has a lot of autonomy, a lot of control, a lot of power. In the past ten years, we have conducted workshops involving several hundred dentists. In the course of these workshops, we discovered that the burnout rate among dentists is extremely high.

Why? What causes dentists to burn out? There are several factors. We will focus on the most salient one: dentists are highly skilled, highly trained professionals who almost always perform routine tasks very well and who almost invariably find themselves in a situation where there is almost no one around who is both able and willing to show appreciation for their work. Neither their patients nor their coworkers are in a good position to express meaningful appreciation. Let us first look at the personnel in a dental office. Typically, dentists work with a staff consisting of a receptionist, a hygienist, and an assistant. Very few dentists collaborate with other dentists. While their staff serves an important and vital function, there is no one who has the expertise to say "Wow, what a wonderful job you did in capping that molar."

But certainly the patients are grateful. Or are they? Let's take a closer look. Most patients enter the dental office in a high state of anxiety. Their major concern as patients is to get out of there as fast as possible with as little pain as possible. Most of them do not want to be there—and they communicate this to their dentists in subtle ways. While dentists are certainly aware of their patients' anxieties, the experience of being feared and even disliked is nevertheless very unpleasant. Moreover, most patients are not in a frame of mind to concern themselves too much about dentists' need for appreciation, respect, and approval. To add to the problem, dentists work on the mouth—a situation that not only produces extreme physical and psychological discomfort for patients but one that makes it difficult for patients to communicate (other than to gasp, groan, or emit an occasional "uh huh") through lips swollen with novacaine. In addition, because dentists work in the mouth, patients don't have a very good view of what the dentists are doing, so they are not very likely to utter sounds of approval even if it were physically possible and even if they were in a frame of mind to do so.

How often do patients phone their dentist the day after a visit to say how well their new filling is fitting and how normal their "bite" feels? Indeed, most dentists we've worked with report that virtually the only instances when they hear from a patient after a visit are when the patient has something to complain about.

The experience, hour after hour, day after day, week after week, of pouring in maximal effort for minimal appreciation is extremely taxing and causes the erosion of the spirit known as burnout.

In discussing this situation with dentists, we learned that many of them respond to this lack of appreciation in a manner that is diametrically opposed to what we would have recommended. The most common response to burnout among dentists is to take on more patients! What dentists are doing is using their autonomy to make a decision that seems reasonable. They are saying in effect, "This job is boring, I'm not getting much appreciation, I might as well become rich." So they live in fancy houses, drive fancy cars— and dread going to work in the morning, longing for the time when their real estate investments will allow them the financial freedom to leave the profession entirely.

Of course, we have oversimplified and overgeneralized. But the picture is too accurate to be easily dismissed. In our work with dentists (and other professionals) we have found that, while money is a very useful commodity (and *might* even buy a modicum of happiness!), it is *not* a good cure for burnout.

Indeed, what we have discovered in working with dentists is that the most successful way of coping with burnout is for them to see fewer patients—and spend more time with them. This time can be spent in helping put them at their ease, reducing the anxiety, and allowing patients and dentists to emerge as three-dimensional people for each other. Let us elaborate: in our workshops, when we asked dentists to describe their most typical unpleasant patients, they used adjectives like "sullen," "uncommunicative," "uninteresting," "unresponsive," "uncooperative," "uninterested," etc. "Of course," as one of us quickly pointed out to them, "you are describing me perfectly! Not the warm, charming, exciting, effervescent personality that my friends know and love, but the me that exists in a dental chair when I'm scared, full of novocaine, and have a mouth stuffed with cotton!"

If dentists had spent more time with patients and allayed their anxiety, they would have reaped a huge benefit. They would have begun to see the kinds of things in patients that their friends see and would have added a great deal of variety to an otherwise routine day. Rather than seeing Mrs. Jones as the uninteresting, sullen possessor of a molar that needs capping and Mr. Smith as the uncooperative, unresponsive owner of a cavity in his incisor (who tends to gag while being x-rayed) dentists would be able to see these two as very different people—each interesting in her or his own right.

Moreover, as their anxiety is reduced, patients begin looking at dentists as competent and caring people, begin trying to attend more to what the dentists are doing, and are in a better position to show them some honest appreciation, which is one of the things dentists were lacking.

This was our recommendation to many dentists. In addition, we urged them to meet with one another on a monthly basis in order to share ideas, talk about any especially interesting problems they encountered or work they had done during that month. This provided them with the kind of support and professional appreciation that many people in less isolated professions can get more easily from their coworkers.

While admittedly these recommendations are not always easy to follow, they are an effective coping strategy if properly implemented.

The third and last example of burnout we would like to present comes from yet another unlikely source—the top echelons of the corporate world. To people who don't work in them, corporate settings probably seem the least likely settings for burnout. Let's examine some of the evidence: the high echelons of the corporate world attract many brilliant, energetic, ambitious, and powerful people. These "supermen" and "wonderwomen" have at their disposal more financial resources and political power than any other professional group. Their salaries and lifestyle are legendary, What possible reason could there be for them to burn out?

The answer, it turns out, has to do with some of the very same reasons that make these people the "supermen" and "wonderwomen" that they are in other people's eyes—their high ambition, energy, and intense involvement in their work. Admission to the top echelons of the corporate world is tough. It requires, in addition to such givens as intelligence and leadership ability, a very high level of commitment.

The men and women who "make it" are invariably people for whom work is one of the most important things in life, if not the most important thing. It is what gives their lives a sense of meaning. They identify with their work and with the organization to such an extent that every success and every failure are personalized. Every sacrifice they (or in some cases their families) are required to make seems worth it, if it will benefit the organization and bring with it the desperately desired success.

As long as their involvement, commitment, and hard work are rewarded by continuous success, such high achievers can continue receiving a sense of meaning from their work indefinitely. They burn out when for some reason it is impossible for them to succeed. When inadequate authority or inadequate resources make it impossible for them to accomplish their work goals the way they think they should be accomplished, the frustration erodes their spirit, and they burn out. Not having enough authority, or financial, time, or human resources to perform up to their high expectations can produce extreme stress for these corporate executives. Another source of stress, that is even worse than inadequate resources for success, is failure. Because these people identify so much with their work, they see the organization's failure as their own. They are not only disappointed in themselves and in the organization, they feel as if life itself has lost its meaning.

What Is Burnout?

Burnout is formally defined and subjectively experienced as a state of physical, emotional, and mental exhaustion caused by long-term involvement in situations that are emotionally demanding. The emotional demands are most often caused by a combination of very high expectations and chronic situational stresses. Burnout is accompanied by an array of symptoms including physical depletion, feelings of helplessness and hopelessness, disillusionment, and the development of a negative self-concept and negative attitudes towards work, people involved in the work, and life itself. In its extreme form burnout represents a breaking point beyond which the ability to cope with the environment is severely hampered.

Burnout tends to afflict people who enter their professions highly motivated and idealistic, expecting their work to give their lives a sense of meaning. It is a particular hazard in occupations in which professionals tend to experience their work as a kind of "calling." Burnout involves the painful realization that we have failed— to make the world a better place, to help the needy, to have a real impact on the organization—that all our efforts were for nothing, that we no longer have the energy it takes to do what we promised ourselves to do, that we have nothing left to give. This realization makes us feel that our whole lives have had no purpose. In this respect burnout represents the failure of work as a solution to the existential dilemma.

Burnout is not an isolated phenomenon that characterizes a limited number of individuals. On the contrary, it occurs very frequently to a wide variety of people, especially those working with people in almost all the human services and in all levels of management. Burnout has detrimental psychological effects and is a major factor in low morale, absenteeism, tardiness, and high job turnover. It also plays a primary role in poor management and in the inadequate delivery of health, education, and welfare services. People who burn out develop a negative self-concept and negative job attitudes. Their concern and feeling for the people they work with becomes dulled and frequently they come to treat their clients, colleagues, and employees in detached, hostile, and uncaring ways.

Burnout can be very costly—in wasted training for those who quit their jobs, and in terms of the psychological price paid by those who stay. It is costly for the organizations in terms of lost talent and poor performance, and it is costly for the employees, clients, and patients. As a result of burnout, they wait longer to receive less attention and concern. The quality of the attention they receive is poorer and the experience of obtaining it can be humiliating.

Tragically, burnout strikes precisely those individuals who had once been among the most idealistic and enthusiastic. In other words, if individuals entered a given profession (e.g., nursing) with a cynical attitude, they would be unlikely to burn out; but if those who entered had a strong desire to give of themselves to others— and actually felt helpful, excited, and idealistic during their early years on the job—they would be more susceptible to the most severe burnout. We have found, over and over again, that in order to burn out a person needs to have been on fire at one time. It follows, then, that one of the great costs of burnout is the diminution of the effective service of the very best people in a given profession. Accordingly, everyone is the poorer for the existence of this phenomenon.

The root cause of burnout lies in our existential need to believe that our lives are meaningful, that the things we do are useful, important, and even "heroic." This belief is our way of dealing with the angst caused by facing up to our own mortality. In previous eras, religion filled this purpose admirably. But, for most people in the modern age, religion is no longer adequate. As Ernest Becker argued, in his book *The Denial of Death,* all human beings have a need to feel "heroic," to know that their lives matter in the larger "cosmic" scheme of things, to merge themselves with something higher than themselves. For people who have rejected the religious answer to this quest, one of the frequently chosen alternatives is work. Thus the stakes have become very high. People who choose this alternative are trying to derive from their work nothing less than a sense of meaning for their lives. If they think they have failed, they burn out.

While burnout is often the result of failure in the existential quest for meaning, it is experienced by most people as a far more mundane process. People experience burnout as a gradual erosion of their spirit and zest as a result of the daily struggles and chronic stresses that are typical of everyday life and work—too many pressures, conflicts, demands, and too few emotional rewards, acknowledgements, and successes.[1] Stress, in and of itself, does not cause burnout. People are often able to flourish in stressful, demanding careers if they feel valuable and appreciated and that their work has significance. They burn out when their work has no meaning and stress continuously outweighs support and rewards.

Although its intensity, duration, frequency, and consequences may vary, burnout always has three basic components: physical, emotional, and mental exhaustion. Someone who is physically exhausted after running a marathon, but emotionally exhilarated, is not burned out. Similarly, someone who is depressed but is still excited about a new project is not burned out. Burnout combines the physical, the emotional, and the mental, and it is a state that is difficult to get out of. You cannot say "I am burned out today" and be all fired up the next day. More needs to happen in order to get out of burnout than just the passage of time. Let us describe the three components of burnout in some detail.

Physical exhaustion is characterized by low energy, chronic fatigue, and weakness. People in the process of burnout report accident-proneness, increased susceptibility to illness, nagging colds, frequent attacks of virus or flu,[2] frequent headaches, nausea, muscle tension in shoulders and neck, back pains, and psychosomatic complaints.[3]* Changes in eating habits involve both eating too much ("Eating became the only nurturing and pleasurable thing left for me. So I ate, and ate, and ate.") and eating too little ("I had this big lump in my throat at all times, which no food could go through.").

It is commonly believed that people who are tired during the day sleep well at night; not so for people who are burned out. Burnout victims frequently report the apparently paradoxical combination of weariness and sleep problems.[4] That is, although they are tired during the day, they are unable to sleep at night because of tormenting thoughts or nightmares. The content of nightmares is often related to the burned-out state of the dreamer. For example, we worked with a prison guard who had dreams in which he was chased and shot; a waitress dreamed about dozens of starving and angry diners who were shouting at her for not bringing food ordered hours before—and the restaurant kitchen was closed; a nuclear physicist under pressure to research and publish awoke in a cold sweat, having dreamed that his greatest discovery was in fact an

---

*Throughout this volume we will be reporting correlational data that are based on self-reports: that is to say, the data relate one variable (for example, environmental stress) to another variable (for example, degree of burnout). While such data are of some value, their interpretation is not always crystal clear. For example, it is often difficult to be certain which variable is the cause and which is the effect, or indeed if both are the effects of a deeper cause—that is, do certain stressful activities produce burnout, does burnout sensitize the individual to stress, or do certain occupations attract people who both burn out easily and experience a lot of stress? Usually, common sense dictates the most reasonable sequence; in other words, in most of the data that we will be reporting it makes most sense to assume that specific variables (like certain stresses) are antecedents to tedium.

There is one additional problem with data that are based on self-report. It may be that the results are influenced by such general factors as the honesty of the respondents or, conversely, the respondents' desire to say things in order to put themselves in a more favorable light. For example, if it turns out that there is a correlation between burnout and psychological depression, it is conceivable that such a result is influenced by honesty in that those people who are honest enough to admit to experiencing burnout are the same people who are honest enough to admit to being depressed. While such a possibility exists in much of the data we will be reporting, it is our best guess that this factor accounts for only a small portion of the relationship, and the rest are meaningful. This "best guess" is an informed judgment based upon corroborating evidence from hundreds of hours of interviews, and discussions with individuals at workshops. We feel therefore that the paper and pencil tests, while in themselves somewhat sterile, are bolstered by "flesh and blood" interactions with people currently experiencing burnout.

error; a teacher dreamed about forgetting to come to his class's final exam.

Many people attempt to combat burnout by physical and chemical means such as barbiturates, tranquilizers, hallucinogens, cigarettes, and alcohol. ("When I get home from work I can't face anyone before I have had a double martini.") Some try overeating. "All I can do at the end of a day is collapse in front of the TV and eat a large bowl of ice cream," a burned-out teacher told us. This is a poor solution; after several months, she was obese as well as burned out. Indeed, all of these coping strategies provide only temporary relief, leaving the individual with an even more overwhelming sense of weariness and despair.

Emotional exhaustion, the second component of burnout, involves primarily feelings of helplessness, hopelessness, and entrapment. In extreme cases these feelings can lead to emotional breakdown or serious thoughts about suicide.[5] In some people the emotional exhaustion of burnout causes incessant, uncontrollable crying; in others it causes paralyzing depression. People who burn out feel that they need all of the little emotional energy they have left to keep going through the motions of daily life. Managers who reach this stage often don't care any more about their goals or the people they manage. Human service professionals often feel they have nothing left to give to anyone. A social worker said, "Sometimes I feel like telling my clients, 'Who cares? You think only you have problems? What about me?'"

"A few years ago," said a lawyer, "I not only liked my work and was very involved in it, but I also had a very active social life. Now I feel my job is a dead end. My emotional resources are drained. My best friends irritate me, I do not know my children, and I do not have the emotional energy to be their friend. I find it hard to be polite and tolerant of my clients. All I want is to be left alone." People can feel emotionally depleted and yet frequently irritable and nervous. Family and friends become just one more demand. Futility and despair increase. Enjoyment from work and from people diminishes and is replaced by loneliness, discouragement, and disenchantment.[6] "I felt like my soul was dying," recalls a welfare worker.

Mental exhaustion, the third component, is characterized by the development of negative attitudes toward one's self, work, and life itself.[7] Burnout victims often report dissatisfaction with their work and way of life and a lowered self-concept; they feel inadequate, inferior, and incompetent. "My hands are tied and I feel useless and impotent," wrote a manager of a large public agency. "I never have enough information for making decisions in my work. I cannot deal effectively with the requirements of my job. I feel worthless, like a total failure, and I resent my subordinates who witness this failure."

In addition to developing negative self-concepts and pessimistic views about their own work, people who burn out also develop negative attitudes toward others. They often discover in themselves coldness and nastiness they never knew existed. In people working in the human services, the negative attitude change associated with burnout is at times manifested in the development of dehumanizing attitudes toward the recipients of their services.

Dehumanization is defined as a decreased awareness of the human attributes of others and a loss of humanity in interpersonal interactions.[8] People stop perceiving others as having the same feelings, impulses, and thoughts as they have and thus in effect deny that others share basic human qualities with them.

As a result of the process of dehumanization, people are less likely to perceive and respond to the unique personal identities of other people and are more likely to treat them as if they were not quite as human as themselves. Burned-out professionals may come to see their clients, employees, patients, or students as aggregates of problems rather than as individuals. "They are all just animals," a prison guard said. "None of my employees has the kind of commitment to the organization that I had when I started, and I am sure none of them is going to make it," a corporation executive said. "I no longer want to work with losers," said a welfare worker. "If they have been victims of society for so long, they probably deserve to be." Ironically, people who dehumanize others eventually come to dehumanize themselves as well.[9] They experience fewer emotions, less empathy, fewer personal feelings, and less satisfaction in their work.

In studying the characteristics of staff burnout in mental health settings we found that the longer the staff had worked in the mental health field the less they liked working with patients, the more they avoided direct contact with them, the less successful they felt in their work, and the more custodial rather than humanistic were their attitudes toward mental illness. They stopped looking for self-fulfillment in their work, good days became very infrequent, and the thing that made work worthwhile was the money and security it provided.[10]

Other psychologists mention such symptoms as cynicisim, negativism, and a tendency to be inflexible. As a result of burnout, workers start discussing clients in intellectual terms and jargon and thereby distance themselves from emotional involvement; they rarely communicate with others; they become loners and withdraw.[11] As a result of investing a great amount of time and energy in patients and meeting with repeated failure, staff members feel defeated and hopeless. In some situations, if, after much hard work on the part of the staff member, a patient regresses, especially after some initial success, the professional becomes bitter or angry and grows indifferent or uninterested in the patient.[12]

A newly appointed college professor promised herself she would be more caring and helpful than her own teachers. Consequently, she made herself available to students, encouraged them to come to her office, and allowed them to call her at home. The students responded enthusiastically. They were in her office at all hours of the day and called her home at night. They would find her in the supermarket, the movies, and the swimming pool. There was no escape from them. It was too much. After a while, she decided to see people in her office only. Gradually her office hours became shorter. Now she sees students by appointment only. Her door, like all other doors in the department, is locked. She developed the usual "undergraduatitis" (i.e., student phobia) that so many burned-out college teachers show signs of: "I find myself crossing the street whenever I see people in their twenties approaching. I don't think I like teaching anymore."

The negative attitude change associated with burnout is not limited to dealing with students, patients, or employees. It affects our feelings toward everyone associated with work, especially those that we come in contact with on a daily basis. A burned-out physician said, "Everything my colleagues do gets on my nerves: their vocabulary, the way they talk, the way they walk, and the way they think. They all seem so stupid to me now, and to think that I once thought they were an exciting, stimulating bunch is quite inconceivable."

The painful disillusionment with work as an avenue for finding meaning in life is at the core of the negative attitude change and mental exhaustion of burnout. When people are unable to derive a sense of significance from their work they experience feelings of personal failure and negative attitude change toward themselves (for not being good enough, strong enough, or knowledgeable enough to get the job done), toward their clients (who were supposed to provide that sense of significance by improving, learning, or healing), and toward colleagues (who might have helped by providing support and challenge, but did not).

It is difficult, if not impossible, to keep such bitter disappointment in one's quest for meaning limited to work. Typically, people who burn out not only feel disillusioned with their work, they feel as if their whole life has lost its meaning. All too often these feelings spill over to affect their attitudes towards their family and friends as well. The result is marital conflict and deteriorating personal relationships.

Dissatisfaction with work leads people to arrive late, leave early, extend work breaks, or avoid work entirely.[13] It can also lead to an "I-don't-give-a-damn" attitude in people who once were very idealistic and committed to their work. Katherine Armstrong, who studied burnout among personnel treating cases of child abuse and neglect, identified such symptoms of burnout as daily resistance to going to work, clock-watching, postponing client contacts, resisting client phone calls and office visits, stereotyping clients, and inability to concentrate on what the client is saying, feeling intolerant of clients' anger, feeling immobilized and helpless, feeling cynical about the clients, and blaming them for their misfortunes.[14] John Jones discovered that burnout was reliably correlated with anonymous theft admissions, dishonesty, and other counterproductive behaviors by employees.[15]

Nurses working in intensive care units (which tend to have very high levels of staff burnout) were found to be significantly more depressed, hostile, and anxious than nurses in less stressful units.[16] They showed high incidence of dropout and absenteeism due to minor illness and vague somatic complaints (such as headaches, upset stomachs, and fatigue). Nurses in high-emotional-risk settings also had a high incidence of hyperactivity and restlessness. They frequently requested transfers to other work sites, depersonalized their patients (treated them as nonpersons), and experienced inter-staff conflict.

Some people's reaction to burnout is primarily somatic; others' may be more emotional. But for the experience to be labeled "burnout" it has to have a certain degree of all three components. Only a few of these symptoms or only occasional symptoms can serve as warning signs. They are an indication that it is time to examine and evaluate your priorities at work and home, the stresses from the environment, and the adequacy of your coping strategies. If you experience high levels of all these physical, emotional, and mental exhaustion reactions, chances are good that you are in the midst of a severe burnout crisis. At the end of the book we have included a self-diagnosis test that can help you identify your level of burnout.

It is not hard to recognize danger signs in other people. We first asked participants in our workshops to diagnose their own levels of burnout. We then asked them to estimate the degree of burnout reported by one of their close colleagues. The correlations between the self-diagnosis and the burnout assessed by close colleagues was highly significant.[17] In other words, people's burnout is almost never a secret from their colleagues; if people are burning out, whether or not they know it, others around them are quite aware of it.

Becoming aware that you are burning out and identifying the major causes for the burnout are the first steps towards effective coping.

The timing, manifestations, and consequences of burnout depend both on the individual and on the environment in which the individual works. In every occupation there are some people who burn out faster than others. And there are occupations in which burnout occurs faster than in others. In certain occupations burnout often occurs shortly after entering the job, sometimes within the first year. A nurse who works with burned children told us that after a few months she, and most other nurses on the ward, could not tolerate the emotional burden of their work, and asked to be transferred. Reported turnover rates among nurses as a whole have been exceptionally high. The National Commission for the Study of Nursing and Nursing Education states that 70 percent of staff nurses in American hospitals resigned from their jobs during a typical year.[18] In the child protection field certain departments turn over workers at 50 to 100 percent each year.[19] Poverty lawyers claim that within two years most newcomers burn out. The same was reported for such diverse professions as inner city teaching, social work, flight controlling, and television producing. People in the human services who live on the job (working in residential treatment centers, etc.) tend to burn out within a year or two. Other professionals, such as doctors, dentists, managers, teachers, and private entrepreneurs, typically report longer periods of time—four to five years—before the onset of burnout.

How Do People Handle Burnout?

People deal with burnout in different ways. Some burned-out workers leave their professions. Quitting one's career, especially after long years in training, is almost always associated with a sense of failure, guilt, and waste. It is also costly for the organization and for society as a whole.

Other people leave one job but stay in the same profession or in the same organization. Typically, people quit one place of work only to find the same problems in a new job. Not surprisingly, after burning out in a series of jobs they often develop a chronic sense of hopelessness and failure.

Still others climb up the administrative ladder as a way of escaping a job in which they burned out. We have come into contact with many instances of caseworkers who burned out in their work with clients and went back to school to receive a higher degree so they could become administrators far removed from any direct contact with clients. On the surface this may seem like a reasonable solution. However, we have found that there is nothing quite as burnout producing as a burned-out worker who is now supervising other workers. Picture the scene: a young caseworker full of enthusiasm and idealism about the work he is starting. What could be more devastating for him than to be saddled with a supervisor who instead of encouraging that idealism says, "I've been here longer than you. Just wait, you'll find out!"

There are also those who never quit, even if they are totally burned out. These people are usually motivated by a strong need for security, and when a job offers them tenure and acceptable retirement benefits frequently they choose to stay. These people are known as "dead wood." Ichak Adizes, who wrote about dead wood as a type of mismanagement style, wrote "The deadwood is apathetic. He waits to be told what to do. . . . He is mostly worried about how to survive until retirement and how to keep intact the little he has. He has no complaints about anything. He fears that any complaint will reflect on him."[20]

In our experience people do not become dead wood until they experience failure in their quest to achieve some idealistic goal. Then, the heart seems to go out of their work. As dead wood they do as little as possible for so long that they seem to become part of the organization's physical structure. They just exist, invisible, until they can live off their pensions. No one knows what they do because their interaction with other employees is minimal. Their response to most inquiries takes the form of: "I don't know, I just work here." In one department of social services we heard a story about a "phantom" probation officer. No one knew who he was, what his schedule was, or what he was doing. However, his reports, all similar and all short, were always presented on time. People who become "dead wood" lose their motivation for change and improvement to such an extent that even when offered a more satisfying position, they typically refuse to take it.

There is another way of surviving burnout. Such a crisis can be a trigger for personal growth. The myth of Sisyphus tells how, as punishment, Sisyphus was condemned to push a large stone to the top of a mountain whence the rock would roll down again. The gods thought that "there is no more dreadful punishment than futile and hopeless labor." Albert Camus wrote, "If this myth is tragic, that is because its hero is conscious. Where would his torture be, indeed if at every step the hope of succeeding upheld him? The workman of today works everyday of his life at the same tasks, and this fate is no less absurd. But it is tragic only at the rare moments when he becomes conscious."[21]

Although this consciousness *is* tragic, it can also provide the opportunity for personal growth. Burnout can be a stimulus for becoming aware of problems, for examining demands imposed by work and home. It can spur us to build support systems and improve coping strategies. It can be an opportunity for reorganizing priorities and for learning about strengths and weaknesses. It can be an impetus for expanding skills and abilities. "This experience [of being burned out] involved incredible pain and suffering," said a television producer, "yet, it was very important for me as a learning experience. It forced me to examine my priorities. I became aware of the things which were most stressful for me, and the positive things I could not do without. Now I see both my vulnerabilities and strengths very clearly, and I have a more realistic view of myself. I have a deep conviction that I will not repeat the mistakes of the past. And I realize how much strength I could find in myself."

Burnout is a complex human experience that is affected by the variability of human nature. The case study method can do more justice to this richness than can abstract descriptions. Accordingly, we will present six detailed case studies to illustrate the major responses to burnout: a case of a broken spirit, a case of leaving the profession forever, a case of a prisoner in a gilded cage, a case of dead wood, a case of quitting up the career ladder, and a case of burnout as a trigger for growth. These case studies all describe normal, well-adjusted people who had typical clusters of symptoms as a result of both a chronic presence of unmodifiable negative features and a consistent lack of positive features in their work environments.

A Broken Spirit

Charlie was a creative, energetic, and ambitious man. When he graduated from college he wanted to develop his own fashion design business and was sure he was going to "make it big." He loved the creative aspect of the job; the business end of it seemed like an exciting challenge. But things did not happen quite as fast as he planned, nor in quite the right way. He found himself caught in the trivia of managing a business with little time for creative fashion design. He felt he could not trust his employees to do anything right, so by himself he advertised his products, handled the books, answered the phone, ordered materials, made sure the designs were done properly, and collected unpaid bills.

Ironically, when Charlie began to gain a reputation for producing well-designed high-quality garments, his life actually seemed to get worse. All of his energies and most of his earnings went back into expanding the business, while his family had problems making ends meet. There was never a sense of achievement and success because, as Charlie described it, "In this type of business you are only as good as your last product, and no one will ever remember the excellent samples you produced in the past."

Anxiety and anger changed Charlie from a friendly person to a man suspicious that everyone was out to ruin him. He was constantly anxious that something would go wrong at work, and something almost always did go wrong. Every day brought another crisis to claim his attention. He entered his office at six o'clock in the morning and got home late at night, only to continue working on his books until the early hours of the next morning. He hardly ever saw his family and would never take a day off or a vacation. He felt guilty about his family and resented the fact that they made him feel guilty.

After four years, Charlie had spent all of his physical, mental, and emotional resources on his business. He felt as though his nerves were tied into one large knot. Not even the increasing doses of tranquilizers his doctor prescribed could calm him down. He hated the government for the taxes it imposed, he hated his incompetent employees, he hated the competition, he hated his patrons, and he hated himself.

He couldn't sleep and couldn't eat. There was never time for laughter nor for releasing tension. Charlie collapsed and was brought to the hospital in a state of complete exhaustion. He was kept in the intensive care unit for five days. When he was released from the hospital he was ordered to rest for several weeks.

After his recuperation he moved with his family to the suburbs. Charlie felt he could no longer handle a job with either creative or managerial responsibilities. He took a position as clerk in a big clothing company and never regained his ambition or his creative spark. His ability to cope with the world of work was severely hampered, his spirit broken.

The Wrong Career

Some people believe burnout indicates that they have chosen the wrong career. Teachers, for instance, may realize they hate teaching soon after first standing alone before a class of pupils. Carol was such a teacher. Her family had expected that Carol would be an elementary school teacher because "Carol is so good with children" and "Elementary school teaching is a good profession for a woman." Carol never questioned this career choice until her last year in college. At that time, when she first became a student teacher, some doubts entered her mind. The whole situation—the lively, noisy children, her insecurity and lack of control—was extremely frightening and unpleasant.

But it was difficult to quit so close to graduation so she finished college. After two years of teaching she realized that she could not go on. She felt unable to fulfill the great, and sometimes conflicting, expectations of the children's parents without more support from them or from the school administration. Standing in front of the class she felt weak, helpless, and miserable. When the school day was over she was physically and emotionally drained; she said she needed "someone to scrape me off the floor." She could not find energy in herself for anything but coping with the daily stress of teaching. Her social life deteriorated, she spent most of her time alone in her room, she was frequently sick and almost always depressed.

Carol realized that unless she wanted to spend the rest of her life in misery she had to get out of teaching. She became a secretary in a manufacturing company and discovered a new contentment with her life. She "thanked God three times a day for not being a teacher," and wondered how she could have endured it for as long as she did.

A Gilded Cage

Some people quit their jobs when they realize that they are burned out and have made the wrong career choice. Others stay, particularly those who cannot financially afford to quit and those who believe that quitting would waste their investment in their careers.

Michael was one who had serious doubts about his career choice but could not afford to quit. He was a pediatrician who chose his profession because he loved medicine and loved children. After finishing medical school he started his own private practice and what he hoped would be a successful and exciting medical career.

As the years passed, it gradually dawned on Michael that running a medical office can be very lonely. His office included two nurses and a receptionist but no other pediatricians who could truly appreciate his work and skill. He found few challenges. Most work was routine and after a while became boring. He had not envisioned medicine as endless cases of flu and diaper rash. He believed he was capable of practicing far better medicine than he did, but since his work was so routine, he began putting less and less into it. He found himself losing interest in his young patients and in medicine itself. Not only did he lose enthusiasm, energy, and satisfaction from his work, he also knew it was affecting his home life and his view of himself.[22]

Before he knew it, Michael was 50 years old. His success made it difficult to change what he was doing. He had to pay for a house in the suburbs, two cars, yearly vacations, and private universities for two children. Money had become the only part of his work that was gratifying. Rather than find outside activities to balance his work, he had expanded his office and started seeing more patients.

As his schedule became more crowded, Michael had less time for conversations with his young patients or their parents, and so he had less personal contact with them. Chatting with his patients, which would have added variety to his daily routine, seemed like a waste of time. And time was money. Michael experienced bouts of severe depression, and started questioning the value and purpose of his life. He felt trapped in his own gilded cage. But he stayed in it, longing for the day when he could live off his investments and forget about medicine.

Dead Wood

Joseph had been a clerk in the same large organization for twenty-three years and now had "only" eleven years left before he could retire. He counted the years, the months, and the weeks until his retirement. Soon he would start counting the days.

It had not always been like this. When Joseph started working in the organization he was "bright-eyed and bushy-tailed," enthusiastic and ambitious. Because he was an employee who could be trusted, a disproportionate amount of work was assigned to him. At first he did not mind because he was sure his extra work would be appreciated. But he only heard from his superiors when things went wrong or when he crossed the authority lines. In time he felt discouraged and defeated, "like a little useless bolt in the machine." He started having nightmares and anxiety attacks, and once contemplated suicide.

One day he felt he simply couldn't take it any more. He had no energy left in him for fighting, and felt that the odds were against him anyway, "so what's the point?" He decided to give up. Since he needed the job, he decided not to quit, but he was not going to put in any effort either. He would do the absolute minimum required in order to keep his job, and nothing else.

Joseph loathed his work. He felt as if something in him died every day when he climbed the broad stairs to the building that housed his office. He punched his time card exactly at eight and again at five, but no one knew what he did between those hours. Joseph avoided contact with his coworkers. His manner was polite but distant. He developed a way of making himself invisible that is easy in a large, complex organization. He looked busy at his desk and when approached with a question or request, his answer was always "I am really sorry but I can't right now, I'm very busy." People eventually stopped making requests of him and only a few still wondered from time to time what exactly he was busy doing.

People who knew him away from work described Joseph very differently. They said he was interesting, lively, and knowledgeable about music; he read a lot and could spend hours with his coin collection. He enjoyed time with his friends and with his family. But Joseph hated his work. He had only one goal left: to make it to retirement, doing as little as possible without being fired.

Quitting Upward

Some burned-out people choose not to leave their organizations but rather to go up the organizational ladder. Jeanne chose this quitting upward path. All her life people had told Jeanne their most private problems because she was genuinely interested and concerned. Becoming a social worker in a welfare department was a natural career choice for her.

To her first cases she gave all of herself—time, attention, and action. But each client was followed by another one with as great a need and as terrible a story. Jeanne gradually realized that all her effort could never have a significant impact on either the lives of the welfare families or the causes of their poverty. Bureaucratic inertia, endless paper work, and poorly planned policy changes were pressures that added to her eventual burnout.

Her morale was low. She comforted herself with food and gained a lot of weight, which only depressed her more. She was absent from work as often as she could manage without being fired. She came late to the office and prolonged field visits by stops at local stores. She minimized interaction with her clients, cutting short their appointments, not listening, and avoiding eye contact while talking with them. She began to dehumanize her clients, calling them "society's losers," blaming them for their living conditions, and making fun of them to her coworkers.

As her attitude toward her job changed, so did her view of herself. She realized she was growing cynical and disillusioned and that she hated people in general and herself in particular. She knew she had to do something to change her life.

Jeanne went back to school to get her master's degree, then returned to the welfare department as a supervisor. In that position she would never have to interact with poor people again. She liked the power her new position provided and liked the paper work. "Papers have no emotional demands and no physical needs. They are never irate and are very easy to put aside." Jeanne felt detached from the young social workers who were starting their careers with her old enthusiasm. She was more comfortable with other supervisors who had chosen the path up.

A Trigger for Growth

Harriet was 41, married, and the mother of two girls. She was a successful actress, receiving leading roles and positive reviews, but her work was not easy. She found some roles to be emotionally draining, especially because her approach to the theater involved using her own experiences to deepen her involvement in a role. She became upset when she had to work with people who were not as serious about the theater as she was. When she started acting in a one-woman show, which she both wrote and produced, Harriet's involvement in the theater became all-encompassing. She was appearing six nights a week and she hardly ever saw her family.

When Harriet was rehearsing, she experienced guilt about neglecting her duties as wife and mother. She saw the theater as an impediment to her family life. When she was at home, time pressures and endless housekeeping tasks kept her from enjoying her family. She began to see them as interfering with her professional life. "All my interaction with my children involved orders: 'Close the door.' 'Practice the piano.' I didn't like being a mother. I resented the children's intrusions."

After months of trying to balance her roles as mother, wife, and professional, Harriet was experiencing severe symptoms of burnout. "I felt a tremendous burden on my shoulders. I was exhausted all the time and frequently depressed. I had no energy at all, and yet I was physically tense, irritable, and upset." Driving in this state of agitation, Harriet hit a parked car and was slightly injured. Just then remodeling work began on her kitchen, and her younger daughter came down with the flu. Harriet felt she couldn't take any more. "I got a migraine headache. There was an enormous amount of tension in my body. Later I developed laryngitis. I couldn't talk, and I didn't want to talk to anyone. I found myself crying a lot. I got to the point where I couldn't leave the house."

Harriet did not run from her crisis. "My style is to throw myself totally into what I do and to experience everything to the fullest. I want to get anything I can out of it." She wanted to face the pain, understand it, and learn from it. She let herself feel the fear, the anger, the frustration, the craziness.

Harriet realized she needed time to regain control of herself and her life, so she canceled several of her scheduled appearances and went away alone for a few days. She spent that time examining her roles as a mother, a wife, an actress, and a person. She examined the demands she thought were imposed on her by these roles and the rewards they provided. She knew she had to reorganize her priorities and one of the first was learning to take care of herself. She had to learn to assert herself, to set limits on how much she could do, and to ask for what she needed.

A few weeks after the crisis Harriet started preparing for a new one-woman show. Writing and rehearsing the show was the highlight of her days, but she had learned how important her family was. "It is my family that grounds me and gives me strength and energy to go out and experiment." To avoid conflicts, she tried to keep her professional life separate from her personal life. When she was working she was totally immersed in her work. When she was with her family she paid complete attention to them—not just to the household tasks, but to the joys and pleasures of life with her husband and children as well. The balance between the creative outlet that her work provided and the security that her family provided made her feel actualized. "I feel I am on the right track," she said, "I feel strong. I feel I could do anything." Easier said than done. Harriet's crisis was probably not the last time she would develop symptoms of burnout. But in the future she may know what the signs mean and be better able to cope with them. For Harriet the experience of burnout became an experience of growth.

In all six case examples the individual took some action in response to the events that caused burnout. These actions can be called *coping strategies*. Coping strategies will be discussed in great detail in subsequent sections of this book. For now it is important to point out that some coping strategies can be useful, others can be disastrous, and still others fall somewhere in between, where they serve merely to delay the inevitable. For example, Charlie's coping strategy after his hospitalization involved a total rejection of his creative abilities and skills. We can conclude that while this prevented a further disaster it was almost certainly not the best strategy for Charlie because his present occupation does not begin to fulfill his potential.

Carol seemed to have coped adequately because she probably would never have been content as a teacher. For people who discover that they were not made for a certain occupation, getting out may be the best solution. On the other hand, we have encountered numerous individuals who were gifted and excited about their professions, but were burning out because they happened to work in organizations that did not provide the proper environment or reward system for their efforts. In these cases a lateral job change—continuing in their professional activity in a different organization—is a much better coping strategy than leaving the profession.

In still other cases the problem is not specific to a given organization but is indigenous to the work itself. Here much more subtle and complex coping strategies would be called for. These will be discussed subsequently.

Whether a particular coping strategy is useful or disastrous can be determined by its consequences. Does the individual, as a result of the actions taken in response to burnout, get a sense of meaning from work, or not? In Charlie's case the answer, obviously, was no. In Harriet's case the answer was obviously yes. All the other cases fell somewhere in between.

Let us now move from the arena of concrete examples to the more general recommendations. As we do this, we are also, in effect, outlining the progression of chapters in this book.

The major strategies for dealing with burnout consist of: (1) being aware of the problem, (2) taking responsibility for doing something about it, (3) achieving some degree of cognitive clarity, and (4) developing new tools for coping, improving the range and quality of old tools.

As mentioned previously, one of the major escalators of burnout is the dual feeling of hopelessness and helplessness, the feeling that "there are too many things in my life that I don't like and that are beyond my control. I feel helpless about it and I have given up all hope of ever being able to change those things." There are two things involved here: one is the *actual* reality of the situation and the other is the perception of the situation on the person's part. In our work with people experiencing burnout, we have found that in almost all cases people have far more control over at least some aspects of their life and work situation than they realize. Once they begin to understand that they have some modicum of control, the feelings of hopelessness and helplessness begin to diminish even before they begin to assert that control. Two people can be working at the same place doing exactly the same job, and yet one can be feeling utterly helpless and hopeless, while the other feels there is both help and hope. The first person experiences intense burnout; the other does not. For example, suppose some dentists felt that they could not spend more time with their patients because they needed to earn $150,000 a year. Such people would feel trapped in that gilded cage and would consider their plight far more helpless and hopeless than it really was. For, in reality, they could unlock that cage by simply settling for less money. In some occupations there is less autonomy. Nevertheless, we have found that almost everyone has more power than he or she realizes.

Some people have learned to develop good coping strategies on their own and thus have avoided or diminished burnout. Others need help—the kind of help we have provided for thousands of people through our workshops and the kind of help we hope this book can provide.

Adequate coping consists first of awareness of the fact that there *is* a problem. There are people who hide from the problem and try to avoid thinking about it. These are people who believe that the way things are is the way they have to be; they also believe that the way things are in their own jobs is the way they are in all jobs. "That's life" is a slogan that may reduce pain slightly, but it also prevents finding a solution. This generalized cynicism masquerading as a philosophical outlook makes it impossible for people to develop an accurate perception of what is happening to them.

Other people who are somewhat aware of the problem tend to think that it is all their own fault. This awareness is usually only partial and it is almost always misdirected and, therefore, dysfunctional. Take the example of the nurses presented earlier. When nurses who work in very painful, demanding jobs begin to burn out, they either develop a cynical attitude or they begin to feel guilt and shame about the way they have come to feel towards and treat their patients as a result of their burnout and try to hide these feelings from everybody else. Both the cynicism, on the one hand, and the internalization of the guilt and shame, on the other hand, increase their burnout. Becoming fully aware of the problem includes becoming aware of the locus of the cause. Awareness temporarily increases the pain until action is taken.

To summarize, one part of achieving awareness is the simple realization that there is a problem; the other part is realizing that the problem is largely a function of the situation rather than of one's own dispositional inadequacy.

Once a person becomes aware that the problem is largely situational, then the coping strategies shift from "What's wrong with me as a person?" to "What can I do about changing my environment to make it more pleasant and easier for me to accomplish my personal and professional goals?" But in order to effect a change, a person must be willing to take responsibility for changing the environment. This is usually difficult. While many are willing to take responsibility for something that seems to be *their* fault," they are reluctant to do something about situational or institutional problems. Somehow if it is a situational problem, the organization should do it. This is not an unreasonable wish—unfortunately they cannot count on the organization to take remedial action. Occasionally an extremely enlightened organization might do so, but this is a rare exception. People can assume more power and control over their lives by realizing that there is more they can do to gain control over the environment than they realize. We have found that beginning to take responsibility for effecting a change in a difficult situation, is therapeutic in and of itself simply because it reduces the debilitating effects of the feelings of helplessness. Moreover, there are specific actions small groups of invididuals can take that can make real and concrete changes. These will be discussed in subsequent chapters.

When people are aware of the existence of a problem and are ready to take responsibility, the third thing necessary is cognitive clarity. People who are burned out and are working in bureaucratic organizations usually cannot easily discriminate the things that can be changed from the things that cannot. Burnout often manifests itself in people who assume that everything destructive and dehumanizing can be changed. These people invariably end up banging their heads against the stone wall of an unresponsive bureaucracy. Some aspects of a bureaucracy simply *cannot* be changed. After trying and failing, they begin feeling hopeless and helpless and come to believe that *nothing* can be changed. There are also people who believe from the outset that nothing can be changed. These individuals quickly develop a cynical attitude and never attempt to change anything. They simply put in their time.

In actuality, there *are* things that cannot be changed or that would be very difficult to change. In some cases, it is probably not worth the effort to try. But there are many aspects of a difficult work situation that *can* be changed with little effort. Part of what we mean by the achievement of "cognitive clarity" is the development of an ability to distinguish between those aspects of an organization that can't be changed and those that can. This allows individuals to channel their efforts where there will be a great likelihood of important progress. Again, not only will the change itself be beneficial, but the mere process of being able to effect a change will reduce the feeling of helplessness and hopelessness and thereby reduce burnout even though the situation remains far from ideal.

In one social service agency with which we worked, for example, we found that the crying need among many of the workers, and a major source of unease on the job most often mentioned by them, was that people high up in the hierarchy weren't aware of the great effort they put into their work. Consequently, they did not feel that their work was appreciated. But, in the kind of bureaucracy that existed in that social service organization, to expect appreciation from high-level officials was very unrealistic. It would have taken a major organizational change to bring about systematic expressions of appreciation from above. Our major intervention was to teach workers on the same hierarchical level to reward each other and to respect and value the appreciation of their peers. We taught them ways of paying attention to and acknowledging the good work of their peers and developed a system of peer review and communication. This simple intervention proved to be very effective.

Time and again we have found that, in a given organization, individuals hunger for appreciation. People who feel unappreciated almost never reach out to show appreciation of someone else's work. Our experience has shown that one of the best ways for individuals to encourage others to pay attention to their work is to start acknowledging the good work of others. When individuals, on their own, reach out to give each other needed support and needed appreciation, the reaching out mushrooms and grows exponentially. Moreover, peer appreciation (which is easy to institute) reduces the need for approval from above (which is frequently difficult, if not impossible, to institute).

There are other discriminations to be learned: for example, people must learn to make a clear discrimination between the concrete demands of the job and the demands they place on themselves that they sometimes erroneously attribute to their "supervisor" or their "organization." Thus, some people regularly overwork, assuming that this is a demand placed on them by their organization. But if they examine the situation closely, they would realize that they were much harsher taskmasters than their employer. They would then realize that they *did* have more control than they realized— and would have to deal with the issue of whether or not they wanted to exercise that control.

Some of the major tools necessary for coping have already been alluded to. For example, in order to see the specific problem, we need to develop some diagnostic and discrimination skills. In the above illustration, the realization that peer review could be an adequate substitute for supervisory praise requires the development of the skill to look for and find alternatives. Similarly, we need practice in looking inward to be able to articulate clearly what our own needs are in a given situation. If a solution involves meeting with other people to discuss problems and solutions, we need to develop certain skills such as "active listening" and clear communication. It is important to realize that these skills are both *essential* and *easy to master.* This will become clearer as you delve more deeply into this material in subsequent chapters.

One of the major reasons for mentioning the sequence of strategies for dealing with burnout is to make the point that earnest awareness is not enough. But it *is* a good first step. As with any problem (alcoholism, obesity, etc.) it is important to be aware and to desire change, but much more is needed to reverse the problem. This can better be illustrated than explained. Several years ago, we conducted a series of burnout workshops for executives in Israel. One of the participants (whom we'll call Dov) was a vice-president of one of that country's largest oil companies. We returned several months later to conduct a more intensive follow-up workshop for alumni of the previous one. We were amazed to find Dov in attendance, because a few days before the start of the workshop, Israel had been hit with a major energy crisis. We were certain that Dov, a self-confessed "workaholic" who had previously told us that he was indispensable to his organization, would be burning the midnight oil helping to solve the crisis. What was he doing at our workshop?

He informed us that several months before the first workshop he had suffered a serious heart attack. His physician ordered him to stay home from work for sixty days to recuperate. While taking long walks in the woods near his home he noticed the trees, the birds, the sky—seeing them as if for the first time. He realized that he was burning out on his job. He became deeply aware of the fact that he was now in his fifties, that he had poured much too much energy into his work. He was working harder and enjoying it less. He vowed that from then on he would pay more attention to things that *he* wanted to do—spend more time on himself and with his family—and cease being a workaholic. "I was excited about this discovery," he told us, "so excited that I could hardly wait to put it into effect. In fact, I was in such a hurry to put it into effect that I ended my convalescence two weeks early and returned to work! And within a very short time, I was back to my usual fourteen-hour day."

A few months later, he came to the initial burnout workshop, without expecting much to happen; he was thoroughly convinced that he was too old to change. In the workshop, however, he increased his understanding of the phenomenon and picked up a few useful skills. Mostly, he came to realize that an awareness of the problem was not enough. Not even his own heart attack was enough to induce him to make the sustained effort necessary to change his life.

The ultimate proof of his change came when the oil crisis happened to coincide with the date of the more intense workshop. The old Dov would have given up the workshop, convinced that he was indispensable. The new Dov had rearranged his priorities so that he and his needs came first. More importantly, he had given up the ego-gratifying conceit that he was indispensable and had trained others to be able to assume more responsibility as he became freer to delegate it. In effect, he became a more successful executive, was more useful to the company and certainly more useful to himself and his family by learning to get gratification from delegating authority rather than from behaving as if he needed to do everything himself. Thus, as frequently happens, as Dov cured his own burnout, he was not the only beneficiary; his organization, his subordinates, as well as his family and friends, benefited from his reorientation.

While burnout can be an extraordinarily painful and distressing experience, as with any difficult event, if properly handled it can not only be overcome, it can be the first step toward increased self-awareness, enriched human understanding, and a precursor of important life changes, growth, and development. Accordingly, people who have experienced burnout and have learned to overcome it almost invariably end up in a better, fuller, more exciting life space than if they had not experienced burnout at all.

TWO

Two Paths: Burnout Versus Peak Performance

M OST highly motivated professionals start their careers with high expectations. Above all they expect that the work they do will make a significant contribution to individuals or society and will give meaning to their own lives. When they work in a supportive and challenging environment, one that has relatively few hassles and stresses, they can achieve peak—or close-to-peak— performance. This, in turn, strengthens their initial motivation. The result is a positive loop that can be sustained indefinitely (see Figure 2–1).

On the other hand, when the same highly motivated individuals confront an environment in which rewards are minimal and the many stresses unmodifiable, an environment in which failure is virtually inevitable, the result is burnout. Because they care so much, and because being successful has such existential significance for them, failure is a devastating experience. Burnout, in turn, reduces their motivation for work. The result is a negative loop that turns some people into "dead wood," makes some people quit their jobs,

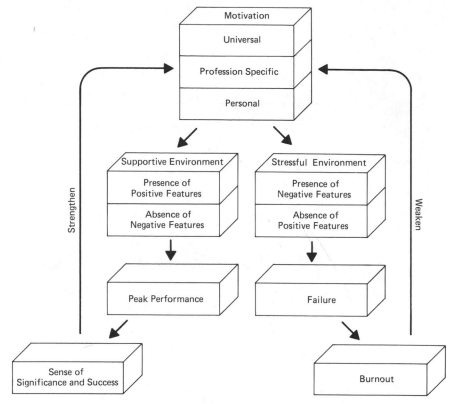

Figure 2–1   *Two Paths: Burnout Versus Peak Performance*

Source: First appeared in A. Pines, "Who Is to Blame for Helpers' Burnout? Environmental Impact," in C. D. Scott and J. Hawk (eds.), *Heal Thyself: The Health of Health Profession-als* (New York: Brunner-Mazel, 1985).

and causes others to leave their careers altogether and look for work in a field that does not involve emotionally stressful work. Thus, the crucial factor in determining whether a certain highly motivated individual will burn out or reach peak performance is the work environment.

It is important to note, again, that what we are about to say does not apply to those professionals who start out alienated or cynical. Of course such people can be and often are unhappy in their work. But their unhappiness is not burnout.

The initial expectations highly motivated people have of their work fall into three major categories: universally shared, profession-specific, and personal expectations. Universally shared expectations include being able to feel that work has significance, having the autonomy to do things the way they ought to be done, finding opportunities for continuous growth, being part of a social network of able colleagues, and receiving adequate monetary compensation for the work. Profession-specific expectations for human service professionals include a desire to work with people, to help those who need help, and to have a positive impact on their lives. For executives and managers these expectations include wanting to make the organization the best that it can be, and to be appreciated for doing so. Personal expectations are most often inspired by an influential person, or by some experience that creates in the individual an idealized image of the chosen profession. Frustrated expectations in any of these three categories can be a common and powerful cause of burnout. In this chapter, we will discuss universally shared work expectations. Profession-specific and personal expectations will be discussed in the next part of the book.

As we noted earlier, every person wants to feel significant: "He must desperately justify himself as an object of primary value in the universe; he must stand out, be a hero, make the biggest possible contribution to world life, show that he counts more than anything or anyone else."[1] One of the primary expectations for highly motivated people is achieving a sense of significance and purpose in their work. Furthermore, in our culture, work provides status and a sense of identity as a full-fledged member of society. The difficulties many people have in adjusting to retirement attest to the important function that work serves in providing a sense of identity and structuring time in a meaningful way.

Even when people have jobs that are stressful or do not pay enough, if their work provides them with a sense of meaning, people will not burn out. Professionals in the human services often report that in spite of the tremendous emotional stress involved in client contact, this is not what causes their burnout, because that contact is also the most significant aspect of their work. Rather, it is the bureaucratic hassles, the senseless rules, and meaningless paper work that cause burnout. "I like my field work," is a common statement. "It is the reason why I chose this work in the first place. Going back to the office and having to waste long, desperately needed hours filling out dozens of forms that no one will ever read is what burns me out."

David Harrison found that burnout among protective service workers occurred in large part because the work lacked significance and opportunities for growth. As an example he reports that social workers often complain that their clerical responsibilities are over-emphasized and their helper roles are underemphasized in governmental agencies.[2]

A sense of meaning can be derived from the feeling that one's work makes a significant contribution to the organization in which one works, to people in need, to society-at-large, or to the future welfare of the world. In every case it serves to motivate professionals, and helps them put in perspective (and thus handle better) the daily stresses and hassles in their work. For the professionals in our studies, no matter what their particular field of work, the feeling that no matter how hard they tried they could not have a real impact was one of the most powerful causes of burnout.[3]

Similar findings were reported by Barry Farber, who studied the process and dimensions of burnout in 60 psychotherapists. He found that most therapists (73.7 percent) cited "lack of concrete indicators of therapeutic success" as the single most stressful aspect of their work. In addition, 25 percent of the therapists in his sample admitted to occasionally feeling disillusioned with the therapeutic enterprise. Among highly committed professionals such as these psychotherapists, the absence of concrete evidence of success causes feelings of insignificance, disillusionment, and helplessness, which are the hallmarks of burnout.[4]

"There is in every organism, including man, an underlying flow of movement toward constructive fulfillment of its inherent possibilities, a natural tendency toward growth," wrote the humanistic psychologist Carl Rogers.[5] Abraham Maslow maintains that people's drive toward actualization of their human potentialities is a central part of their personality. The self-actualization drive promotes expression of people's unique characteristics. It is the highest need in a human's hierarchy of needs, and one that can be satisfied only after the satisfaction of the lower-order needs (physiological needs, needs for safety, security, love, and esteem).[6]

Not every job provides opportunities for growth and self-actualization, and not all people expect to find such opportunities in their work. Yet for highly motivated professionals, especially those who spend many years in professional training, job satisfaction often results from a feeling of psychological growth.[7] Such professionals often expect their careers to provide them with both continual challenge and opportunities for self-actualization. When their work does not allow for the expression of their talents and skills, they suffer severe frustration. Burnout, turnover, and low job satisfaction occur when the work does not encourage or allow growth.[8] In a sample of 724 human service professionals we found that the more self-actualized people were, the less likely they were to be burned out.[9]

Most highly motivated professionals expect to be able to do things their own way, to have a reasonable degree of control over their work environment, and to be paid enough to have independence and control over their lives outside of work. Thus, for highly motivated people, lack of control over their work can be a particularly stressful experience.[10] Studs Terkel, in his book *Working*, reports that being oversupervised was a major source of stress in most work settings.[11] Being fired from a job is one of the most extreme forms of loss of control. Reports show that depression, suicide, sexual impotence, and even child abuse accompanied the high unemployment of the 1970s.[12] Unemployed men show more signs of both psychological and physiological distress than do their employed counterparts.[13] When unemployment rises by 1 percent, 1.9 percent more people die from heart disease, cirrhosis of the liver, and other stress-related diseases over the next six years. Martin Seligman demonstrated how people actually learn helplessness when they repeatedly undergo negative experiences over which they have no control.[14] The negative effects of lack of control and the positive effects of control were documented even in relatively brief laboratory experiments. Researchers have found that the sense of being able to control stresses (such as an electric shock and a loud noise) increased people's ability to endure them. People who manage to assume control, after having lost it temporarily, feel better emotionally and physically, and are more able to change the world around them.

Everyone who works has the hope, if not the expectation, of earning enough money to provide a degree of financial independence and a sense of security. Unfortunately, people define "enough money" by comparison with a reference group similar to and slightly above themselves. Psychiatrist Martin Lipp notes:

> The ideal income tends to remain elusively at ten to twenty percent above the current income, even at the very highest socioeconomic strata. Depending on income as the primary source of job satisfaction therefore tends to lead consistently to frustration: it's never enough. Paradoxically one's income becomes increasingly satisfying in inverse proportion to the importance attached to it. If you get pleasure from other aspects of your work, you are far more likely to be content with your income no matter how high or low it may be.[15]

While highly motivated professionals expect to be paid adequately for their work, money in most cases is not one of their primary reasons for getting into their profession. In addition, our research has found that there is no simple and direct relationship between burnout and satisfaction with pay. In two different studies we also found that there was no correlation between satisfaction with pay and overall job satisfaction, liking of the job, and liking of the particular caseload one was responsible for.[16] Money does matter, but only when it is perceived as a symbol of the recognition (or lack of recognition) for work well done.

Work-related social contacts are an important aspect of work, even when individuals are happily married, with a stable and supportive network of family and friends. Most people share an explicit or implicit expectation that their coworkers will be stimulating and friendly, will provide them with professional support, appreciation, and challenge, will share their world view, and will be fun to be with.

Research shows that good work relations have a positive effect on both job satisfaction and people's general sense of well-being.[17] On the other hand, a poor relationship with one's boss, subordinates, and colleagues is a major source of stress at work.[18] A number of experts in organizational psychology have suggested that good relationships among members of a group working together are a central factor in individual and organizational health.[19] Similarly, the work environment can be a clearinghouse of friendships and camaraderie. Friends make a job pleasurable, and enjoyable social contacts are an important source of job satisfaction.[20]

In a study involving 76 mental health workers Pines & Maslach found that when work relationships were good, staff members were more likely to express positive attitudes toward the institution and toward the patients, to enjoy their work, feel successful in it, and look for "self-fulfillment" in it.[21]

Supportive Versus Stressful
Environments

Work environments can significantly affect the burnout rates of highly motivated people by helping or preventing them from reaching their goals and with those goals their peak performance. Given the high costs of lost motivation, turnover, tardiness, absenteeism, poor delivery of services, and so on, organizations have a high stake in trying to prevent burnout. Unfortunately, some organizations use the burnout process itself as a screening device. A prominent executive once told us: "Let them burn out and quit; there are three people out there eagerly waiting for each position opening up, who will be willing to promise to remain forever both cheerful and grateful." The fact that burned-out professionals are more likely to quit their jobs than to be fired demonstrates the fallacy of this reasoning.

This type of reasoning is not limited to organizations. In most discussions about burnout the finger of blame has been pointed at the burnout-victims. "The reason they burn out," the typical argument goes, "is because there is something wrong with them." And the ready proof. "Why are there people in the same job who even after many years love their work and show no signs of burnout?" What these critics try to do is find personality deficits in the burnout victim. But, as we have shown, a worker who is "burnout proof" is often undesirable because he or she lacks idealism. Moreover, while personality differences certainly exist, this is, in reality, a minor aspect of the problem; it is much more useful to focus on the environment as the primary cause of burnout.

How is it possible to test what has more effect—a worker's personality or the work environment? One way might be to put the same worker first in a supportive environment and then in a stressful one and observe what happens. If burnout is primarily a function of individual dispositions, the different environment should make very little difference. On the other hand, if burnout is primarily a function of situational determinants, the same individual can be expected to burn out in the stressful environment and flourish in the supportive one. This kind of controlled experiment could never be carried out for obvious ethical reasons.

But there are naturally occurring cases in which the same individual ends up working in two environments that differ radically in terms of the relative presence of positive and negative work features. These kinds of cases are important because they demonstrate the effect of the work environment independently of the individual. The following case study of two special-education classes for severely handicapped children, both taught by the same teacher, demonstrates this point well.

Both classes served similar middle-class suburban neighborhoods under the auspices of the same county government and within the limits of the same budget. Yet the work environment and, as a result, the staff burnout in the two classes were vastly different.

Karen, a special-education teacher, had always liked children and for as long as she can remember thought about becoming a teacher. She chose special education because she felt that in this area of teaching she could have a greater impact on the children she worked with. For five and a half years she worked in a small school for retarded children, leaving because of personal reasons unrelated to the work environment.

The physical layout of the school had been designed by the teachers, who knew what they and the retarded children needed and helped the architects plan the school accordingly. The new building had spacious classrooms filled with sunlight. One wall in every classroom was all windows. Outside the windows were play areas so that some children could be outdoors while others remained inside. The play areas were fenced so it was safe for the children to wander. Another wall in each classroom was mirrored so the children could see themselves, helping them to develop an accurate self-image. There were big movable cabinets so the rooms could be divided as needed. The walls separating the different classrooms could be moved to make the entire school into one large space. The colors of the rooms were bright and cheerful; the colors for each classroom had been chosen by the teachers. The furniture was all new and color coordinated. The school was well equipped and there was enough space both to store equipment and to use it properly.

In the middle of the school was a big activity area that could be used for social events such as parties, plays, and joint lunches. The support staff—speech therapists and physical therapists—had their own rooms so they could work individually with children without disturbing the rest of the class. There was a staff room where the teachers could take their breaks. It was close enough to all the classrooms so when a crisis occurred the teachers were immediately available.

The children seemed to enjoy very much the physical environment of the school and to feel safe in it. They were free to move around the entire school area and to visit other classrooms. As a result, they became close to other children and to other staff members. The open contact among all the children and all the teachers made the school feel like a home. The physical environment enabled teachers to be more responsive to the children's individual needs, and the children felt and appreciated it.

Since the school was in one building, it created a sense of community among the children and the staff. The teachers could watch out for each other's children. Even when children left their own classroom, other teachers could keep an eye on them.

After two and a half years and many hours spent in staff meetings, the teachers got together and decided to teach as a team. All the children were divided into groups according to their age and ability ranges. Each teacher then chose an area of special interest to teach. There was a lot more variety and challenge in the team teaching because of the different age and ability groups and because the staff could go deeply into areas they liked. The teachers had total control over the acceptance of children to the school and their assignment to the different educational programs. For example, when a child who was sent to the school was clearly misplaced, the teachers had the power to modify the placement decision. Staff members had autonomy and the support of the administration and of colleagues and felt that their work enabled them to grow as professionals and have an impact on the children they were teaching.

When Karen had to leave this school, she was heartbroken. And indeed, she soon discovered that work environments can be very different.

Karen's new class was housed in a little theater building on a regular elementary school campus. Two special-education classes had to share one room that was the same size as the classroom she herself had in the other school. But she had to share this space with another teacher so she actually had half the space. The other teacher resented Karen's intrusion into what she considered "her" space.

The building was old and seemed dark and dirty, even though it was cleaned regularly. The floors were scratched and the furniture consisted of mismatched discards from other classes. The overall atmosphere was depressing. Even though Karen had a budget similar to the one for her previous class, she saw no point in purchasing equipment because there were not enough storage cabinets and no space to put things away. The playground was a considerable distance from the classroom. It was not fenced and was next to a busy parking lot. The staff had to watch the children constantly. "It was frightening," said Karen, "because it took a child only a second to run to the street." Even though there was a teacher's room on the school grounds, it was too far away from the classroom and Karen was reluctant to go there lest something happen in her absence.

The support staff did not have their own space and had to work with children in the classroom; as a result there were often many people in the classroom: an occupational therapist, a speech therapist, a physical therapist, and the two physical education teachers. The therapists complained about having to work amid so much noise and so many distractions. But the administration was unresponsive to their complaints. The noise was indeed loud and pervasive. Karen felt she was under observation all the time, with many people offering her unsolicited advice on how to teach her class. Their presence added a lot of stress to a situation that was already unbearable.

The staff recognized the need for modifications in the classroom and wrote long letters to the school administration and the department of education requesting change; they even located other classrooms better suited for the children's needs. They did not receive a reply.

Placement decisions were made by the administration in a haphazard way without concern for either the children's or the teacher's needs; the staff had no say about which or how many children would be placed in their classes. For example, on one occasion, when Karen was barely holding things together, out of the blue, the school bus driver informed her that she would be getting another child the next day.

Within six months, Karen was exhausted—physically, emotionally, and mentally. "I would come home from school and collapse. I began to experience back problems. I felt depressed, trapped, inadequate, and scared. Teaching was something I had loved, and something I had been good at. I was afraid I would never love it again. I was sure this was the end of my teaching career."

Karen's doctor suggested that she take some time off from work. She started by taking a month off. But after a month she felt that she still needed more time—so she took two additional months. During this time she started looking for other jobs and talking to other teachers who had left the same school before her. Most of them had changed jobs even though it meant a decrease in salary and benefits. They felt it was well worth it.

The quality of life in any work environment is influenced in part by the larger context within which it is situated: the national and local culture, the particular social, political, and economic climate, as well as the physical location. A special-education class in Israel in certain ways is very different from a similar class in the United States; teaching special education in the 1960s was probably rather different from what it is today; teaching a special-education class in an inner city ghetto is quite different from teaching such a class in a suburban neighborhood; teaching in a private school is different from teaching in a public school.

In addition, every discussion of burnout has to include a consideration of both the professionals and, in the case of human service professionals, the recipients of their services. Just as certain attitudes and vulnerabilities can make some people burn out faster than others, certain personality characteristics or problems of the service recipients can make helping them more stressful and thus more likely to produce burnout.

Yet, as the example of the two special-education classes shows, even the same person, working with children exhibiting similar problems in two schools similar in function, location, budget, and sociopolitical environment, will burn out in one and not in the other.

The example of the two classes, supported by extensive research, suggests a number of psychological, physical, social, and organizational features of the work environment that play an important role in either promoting or preventing burnout (see Table 2–1).

The *psychological* dimension of an environment includes those aspects that affect the worker's emotional well-being such as the sense of meaning and the opportunities for personal growth provided, and those that impinge on the cognitive sphere such as the variety provided by the work and the frequency of overload.

The *physical* dimension of an environment includes such fixed features as space, architectural structure, and noise, and the flexibility to change fixed features and adapt them to one's own taste and needs.

The *social* dimension of a work environment includes the people coming in direct contact with the individual including service recipients (their number and the severity of their problems they present); coworkers (work relations, work sharing, and availability of time out); and supervisors and administrators (feedback, support, and challenge they provide).

The *organizational* dimension of a work environment includes such bureaucratic difficulties as red tape and excessive paper work

TABLE 2-1

Work Environment Features That Are Burnout Correlates

PSYCHOLOGICAL	PHYSICAL	SOCIAL	ORGANIZATIONAL
Cognitive:	Fixed:	Service recipients:	Bureaucratic:
Autonomy	Structure		Red tape
Variety	Space	Numbers	Paper work
Overload	Noise	Problems	Communication problems
		Relations	
Emotional:	Flexibility to change fixed features	Co-workers:	Administrative:
Significance		Work relations	Rules and regulation
Actualization		Sharing	Policy influence
Growth		Time out	Participation
		Support	
		Challenge	Role in the organization:
			Role conflict
		Supervisors and administrators:	Role ambiguity
			Status disorder
		Feedback	
		Rewards	
		Support	
		Challenge	

Source: A. Pines, "Changing Organizations: Is a Work Environment Without Burnout a Possible Goal?", in *Job Stress and Burnout,* edited by W. Paine. Copyright © 1982 by Sage Publications, Inc. Reprinted by permission of Sage Publications, Inc.

and such administrative features as the relative flexibility of rules and regulations and the role of the individual in the organization.

We will be discussing these four dimensions in detail through the next three chapters. For illustrative purposes, we will show how they influenced Karen's experience in the two schools.

In the first school, teachers had a lot of autonomy. As you will recall, they designed the school, they could affect placement decisions, and they eventually decided on their own teaching style. In the second school, one of the most stressful aspects was the fact that the teachers had almost no autonomy. The administration ignored the teachers' repeated complaints about the classroom and allowed the teachers no say in the placement of children.

One of the positive aspects of the team teaching in the first school was the variety it provided the teachers, because of the need to relate to different age and ability groups. This variety enhanced the teachers' challenge and interest in work.

There are two kinds of overload, quantitative (having too many tasks to accomplish per unit of time), and qualitative (having tasks that are too difficult). As we have seen, in the second school, the work imposed both qualitative and quantitative overload. Karen had too many children, and some of those children had very serious problems she was never trained to treat. Karen's feelings of inadequacy about treating the special problems presented by the children were amplified by the fact that there were so many of them.

In the first school, Karen felt that she had a major impact on the children's lives. She felt she was doing more than teaching facts—that her work was extremely significant. This gave her life a sense of meaning and purpose. In the second school she felt inadequate, helpless, hopeless, and scared. She could hardly deal with the children's physical needs and felt she failed to fulfill the teaching objectives imposed on her, as well as her own goals as a person and as an educator. She felt that no matter how hard she tried she could not improve her work situation and have more of an impact on the children under her care; this feeling of futility and despair was a major cause of her burnout.

The team teaching in the first school provided the teachers with opportunities for self-actualization and growth by enabling them to teach the subjects they themselves liked most, and challenging them to teach all the children in the school—children who presented different problems and who were in grade and age levels they may have been unfamiliar with.

The physical structure of a work environment affects professionals directly by supporting or thwarting their work-related goals. Since the children in Karen's special-education classes needed a lot of one-to-one work, the windows near the outside enclosed play area at her first school were very important. They enabled her to keep an eye on the rest of her class while she was working with one child. The play area was enclosed so Karen didn't have to worry about children running into the street.

The structure of a work environment can also influence the person-environment fit by making desired social interaction easier or more difficult to achieve. Given the openness of the first school building, children felt free to move around and go to other classrooms; as a result they developed close relationships with children in other classrooms and with other staff members. Many experts are convinced that vandalism is a symptom of stress caused by physical designs that destroy social networks. When people don't have a sense of belonging and mutual support, they will not care about their space. And indeed, the example of the two classes indicates that whereas the first class felt "almost like a home," and the children liked it and cared for it, the second class was a very stressful environment to which the children responded with wild and destructive behavior. "They would run around, climb on tables, run to the other side of the room and disturb the other class. When they got angry they would throw toys and break them."

In Karen's second class, lack of space had a very negative impact on both the teachers and the children. Sharing classroom space with another teacher and with all the support staff resulted in the teachers and therapists feeling resentful. The children, who needed a lot of space, felt trapped in the small classroom. "No matter what they did they were in somebody's space. Everybody was always tripping over toys." The crowded, inadequate space increased the tension and stress experienced by students and staff.

The incessant noise in the classroom was distracting and unpleasant. It was a chronic stressor that added to the noxious environment. Karen reported that often the screams of the children and the other noises would continue ringing in her ears hours after she left school.

Some people are more sensitive to noise than others; some like large, open areas whereas others feel comfortable in small, enclosed areas. The best work environment is one that is flexible enough to accommodate the individual, rather than forcing the individual to accommodate. In the first school, flexibility to change features was maximized: The physical layout was designed by the teachers; movable partitions enabled teachers to change the sizes of classrooms and even to open the whole school into one large space.

The quality of interactions between the professionals and the recipients of their services is affected by their number, the severity or complexity of their problems, and their interpersonal relations. On all three scores the second classroom was significantly more stressful than the first.

In the first school, the supportive and challenging relationship among the coworkers was one of the most positive features of the work environment. In the second school, the necessity for two teachers to share the small building produced stress and resentment which contributed to their dissatisfaction and burnout.

Work-sharing can help professionals defuse many work stresses and increase challenge, variety, and power. In the first school, team teaching meant that teachers could choose areas they particularly loved. Because the teachers worked as a team they also had complete control over assigning children to the program, control they would not have had otherwise.

In her second job Karen reported that after working straight through for five hours, she felt that she "couldn't breathe." In contrast, one of the things that made work in the first setting so enjoyable was that the school structure enabled teachers to supervise each other's children and thus made it possible for them to take time out whenever needed. The proximity of the staff room to all the classrooms allowed teachers to return to their classes immediately if a crisis did occur.

Support and challenge are two of the most important functions coworkers can provide for each other. The example of the two schools shows how these variables can determine whether a work atmosphere will be hostile, stressful, and burnout producing or friendly, supportive, and growth enhancing.

Supervisors and administrators can influence the well-being of workers by providing immediate and appropriate feedback, by adequate distribution of rewards, and by providing support and challenge. Karen and the teacher who shared her classroom wrote several letters requesting a room change and changes in assignment of children. But the bureaucracy did not respond. This lack of administrative support increased Karen's stress.

The problems mentioned most often as causing burnout among the bureaucratic features of the work environment are red tape, excessive paper work, and communication problems. The fact that after her exhausting work day Karen had to deal with a considerable amount of paper work was for her the final straw.

Administrative influence is often transmitted via rules and regulations. When these are rigid or appear excessive, senseless, or arbitrary, they increase the likelihood of burnout. A related cause of burnout, as Karen's case demonstrated, is the inability to participate in and influence policy decisions that affect one's work and well-being.

In addition to the policies and practices of the organization, there are aspects of the individual's place in the organization and how he or she relates to it which also contribute to the likelihood of burnout. They include role conflict, role ambiguity, and what organizational psychologists call "status disorders." In Karen's case, role conflict resulted from the demands imposed on her by her three roles—as a teacher with clear educational goals, as a caretaker who had to attend to the physical and psychological needs of severely handicapped children, and as a clerk with a massive load of paper work. Part of Karen's stress resulted from an ambiguity in her role definition. Was she first and foremost a teacher? a counselor? a bureaucrat? The fact that her status within the educational system and within the school system did not reflect her many responsibilities was an added stress.

As you have no doubt noticed, some of the features of the work environment presented in Table 2-1 are positive (such as significance, autonomy, challenge, and support) and some are negative (such as overload, role conflict, red tape, and paper work). Until recently, research in this area has concentrated on the presence of negative work features, and has largely ignored stress reactions that result from the lack of positive features. Two studies emphasized the importance of lack of positive features in the work environment as a source of stress and burnout. Both studies demonstrated that lack of positive work features is significantly correlated with burnout and work dissatisfaction, independently of the presence of negative work features.[22] Thus, organizations seeking to minimize the threat of burnout can try to maximize the positive work features as well as minimize the negative ones.

This recommendation sounds obvious. But it is easier said than done. At the same time, it is not as difficult as most supervisors and managers seem to think. All work features are dynamically interrelated. In addition to their independent effects, they also interact with and affect one another. For example, participation in decision making (the organizational dimension) is likely to have a positive effect on perceived autonomy (the psychological dimension). Similarly, good relations between coworkers (social dimension) can reduce the negative impact of crowding (physical dimension).

Returning to the two paths leading a highly motivated worker either to burnout or to peak performance (described in Figure 2-1), we can see that the main feature distinguishing between the two paths is the nature of their work environment (supportive vs. stressful). What enables a highly motivated worker to reach his peak performance is the presence of these positive work features and the absence of unmodifiable work stresses. The conclusions drawn from Karen's case apply to all professionals and all work environments.

The work environment of a multinational corporation, for example, may be very different from that of a special-education class, yet it can be similarly analyzed in terms of such positive features as autonomy, significance, challenge, and support or, conversely, such negative features as overload, red tape, and excessive paper work.

Karen's case demonstrates how a highly motivated individual, when working in a supportive environment, achieved peak performance, and with it a sense of significance and success. These, in turn, strengthened the initial motivation and created a positive motivational loop that could have been sustained almost indefinitely. The same highly motivated individual, when working in a highly stressful environment, inevitably failed. Karen's failure and the emotional turmoil surrounding the failure caused her burnout and the negative motivational loop that eventually made her quit her job and leave her career in special education. Currently, Karen is happy and successful working in a kindergarten she owns and operates together with her husband.

The Individual and the Environment

Why do some people quit, others stay, and yet others grow with the experience of burnout? The specific answer depends on a complex combination of variables involving the person and the environment. Karen decided to quit because she saw no way to influence her work situation and had no strength to go on. Someone else in her situation might have lasted a bit longer; many people would have given up much sooner.

The reasons people have for choosing a particular occupation and the factors that qualify them for it, when combined with the situational stresses characteristic of that particular occupation, determine to a large extent people's response to burnout. In Karen's second school, for example, all the teachers burned out and quit within a year.

A similar response to stress comes from a very different field of work—corporate management. One of the most consistent findings in every management workshop we have conducted has been that managers need, above all else, a sense of control and freedom on the job—an ability to do things the way they think things should be done (and to be successful and recognized for their contribution). Situations in which that freedom was undermined became intolerable for them and most said they would rather quit than stay. Managers who are not willing or able to accept the lack of autonomy as inevitable are unlikely to end up as dead wood in the organization.

On the other hand, in many service organizations we found workers experiencing prolonged burnout but staying on as dead wood, because working for the government provided them with the security of a good pension plan. Their need for security was greater than their need for control and autonomy.

One might ask whether this difference is the result of personality or environment. That is, does the government agency attract the kind of people who have a high need for security and a low need for autonomy—or does being locked into a bureaucratic organization with a good pension plan create a dulling of one's need for autonomy, and produce a need for security at all costs? Our research indicates that both factors are at work. While people with a high need for autonomy are naturally attracted to work environments where autonomy is encouraged, it is also the case that the environment can expand or curb these tendencies. Thus people with a high need for autonomy who find themselves in a position where they cannot exercise that autonomy, if they remain, may find their need for autonomy diminishing and their need for security increasing.

People experience burnout differently and react differently to the experience because people are different. They are born with different genetic dispositions, have different childhood experiences, and different education. These differences are manifested in the way people try to make sense of their existence in the world. For some, the most meaningful thing in life is autonomy, for others it is security.

People also approach the inevitable stresses of life and work in different ways. Some people view the world as dominated by evil forces and believe they must always be prepared for the worst. Other people believe that, despite minor setbacks, things will eventually turn out for the best. For them the important thing is being happy and experiencing life to its fullest. Because they can recognize the real tragedies, trivial problems are not exaggerated or perceived as traumatic. The process involved here is *cognitive appraisal*.

According to psychologist Richard Lazarus, all emotions are shaped by cognitive appraisals of events in terms of their significance for our well-being.[23] Appraisal takes five key forms. An event may be (1) relevant or irrelevant to one's well-being, (2) already harmful, (3) potentially harmful, (4) challenging, or (5) potentially positive in outcome. The same set of circumstances can produce quite different patterns of response to stress in different individuals, depending on their history and characteristics. For example, one person may cope with terminal illness by denial and another by becoming depressed; one person may handle an insult by ignoring it and another by getting angry and planning revenge.

While individual differences do exist, the major causes of burnout reside in the environment. Organizations can encourage choices of moving upwards, lateral job changes, or quitting altogether—depending on the stress they impose, their flexibility, and the rewards they provide. Money is important for most people, but there are other rewards that assume even greater importance in this context. If the rewards in the form of support, challenge, and recognition are very high, people may remain in extremely stressful occupations. Similarly, the availability of jobs in a certain field enables people with a high need for variety to change their job setting with the first signs of burnout.

The major point is this: while people do differ from one another in how they respond to stress, almost everyone will experience burnout if severe, uncontrollable, and unmodifiable chronic pressures are placed on them without adequate support, regardless of individual differences in such things as cognitive appraisal. Similarly, our own work has demonstrated over and over again that when the environment changes for the better—becomes more supportive, less stressful, more exciting, more enjoyable, more appropriate to one's skills—such changes have important positive effects on almost everyone, regardless of individual differences. Thus our analysis of the causes and cures of burnout has focused and will continue to focus on the environment—not because we think individual differences are uninteresting or unimportant, but because almost all individuals can be affected by environmental changes regardless of their personality characteristics or cognitive styles. In short, looking toward the environment for solutions has more practical utility for understanding and reducing burnout.

The environment consists of all the settings in which the individual functions, including the occupational, organizational, social, home, and recreational environments. As much as individual environments differ, common stresses can be identified across occupations.[24] In our workshops for members of one occupational group, we would ask everyone to write down the three most stressful and most rewarding aspects of their work, and look for commonalities with the lists of others.

Every occupational group was able to identify quite easily common stressful and rewarding features of their work. For corporate managers, as we saw earlier, the most stressful aspects of work were lack of autonomy and recognition. For people in human services, the shared pressures were the result of not being able to help the sick, the needy, and the maladjusted. In large organizations, clerks and administrators noted mainly pressures resulting from overload of paper work and administrative inertia. Fire fighters, police officers, and military personnel reported burnout caused by dangerous work situations and lack of support from the public or the system. Many working women described guilt and anxiety over conflicts between their work and home obligations. People in business were often stressed by competition and by the need to make important decisions without sufficient time or information.

Once again, the broader theme of almost all occupational stress can be seen as the need to feel that work is meaningful and significant. The most stressful aspects of the job are the obstacles that prevent us from achieving our existential goals. Since people in a particular occupational group tend to have similar existential goals that made them choose that profession, they also have similar stresses. Because, for managers, having an impact and recognition are the things that give meaning to life, their absence is stressful. Because, for people in the helping professions, helping gives a sense of meaning to life, not being able to help is most stressful.

Just as habitual ways of looking at the world mediate the effects of burnout for the individual, the four levels of the work environment—psychological, physical, social, and organizational—mediate their effect for the organization.

While the main difference between Karen's two schools was on the physical dimension, in other organizations differences in the psychological and social levels are reflected in the problems individuals face and in the prevalence of employees' burnout. Two family service agencies we worked with had a similar number of psychiatrists, clinical psychologists, social workers, and trainees. Both were located in suburban communities and served a similar clientele. In one agency most employees did not stay longer than two or three years. There was a high level of absenteeism; employees came to work late and left early. Their home visits tended to be very short; the route to them was as long as possible. The atmosphere in the agency was hostile and competitive. Staff members were reserved and cautious, especially about admitting less-than-perfect knowledge. Even students who interned in the agency were criticized for asking questions. No one dared admit not knowing how to deal with a case, and staff meetings were called "crocodile sessions" because of the prevalence of harsh nonconstructive criticism. In the other agency professionals stayed for many years. They thought of the agency as a "home," a warm, supportive, and exciting place. Even the chief psychologist presented cases to the staff for suggestions and feedback and at times admitted being troubled or confused.

Almost everyone will burn out given the "right" combination of environmental conditions. In some instances, the primary causes of burnout reside in a stressful organizational setting; in others, the causes can be found in a combination of stresses particular to a certain occupation. In all cases, the people who begin with the highest ideals (unless they somehow manage to develop effective coping strategies on their own) are likely to experience the most severe burnout. The prerequisite for burnout, initial idealism and excitement, differentiates it from simple job alienation. Alienation can happen to people who have never expected anything from their work except a paycheck. Thus, assembly-line workers are prone to experience alienation but not burnout. Burnout most often happens to people who initially cared the least about their paychecks.

Burnout is different from clinical depression. At the early stages of burnout on the job people are often happy and productive in their other spheres of life. Depression, on the other hand, is pervasive. In depression the individual and the individual's personal history are the source of symptoms and the focus of therapy. In burnout the search for causes of symptoms and modes of coping focuses on the environment. In all but the most extreme cases, in which the individual burning out becomes depressed, the experience is seen from a social rather than an individual perspective.

People who are burned out feel exhausted, but, of course, burnout is more than simple fatigue. Obviously people who work hard are going to get fatigued. For example, we once interviewed a high-ranking Israeli combat officer who held a very exciting job of great power, challenge, and significance. He told us that at the end of his full day (frequently lasting from twelve to twenty hours) he felt totally exhausted, and yet he referred to it as "a good exhaustion," full of a sense of accomplishment—he felt like a juggler who manages to keep twelve balls in the air all at once. Obviously this is not burnout.

Why? He was clearly not experiencing the key elements of burn-out—feelings of helplessness, hopelessness, and entrapment. Even the stress of knowing that a mistake could cost many lives caused excitement rather than anxiety. It increased his belief in the importance of his work. Indeed, people burn out not only from being overloaded with too much work; they also burn out from being underchallenged, from being overtrained, from not feeling well utilized. In each case the main cause for burnout is the feeling that the work no longer gives life a sense of meaning and purpose.

PART TWO

Causes of Burnout

THREE

Burnout
in Management

IN a recent workshop for corporate
managers, we repeated an exercise we try to do in every burnout
workshop. We asked the participants to write down their hopes and
expectations when they took their current job. We then asked them
to meet in groups of four (with three of the managers they knew
least) and describe to the other three members of their group what
each had written. Next they were asked to decide on the items (if
any) that all four of them had in common. These shared hopes and
expectations were then presented by a spokesperson from each
foursome to the whole group, and written on a blackboard. Every
spokesperson was asked to indicate if his group had on its list any
of the items already written on the board.

What these managers discovered very quickly was that once the
first three foursomes presented their shared items, all the remaining
items were pretty much repetitions of the first. What they had no
way of realizing was that we received a very similar list from every
group of managers we ever worked with. And that with almost every

group of managers three foursomes were sufficient to produce the entire list. The shared items expressed two main themes—a need for autonomy and personal freedom and a need to be successful and receive recognition for it.

The hopes and expectations mentioned most frequently were:

- Have a significant impact on the organization
- Be able to do my own thing, express myself
- Have the resources needed to do my work well
- Be number one; be a success
- Make the organization the best that it can be
- Prove myself to myself and to the organization
- Be appreciated and recognized
- Have power and status
- Do something significant
- Be adequately rewarded

In the next stage of the exercise, we asked the managers to write down the three most stressful aspects of their work. Once again, they shared those stresses with their foursome and chose the stress (or stresses) that all of them had in common to present to the whole group. Once again, the stresses that were written on the blackboard turned out to be very similar for most of the foursomes. The stresses mentioned most frequently:

- Not enough power to have a real impact
- Inadequate monetary resources
- Inadequate staffing resources
- Political pressures, not enough information
- Administrative and bureaucratic interference
- Inadequate recognition and monetary rewards
- Not enough opportunities for advancement
- Inability to do things the way they should be done

Needless to say, practically every other group of managers we ever worked with came with a very similar list of stresses. But what is more significant is that the stresses were very closely related to their hopes and expectations. More precisely stated—the stresses were frustrated hopes and expectations. Why were the inability to have real impact, the inadequate resources in money and manpower, and the political pressures so stressful for these managers?

Because they wanted to have a significant impact on their organization by doing their own thing, for which they needed to have adequate resources. They didn't just want to do their job. They wanted to be number one. They wanted to make the organization the best that it could be, because they identified with its success, and wanted it to be their own success.

On a deeper level, it seems that these managers expected success at work to do something of great value—to give their life a sense of meaning. When financial, political, administrative, or staffing obstacles prevented them from accomplishing in their work what they wanted to accomplish, the frustration was experienced as a major stress. When such a frustration is chronic, and especially when it leads to failure, the result is burnout.

So we see that managers burn out for the same reason that other professionals burn out: their work experience doesn't match their ideal; they can't achieve in their work what they expected to achieve.

Highly motivated executives don't work hard because of money (even though they, like everyone else, like to get paid well). They don't work hard because of the threat of punishment or censure either. Idealistic managers work hard because they expect their work to make their life matter in the larger scheme of things and give meaning to their existence. They don't need either a "carrot" or a "stick" to motivate them. They are motivated primarily because they identify with their work.

In a supportive environment, where they have the autonomy, resources, and support needed to accomplish their goals without the frustration of bureaucratic hassles and red tape, such highly motivated managers can reach peak performance. Reaching peak performance increases their sense of significance and success, which, in turn, increases their original motivation. However, when the same highly motivated managers are thrown into a stressful environment, where they are overloaded with work, where their ambition is stifled by bureaucratic interference, poor communication, and paper work, where they can't get the resources they need to get the job done well, where they feel stuck below their level of competence, where they feel unappreciated, and where they don't get a sense of meaning from their work, burnout is very likely. This can be clearly seen in situations where failure is inevitable, as, for example, when it is impossible to get the quantity of products demanded if standards of quality are to be maintained. For ambitious executives whose egos are tied to their performance, failure is a powerful cause of burnout.

Human beings have not always looked to work as a path to finding meaning in life, as do so many modern-day executives. In the Bible, work is described as a punishment God gave man for disobeying Him. Similarly, for the ancient Greeks work was pain (the Greek word for work, *ponos*, means pain). It was the Protestant Reformation that lay the foundation for our current view of work. Martin Luther, the leader of the Reformation, thought that work was holy, and a way to worship God.

In the modern view of work, the worship of God has been replaced by an attempt to achieve self-actualization. Jay Rohrlich, a psychiatrist specializing in work with Wall Street executives, claims in his book *Work and Love* that self-definition through achievements at work is a primary goal in our society. The freedom to find personal satisfaction through achievements at work is seen as one of our most basic rights. The joy of control experienced by some ambitious executives is similar to religious fervor. The basis of this approach can be paraphrased as a variation on the classic notion: "I work, therefore I exist." Yet the modern dilemma, as it was articulated by Max Weber, is: "Do we work in order to live, or do we live in order to work?" Is work a goal, asks Rohrlich, or is it a means for freeing time in which "true" self-actualization can take place? The nobility of work is not a working-class concept. An addiction to work happens only among people who don't have to work hard in order to survive.[1]

Work can indeed be very ego gratifying. It enables some people to be "heroes" in a culture-prescribed "hero system" (to use Ernest Becker's terminology). For those people, work can have a transcendent value. A manager who succeeds in becoming the chief executive officer of one of the *Fortune* 500 corporations can get his sense of "cosmic significance" from his executive power; a politician who rises to the top of a political structure can get it from his political power; a businessman who creates a financial empire can get it from his monetary power.

For such recognized "heroes" in our society, having power, money, and recognition can provide enough meaning to life so that they don't need anything else. But this path to "heroism" is not a common one. There are very few places at the top. And many of those who make it to the top still feel empty, because success has not made them as happy as they expected it to. Even for people who are successful in their careers and who get from them a sense of meaning, work is not enough to give life meaning indefinitely. There are several reasons for that. One is that once expectations are fulfilled, and the thrill about the success has subsided, people tend to start taking it for granted, and the success loses its rewarding power. Another reason is that past success is no guarantee of future success. And, as the following case studies demonstrate, failure is a most powerful cause of burnout.

When Susan was hired as the executive director of a victim witness program, she knew it was a political job. It was part of a federal grant to the district attorney's office and involved working with a variety of community groups. Susan was responsible for designing a program to help victims and witnesses of violent crimes. She was given a small budget with which to serve the entire city and pay her staff. The enormity of the job as defined was overwhelming. "Many people had warned me that it was an impossible job," said Susan, "but I felt it was a challenge and a great opportunity."

All the salaries on the grant were low. The staff resented this and projected a great deal of anger onto Susan. As director, Susan had to answer to her staff, the district attorney's office, community and minority groups, the city system, and a policy committee. This committee was composed of representatives from various community agencies and interest groups and there was no agreement among them on the goals of the program. Susan worked sixty hours a week, nights, and weekends. She tried to do everything: business management, financial accounting, reports, training staff and volunteers, community outreach, and service to victims and witnesses. There was simply not enough money or time for everything.

Susan found one of the most frustrating aspects of her job was dealing with the "system." The bureaucracy did not provide candidates for staff positions so Susan had to recruit and select her own staff. The state government made service to victims difficult by complicated forms and requirements. Susan had to provide financial accounting to four agencies responsible for the program. "If the wrong form was submitted, or if a form was submitted to the wrong agency, it took weeks before it was returned and then the whole process had to start again. It often took three additional forms to correct an error. To get anything accomplished in the city took ten times longer than it was supposed to take."

In spite of all these obstacles Susan was committed to the program. She felt it was an important social service and she wanted to help the victims. In ten months the program served 1,000 clients with a staff of three and a few volunteers. But Susan felt that what mattered was what had not been done, although what was expected was humanly impossible, given the resources of the program.

Susan began to develop the classic symptoms of burnout at a high level of management.

> As the pressures and frustrations increased and I felt less effective in what I was doing, my self-concept became more negative. I was a terrible administrator, I wasn't smart enough to do the job, I had let the people down who had helped me get the job. I thought that there was something wrong with me that I was having so much trouble in the situation. The negative self-concept carried over into other aspects of my life, my personal relationships, athletic activities, relationships with my family. Once that sort of concept begins to develop, it almost develops a will of its own and it becomes difficult to let in any information that might allow for a more positive self-evaluation.
>
> I was so fed up with public employment. I was fed up with the way people are exploited or the way I felt I was exploited. I was so tired of having to work with stupid, inept people, and deal with city bureaucracy. I was tired of the politics of community groups and agencies. I was tired of clients who were demanding *everything immediately!*

Susan was mentally, emotionally, and physically exhausted. She resigned.

Whit, a 33-year-old mechanical engineer, provides an example of the causes for burnout in middle management. Whit had chosen his profession because he liked to build things with his hands and was good at it. For twelve years his work at a large oil company gave him ample opportunity for success. The work involved creating new instruments, and improving old ones. Whit loved the excitement of each new challenge. He even enjoyed the stress involved. Sometimes he worked twenty hours straight to meet a deadline. Often he became so absorbed in his projects that he ignored his wife and children. But he believed that his wife understood and supported him. Whit felt respected, successful, and happy with his life. He felt it gave him everything he wanted.

Things started to go wrong when Whit was promoted to a managerial position. It was the natural career step for him, but he had never been trained in management. It was not something he particularly wanted to do, yet it was an important promotion, and he knew that, "in the corporate world if you don't get promoted, you're actually getting demoted."

The first few months on his new job were stressful for Whit because he didn't know exactly what he was doing. But there was something exciting about managing a team to get a project done, and he enjoyed the new challenge. After this brief period of getting acquainted with the new job, he was assigned a project that was beyond his budding skills as a manager: he needed to guide sixty people through a $5 million project in just nine months.

Whit started working twenty-hour-days, the way he had when, as a hands-on engineer, he needed to get something done. But he found that his subordinates didn't care as much about the project as he did, and he also found that they resented his style of management, which tended toward the autocratic. Their dissatisfaction grew with time until they rebelled openly by going above his head and demanding his removal from the project. To his great shock, top management sided with them. Three months before the project was to be finished, he was transferred.

Whit was devastated. He had failed in his work, the thing that meant the most to him, and he had failed royally. Everyone in the company heard what had happened. The embarrassment and humiliation were almost too much for him to bear. When he first got the news about his dismissal from the project, he contemplated quitting the company. But his wife urged him not to, at least not until he found another job. (His professional position, and the high salary that came with it were also very important to her own sense of identity and security.)

Whit, in fact, didn't start looking for another job. His ego was so crushed by his failure as a manager that he couldn't summon the emotional energy he needed to go job hunting. He felt sad and emotionally depleted, had difficulty concentrating, and difficulty sleeping. Life, for him, had lost its meaning and purpose.

At the same company, Whit had reached peak performance and then burned out. Reaching peak performance had given him a sense of significance and success, which in turn had increased his work motivation. He remained in this positive loop for twelve years and probably would have remained in it indefinitely if he hadn't been promoted. Once he began to fail in his new positon, he burned out in less than a year.

David, a 50-year-old training expert at a large government agency, married and the father of six children, provides another example of the causes of burnout in high-level management.

> After thirteen years in the same department, I was told I was going to be transferred to another department the next day! I felt devastated; I felt a total lack of self-worth. I did not trust the person I was transferred to and resented the unfair and inconsiderate way the transfer was done. But I had no choice. I know this is not at all uncommon, but it's devastating when it happens to you. I found it very hard to take. I felt that the company was playing games with my life.
>
> I felt angry, humiliated, and used; they were going to pick my brains and then dump me. The experience was eroding away my soul. I felt like I didn't exist. I was doing my job like a machine, like a warm mannequin, not a person. . . . I felt trapped. That was the worst thing. . . . I wanted to escape at any cost, but there was no way out. The obligations of a large family didn't give me the latitude to simply walk out. And there was the pressure of having put all those years into a retirement system that I knew I was far enough into so that I couldn't go somewhere else. I knew that if I left I was throwing a lot of my future away. . . . The most devastating thing was the feeling of worthlessness. And I couldn't get out of it. I was so miserable, I couldn't see any of my friends. I was in no shape to be a loving husband and father.
>
> At times I thought I was at the point of murder. The pressure builds up and builds up until something has to give and you've got to cash in all your stamps. And then you just do it. You simply have to escape.
>
> We are a good, warm, and loving family, and this is the thing that got me through all this. . . . That's the thing that has held me together. The love and support of my wife and children prevented me from committing an act of violence, either on someone else or on myself—which I contemplated seriously.

Although Whit's involuntary removal as head of the project and David's involuntary transfer to another department are not uncommon in large corporations, they are extreme events in almost any other work setting. In most occupations burnout is not caused by such dramatic single events, but rather by a slow and gradual process of erosion.

David, Whit, and Susan had very different managerial positions within their organizations, yet there was a common thread in the causes of their burnout. David was a first-line manager with most pressures coming from above; the greatest stress (dramatically demonstrated by his transfer) was lack of say about his work. Whit, as a middle manager, felt pressured both by his employees and by top management. These pressures, once again, made him feel that he didn't have control over his work. (His removal from heading the project proved he was indeed right.) Susan, who was an executive director, with supposedly a great deal of freedom and authority, actually felt pressures from all directions, and all at once. The greatest stress was the lack of political power and the bureaucratic interference which made it impossible for her to do her work the way she wanted to do it.

Dan Gowler and Karen Legge, who wrote about managerial stress, see it as the product of three factors: uncertainty of outcome, importance of that outcome to the individuals, and the individuals' perception of their ability to influence that outcome.[2] All three uncertainties are clearly related to lack of control and autonomy. One source of uncertainty and stress that Gowler and Legge see as common to many managerial jobs stems from a lack of clear criteria for success. In many organizations, managerial success is equated with implementation of organizational objectives such as increased profits or business expansion. Attainment of these objectives, however, may depend on external factors—like the health of the national economy, the availability of raw materials, and the development of new technology—as much as on the skill of individual managers. Thus managers may feel unable to control their success through their own performance.

Susan, Whit, and David had in their work all three of these stress-producing factors. They had no control over the outcome of their work, that outcome was extremely important to them, and they felt powerless to influence it. In addition, all three felt that they had failed, even though according to objective criteria, two of them might have been seen as having accomplished impossible tasks, under the circumstances.

Whit, Susan, and David shared other common stresses in their jobs, stresses that are common to all managerial work, and are powerful causes of burnout. All three lacked the resources to get the work done the way they felt it should be done. All three lacked power to make (or influence) decisions affecting their work. All felt isolated and lacked a support network of colleagues who could be relied on when the stress at work got to be too much. All felt insufficiently appreciated and recognized for their work, and as a result were unable to derive from their work a sense of significance.

Susan and Whit had one other thing in common. Both of them can qualify for the title "workaholic." In recent years, the term "workaholism" has appeared frequently both in the popular and scientific literature. The term was coined by Wayne E. Oates, a priest and psychologist, in his 1971 book *Confessions of a Workaholic.*[3] It connotes addiction to work. Typically, workaholics are people for whom work has become a single, all-involving preoccupation. It is the only thing in life that seems to matter to them, the only thing that makes them feel alive. They invest all their time and energy in it, so there is little or nothing left for other people or activities.

Workaholics get their sense of "cosmic significance" from work, as most devoutly religious people get it from their religion. Since they don't need much besides work, many of them never marry, limiting themselves to relationships that won't interfere with their work. When they are forced for some reason (such as pressure from the corporation) to marry, unless their mates are also workaholics, sooner or later the demands of their mates for more time start a pattern of escape from home (coming to work early, leaving late, taking work home).

When both mates are workaholics, their involvement with each other is necessarily limited. Such couples may keep separate apartments, perhaps even in separate cities; they keep different hours and have different sets of friends. Their limited involvement in the marriage leaves them plenty of time to be involved in their careers.

Needless to say, burnout at work is a particularly traumatic event for a workaholic. Since marriage has been firmly relegated to second place, it can't provide the needed support during burnout. A first-line manager, burned out in his job and recently separated from his wife, says:

> I sat all through the night with a gun pointed at my head. I couldn't see a reason to live. My wife left me, and I couldn't blame her. I was really impossible to live with. She needed to get away to save her own sanity. And I felt like a total failure at my job. It all of a sudden

dawned on me that I was trying to do an impossible thing. I couldn't really change anything in the lives of the people I was responsible for. And besides, I no longer felt they deserved help. I couldn't believe I had sacrificed my marriage for them. What a stupid fool I'd been. . . . I felt all alone in the world, trapped in a corrupt and inefficient system . . . my whole life had been wasted. What reason was there for me to go on living?

Burnout is not always caused by external events as it was for Whit, David, and Susan. Sometimes burnout is triggered by a mid-career crisis. Like burnout, the mid-career crisis tends to happen to people who are highly motivated, with high ideals and enthusiasm. It happens particularly to people who have made their career choices at an early age. They start out convinced that as a corporate executive, a lawyer, a doctor, they will make a major contribution to society. By mid-career they realize that their contribution may be far smaller than they had hoped, or they begin to think that society doesn't deserve the sacrifice they are making. They start feeling empty and disillusioned, painfully aware of their mortality and the passage of time—time remaining and time spent.

Someone once said we should look at our lives as days of the week, with each day representing a decade. Well, these people suddenly look up from their work and discover it's Wednesday, or Thursday, or even Friday morning, and they say, "Wait a minute. This isn't what I want!" William Bridges describes it:

> When the dream has been gained, the vice-presidency, the book, the three kids and the handsome home—there is the moment of realization: "O.K., I've got it, now what?" And even: "Is *this* it? Is *this* the destination that I've sacrificed everything for?" The discrepancy between public image and private awareness can be excruciating at this point in life. And what of the person who didn't make it? The denied dream is the other gateway to reality. There one is faced with the nevers. "I guess I have to face the fact that I'm *never* going to be the head of the company . . . *never* going to be the parent of four happy, well-adjusted children." And with that acknowledgment comes the strange sense that one has been chasing a carrot on a stick, that the sunset into which one was riding was painted on the other end of the train car.[4]

Burnout is less likely to happen, and if it happens is less likely to be devastating, if people are aware of its danger, are prepared for it, and take active responsibility for doing something about it. One way to do that is by making the crucial events in our lives as concrete as possible. In our workshops, we ask people to do the following: "List side by side on a piece of paper what is demanded of you at work and what is demanded of you at home. Then consider to what extent these demands are essential, current, legitimate, and reasonable, and contemplate your priorities in responding to them." Let's take the example of Dale, who is a 40-year-old corporate executive for one of the *Fortune* 500 companies on the East Coast, and who has two young children. Dale's lists look like this:

WORK

1. Be a brilliant manager.
2. Don't make any mistakes.
3. Help make the corporation the best that it can be.
4. Keep up with new information about the business.
5. Bring in new business.
6. Pal around with other executives without making it seem like malingering.
7. Get along with top management without making it seem like toadying.
8. Be a good boss to the secretary and the back office support staff.
9. Dress appropriately.
10. Be entertaining, charming, someone other executives like and respect.
11. Be a team player and represent the corporation well.

HOME

1. Be a good husband and father.
2. Support my family financially and of course emotionally.
3. Take care of the yard.
4. Be a role model for the kids and a good disciplinarian.
5. Share chores.

You will notice not only that Dale has many more items in his work column, but that the work column is more specific and well thought out. We would wager that if we had asked him about any of the items on his work list—say, "How can you be a good boss to your secretary?"—Dale could tell us exactly what that meant, from being clear in his instructions, to taking her to lunch for National Secretary Week. But if we had asked him what it meant to be "a good role model" for his kids, it might have taken him quite some time to come up with an answer. This difference reflects a far deeper difference in priority and significance of these two spheres of life.

Dale felt that all the things he does at work are important and that he must exert a great deal of energy meeting these demands if he is going to get to the top of the corporate ladder, which is his paramount concern. Yet, after making the lists and scrutinizing them in a careful and honest manner, Dale realized that some of the demands he listed as imposed by his job were actually self-imposed. In other words, he was making demands on himself as a corporate executive, a boss, and a colleague far in excess of what the corporation expected of him.

Dale's experience is not unique. It tends to characterize high achievers: top-level executives, politicians, lawyers, doctors, scientists, who get involved from a very young age in demanding and ego-involving careers. Unfortunately, many of them don't stop to evaluate their self-imposed demands and priorities until it is too late. Typically, they start their careers very early. They work very hard to get the best possible position. Once they get that desired position they work very hard to be promoted and stay at the top. They typically also get married, and have children. But since their jobs receive highest priority, they rarely have time for their families. It usually takes a dramatic event to shake up this single-minded involvement with work. In our experience, the dramatic event is almost invariably a negative one, such as a major failure, a life-threatening illness, an accident, or a divorce. In all cases, the precipitating event makes them realize that achieving their initial goals may not, in fact, be as fulfilling as they had once assumed.

WHAT MAKES A MANAGER MORE OR LESS LIKELY TO BURN OUT?

Do you always move, walk, eat rapidly?

Do you feel (and openly show) impatience with the rate at which most events take place? Do you find it difficult to restrain yourself from hurrying the speech of others?

Does it bother you to watch someone else perform a task you know you can do faster?

Do you often try to do two things at once (dictate while driving or read business papers while you eat)?

If you answered yes to any of these questions, according to Meyer Friedman and Ray H. Rosenman, you may fall into the Type A behavior pattern.[5] Type A behavior characterizes the high achievers who are disproportionately represented among corporate executives. This behavior is characterized by competition, speed, and high energy. Type A managers usually try to do several things at once, take work home, and exhibit hostile and aggressive behavior toward the people around them. Type B managers, on the other hand, are less ambitious and competitive, and more relaxed—but their performance is generally as good. Type A people identify with their work too much, and consequently view competitive situations as threats to their self-esteem. The perceived threat at work causes feelings of anxiety and hostility. Type A behavior is expressed fully only in situations such as stressful work that demands and even encourages this kind of behavior. Studies of burnout in organizational settings suggest that Type A behavior is highly correlated with burnout.[6]

In her recent Ph.D dissertation, Anna-Maria Garden argues that Jungian personality types can tell us a great deal about burnout.[7] She compared corporate managers to people in the helping professions in order to identify the different personality traits that are most related to burnout in the two occupational groups.

The premise of the Jungian theory of psychological types most relevant to her work is that one is either a "feeling type" or a "thinking type."[8] People who are oriented to life primarily through thinking typically develop strong powers of analysis, objectivity in weighing events with regard to logical outcomes, and a tough-minded scepticism. People whose orientation is primarily feeling typically develop a sensitivity to other people's feelings and needs. They have a need for affiliation, a capacity for warmth, and a desire for harmony.

The distinction between feeling and thinking types also reflects the differences in the experience of burnout in the human services and in corporate management. On one level these types differ in maintaining a personal versus an impersonal stance toward others; on another level they differ in terms of the priority given to achievement and work as compared to people. Indeed, the human services literature on burnout focuses on how burnout affects attitudes toward people, while in the managerial literature the focus is on how job stress affects attitudes toward work success and achievement.

In her study, Garden compared 194 mid-career managers to 81 nurses. She discovered, as expected, that the dominant psychological function in the sample of managers was thinking, while in the sample of nurses it was feeling. She further discovered that as a result of burnout, feeling types were likely to lose concern for others and become more hostile, wile thinking types were likely to become more concerned with others. Yet it is feeling types who, by definition, are more concerned with others. In other words, the orientation that is typically associated with a particular type is also correlated with burnout for that type. In our own work, we found that burnout resulted in similar differences in attitudes toward people when we compared individuals who described themselves as mainly motivated by a need for self-expression and self-fulfillment (most of them in different areas of business and science) to individuals who described themselves as mainly motivated by people (most of them in the human services).[9] Results showed that the more burned out self-motivated people were, the greater importance they attributed to having social support. We interpreted this finding as indicating that support is important to them only when they burn out. But since they did not bother to develop support networks, they didn't have these networks when they needed them most. For people-oriented individuals, support was always important, so they had more support networks available to them when they burned out, and they knew better how to use them as buffers against burnout.

In Garden's research, the more burned out thinking types were, the lower was their achievement orientation. For feeling types there was no correlation between burnout and achievement orientation. Garden interprets these findings as suggesting that the process of burnout is different for the two Jungian types, even though the end state is similar. As a result of burnout, the thinking and feeling types become more like one another. What happens is a lessening of the characteristic orientation of that type and in particular a loss of what previously distinguished one type from another. If feeling types were previously distinguished from thinking types by their caring for others, then this ceases to be a distinguishing or a defining characteristic. If thinking types were previously distinguished from feeling types by their need to achieve, then this ceases to be a distinguishing or defining characteristic.

The literature on executive burnout, similarly, emphasizes the loss of ambition, enthusiasm, and commitment as the primary characteristic of executive burnout: "The challenge becomes humdrum, the bounce goes out of the step, the drive lessens, the will to excel ceases."[10] "Those working within a corporation may suffer from negative thinking and believe that their organization has disappointed them. Their comments are replete with negative, cynical and depressed overtones."[11]

Another part of Garden's work addressed the causes of burnout in thinking as compared to feeling types. She discovered that mental demands at work were correlated with burnout for the thinking types but not for the emotional types. Emotional demands at work, on the other hand, were correlated with burnout for the feeling types.

This is an intriguing, counterintuitive finding—burnout seems to be most strongly associated with the kind of demand each type is naturally adapted to deal with. Why should this be? Why aren't thinking-type managers more burned out by the emotional demands of their work than by the mental demands it imposes on them? Why aren't feeling-type helping professionals more burned out by the mental demands of their work than by the emotional demands the work imposes?

The reason, we would argue, is that for thinking-type managers, mental achievements are expected to provide a sense of meaning to life. For professionals in the human services, who see themselves as "feelings experts," on the other hand, achievements in the sphere of human emotions are expected to provide a sense of cosmic significance. For both types, demands that can not be met in their own area of expertise are most stressful because they make them feel they have failed in the areas which they identify with most and value most. The failure is not only in the task, it is in themselves and in their existential quest.

The Israeli sociologist Aaron Antonovsky proposed a new approach to "health, stress, and coping."[12] Central to his approach is what he calls "the sense of coherence"—a general attitude characteristic of those who consistently enjoy good health—that the world is comprehensible; that one's own life is meaningful, orderly, and reasonably predictable; and that one participates in the shaping of one's destiny.

A related personality dimension that seems to have particular significance for burnout in management is "hardiness." Salvador Maddi and Suzanne Kobasa tried to find out why people who have similar work and life stresses have different likelihoods of getting ill. They studied two groups of managers who were similar in education level, income, family situation, and life and work stresses, yet were significantly different in terms of their frequencies of illness.[13] The managers who didn't get sick despite all their stresses were termed "hardy." They had three identifying characteristics:

1. Involvement—as opposed to alienation—and curiosity toward their environment, which in their eyes always seemed interesting and significant.
2. Control—as opposed to helplessness—and belief in their ability to influence their environment with their ideas, words, and actions.
3. Love of challenge—as opposed to indifference—and view of change as natural and even necessary for growth and development.

All three elements are important for effective coping: By having an optimistic outlook, seeing change as natural and enjoyable, and actively attempting to understand as much as possible about all changes so that the greatest benefit can be derived from them, hardy managers make stressful events less stressful. The three components are interrelated; each depends on and affects the other two. When a hardy manager tries to influence an event (control), the effort usually entails curiosity about the possible consequences (involvement), and a desire to learn everything that can bring about personal growth (challenge).

In contrast, nonhardy managers tend to see their environment as boring, insignificant, and threatening; they feel helpless against powerful forces larger than themselves; they believe that life is best when not disturbed by change; they don't believe that growth is important or possible, and they are passive in their interaction with the world. When stressful events occur, nonhardy managers see little basis for optimism, or for attempting to change the situation. Since their personality does not provide them with an adequate buffer, the stresses have a direct impact on their health.

For example, in response to a threat of being fired, the hardy manager not only tries to change the decision, and to look into other job possibilities (both actions expressing control), but she also tries to find out about the reasons for the decision (involvement) and sees in it an important opportunity to examine the future of her career (challenge). In response to the same threat, the nonhardy manager can't decide what to do (helplessness), tries to avoid the problem by doing other things to keep his mind away from it (alienation), and sees it as a change for the worse (threat).

In our studies we found these same three elements—control, involvement, and challenge—to be important buffers against burnout. But our focus was not on these elements as personality characteristics, as it was for Kobasa and Maddi, but rather as features in the environment that prevent or enhance burnout.

Thus, we view control as the degree of autonomy given to workers to do the work the way they think it should be done. We view involvement as the individual's experience that the work she or he is doing has significance. And we view challenge as the opportunities for growth provided by the work. (You may recall that we discussed these features in Chapter 2 as part of the universal work expectations.) In other words, the same factors that buffer against burnout in the work environment also protect against burnout in the person. What we are arguing is that the degree of hardiness is not necessarily an innate trait; rather, we see it as a teachable way of interacting with the environment. Viewing hardiness as a way of approaching the world *that is learned,* and thus can be unlearned and relearned, offers some hope for those unlucky enough to have been "born nonhardy."

And how does one learn to be hardy: The same way one learns any way of dealing with the world. Culture, it turns out, has a lot to do with it. Different cultures socialize people to perceive the world around them differently, and cope with it differently. Let us look at direct versus indirect coping styles—each of which can be effective in the proper circumstances. In some cultures (such as Israel), there is an emphasis on a direct and active coping style; in others (such as Japan), indirect coping is valued more. These cultural differences have a big influence on the likelihood of burnout.

The comparison between Israelis and Americans provides a dramatic example. Both cultures present the individual with a generally stressful environment but, as anyone who spent time in both countries knows, life in Israel is considerably more stressful than life in America. There are tensions between groups of different cultural origins, different religious beliefs, and different political affiliations. Given the physical and the emotional stresses Israelis face because

of constant warfare and a long military service, and the severe economic difficulties posed by spiralling inflation rates during the years
when we conducted our research, we might have expected that
burnout would be higher in Israel than in America. The data, however, show that Israeli managers report less burnout in their work
than American managers.[14] It is noteworthy that the same results
were found in all the studies in which samples from the two countries were compared. These studies, which involved comparable
groups in terms of sex, age, and profession investigated burnout on
the job and at home. Their data confirmed the same unexpected
result—Israelis report less burnout than Americans.[15] We can think
of several reasons why this might be so:

- Israelis don't expect as much as Americans do to get a sense of
  significance from their work alone (they get it, more so than
  Americans, also from their families and country). Because the Israeli culture does not build as many unrealistic expectations from
  work as the American culture does, Israelis are less likely to be
  disappointed.
- Israelis tend to cope with stress in a more confrontive (active and
  direct) way than do Americans (Americans tend to be more avoid-
  ance-seeking than Israelis, and more dependent on drugs and alcohol.) The Israeli way is better because it is more likely to produce changes.
- The problems of existence in Israel, on the personal and the national level, are so immense that work problems tend to seem
  trivial by comparison. Americans, on the other hand, live in a
  relatively benign culture, where work problems loom large.
- The social structure in Israel provides more support for the individual, and Israelis' social support networks are more stable and
  protect people better from stress.
- The one-month-a-year military service gives the Israeli manager
  an important yearly vacation from work, a vacation that helps the
  manager "clear his head," and examine priorities from some distance.
- There are stronger social norms against admitting the existence
  of personal problems among Israelis. Because of such cultural
  sanctions Israelis are less likely than Americans to report burnout,
  even if they experience it to the same, or even higher degree.
- Israelis report, and experience, less burnout than Americans, not
  in spite of their greater stress, but *because* of it. When an American manager fails in his work, the focus of the blame is most often

dispositional: "How could I have been so dumb?" When an Israeli fails, on the other hand, the blame is assigned most often to the situation or the system: "those stupid bureaucrats," "the lousy government," "the unreasonable time demanded for army duty," or "the crazy economy." Israelis are least likely to blame themselves for failure. Their networks of family and friends also tend to reinforce that outward-directed focus of blame: "Of course it's not your fault. No one could have succeeded under these conditions."

There is no reason to think that Israelis are constitutionally different from Americans. We can say, therefore, that Israeli managers, because of their situation, have learned to deal with problems in a different way. They may have learned how to be "hardy" and defeat burnout.

The comparison between Israelis and Americans brings us back to the discussion of the individual differences mediating between the effects of the environment and the experience of burnout, and to the conclusion that burnout depends on the interaction between people and their environment—as they perceive it and interpret it.

We have discussed three personality dimensions that mediate between the objective world and people's interpretation of it—Type A behavior, "thinking versus feeling" as a primary mode for dealing with the world, and hardiness. There is another dimension that, like the previous three, has special relevance for people in management—motivation for success. This motivation is an implied characteristic for all three personality types, yet it has not been addressed directly.

David C. McClelland, a Harvard psychologist who studied achievement motivation, showed that men with high needs to achieve are more successful, especially in the business world, than those with low achievement needs.[16] McClelland's achievement syndrome includes moderate risk-taking strategies; that is, high achievers are neither too risky nor too cautious. Similarly, people with higher achievement motivation show energetic instrumental activity to attain goals, a willingness to take personal reponsibility for actions, a desire for knowledge about the results of their actions, and a tendency for long-range planning. Our own work suggests that people who employ these strategies in their work, especially with bureaucratic organizations, are less likely to experience burnout.

Our studies also showed that a sense of success and achievement is negatively correlated with burnout.[17] Successful professionals tend to see themselves more positively and to develop less burnout; those who have the frustration of failure are more likely to burn out. The negative correlation between success and burnout does not imply causality. It could be that failure causes burnout; it could be that burnout increases the likelihood of failure: it could also be that certain qualities in an individal or a situation promote both burnout *and* failure at work.

Success and failure are not always judged by objective absolute criteria. Individuals' perceptions of their achievements occasionally have very little to do with objective reality. For example, if an MBA student got 92 percent correct answers on an exam, we might consider that very successful. But if his three best friends got 97 percent on the same exam, he might consider himself a failure. Some people may be successful by others' standards and yet view themselves as failures because they are comparing themselves to someone above them in ability or achievements. It is unfortunate that, for these people, the positive effect of a real success is emotionally lost, since each success can serve as a powerful buffer against burnout. Accordingly, it is important for individuals to learn to acknowledge and indeed bask in their own success before pushing on to other challenges. But there are pressures, such as competition, that subvert this experience of success.

Like our MBA student, people who are caught up in a highly competitive game do not judge their accomplishments relative to their skill or effort but relative to other people's success. They do not evaluate their achievements relative to their previous achievements or to their expectations but to the achievement of others. For example, a successful lawyer told us, "This year I made twenty percent more than last year, but my partners still made a lot more than me." A professor of organizational development said, "I have a nice list of publications and a good prospect of getting tenure in the department, but a friend who graduated with me already has an international scientific reputation. I'll never be as good as he is." Such comparisons can be self-destructive: the achievement is not enjoyed to its fullest because its importance is diminished relative to others who achieve more. The obsession with competition is a stress that some people never overcome. If the achievement of money, fame, or professional excellence is compared not to one's own aspirations and needs but to those of others, no level of success will suffice. This can only add to the pressures that produce burnout.

The drive for achievement can also be self-destructive when it dominates a person's life, as witness this statement by a middle-aged ulcerated executive:

> For years I have been completely immersed in my career. I worked days and nights, weekends and holidays, to establish and develop my private business and to make more money. Almost all of a sudden I realized that I do not know my wife and my children. I don't have any real friends because our social activities were always targeted around potential clients or business partners. I feel as if life passed me by, when I was too busy with the wrong things.

This preoccupation with work can lead to a double pressure: the push for more achievement and the absence of the other rewards in life.

When people are extremely achievement-oriented or future-oriented, attaining success is usually not associated with happiness but rather with disappointment. For example, we once encountered a scientist who worked hard to reach his prominent position and who made a discovery that brought him sudden recognition; he then became severely depressed. In effect, he seemed to be saying to himself: "Is that it? Is that what I have worked all these years for?" In a life dominated by the future, success satisfies only for a moment, and this moment is painful because it makes the price of success evident.

So we see that success and achievement are positive aspects of life that can alleviate burnout and provide the person with a sense of fulfillment. But these are subjective experiences and do not necessarily reflect reality. When the drive for success becomes all-encompassing, it can be a source of stress and burnout. In order to turn success into a positive rather than a negative outcome, we must learn to take some time to relax and enjoy successful accomplishments and to make that experience part of ourselves before moving on to meet the next challenge.

This may be easier said than done for some people. And it seems that these kinds of people are disproportionately represented in the corporate world. Type A people are a good case in point. They know that they "should be able to relax" that they "should enjoy one success before moving to the next challenge" but they can't make those "shoulds" happen. "I'm just not that kind of a person," they reason, "and there is nothing I or anyone else can do about it."

Now, while it is true that being hard-driving, ambitious, and success-oriented may make relaxing difficult, it definitely is not true that there is nothing one can do about it. A fascinating demonstration of this was provided by Type A people. When Drs. Meyer Friedman and Ray H. Rosenman published the first medical statistics regarding Type A behavior (based on thirty years of research), their conclusion was clear and straightforward—Type A behavior leads to premature heart disease.[18] Several years later, the statistics of coronary heart attacks indicated that there was no longer a correlation between Type A behavior and premature heart disease. Why? Type As learned that being in good physical health reduces the likelihood of heart attacks, so they started jogging and exercising with their characteristic vim and vigor, and succeeded in beating their odds. A particular personality structure may make someone more likely to behave in a particular way in response to a particular situation, but it in no way guarantees it.

The discussions of achievement motivation, hardiness, the Jungian types, and Type A behavior focused on psychological factors in executive burnout. Yet throughout this book we have argued that a focus on the environment is more beneficial than a focus on the individual. In support of our contention, research findings accumulated over the past ten years have shown few significant and consistent personality correlates of burnout but many significant and consistent job, work setting, and organizational correlates of burnout.[19]

As we noted before, an emphasis on the environment does not imply that personality traits have no effect. Personality variables play a major role in the choice of a career and in mediating the stresses that come with it. When we look at the organizational environment as a given, differences in personality—of the kind we discussed in this chapter—determine the likelihood of different people to burn out. If, on the other hand, we look at people's personalities as a given, differences in the organizational environment—of the kind we discussed in Chapter 2 and will discuss further in Chapter 9—determine the likelihood that all the people in a particular organization will burn out. Since we view environments as more amenable to change than people's personalities, we prefer to direct our efforts to work environments.

FOUR

Burnout in the Helping Professions

SUE was 32, bright, warm, sensitive. She wanted to "help people" and to "make the world a better place," but, although she received a master's degree in social welfare, nothing in her background or her formal training prepared her for the stresses she would face in her work.

Sue's first job was in a residential program for psychiatric patients who were making the transition from hospital life back into the community. After three years Sue felt she had to leave the job. "I got tired of working with chronic patients," she said. "I was still interested in being a therapist but there was a limit to the amount of therapy that could be done with these patients. Work with them involved mostly maintaining them on medication and helping them to manage in the community. They were very needy people, very dependent, and it was draining. I did see some changes with a few of the young clients, but for the most part the improvement I saw was minuscule." Sue felt she was ready for a change.

Sue accepted a job as family counselor for a police department.

Her unit was responsible for responding to domestic disturbance calls and for training police officers in family crisis intervention. "In the beginning it was really fascinating. It was exciting, pioneering territory. We had a lot of publicity. There were TV shows, newspaper articles, and a film. But there were also many problems.

Sue felt that she needed to distance herself from some of the situations she worked with. "Part of it was in self-protection because some of the things were so grim. I saw so *much* horrible stuff. Not only domestic violence, but child abuse and horrible ways that people lived, going into filthy homes, seeing so many crazy people who weren't coping. It was just too much. After a while I had to shut some of it off."

Sue felt frustration and futility.

> The situations started looking so much alike to me. I could never see changes. It was always the same people, in the same situations. I would get angry when I'd go in. After a while, I stopped listening. I stopped being empathetic. I had to lose my compassion in order to survive emotionally. It wasn't a job where you got many thanks from the clients. It was a vicious circle; because the more angry I became, the less I felt like putting out in the counseling sessions, so of course the less happened with the clients.

Sue also felt isolated and frustrated on her job. She felt there was no flexibility and no encouragement of personal development by the department or by her boss. The atmosphere in the office was one of suspicion; staff members were reporting each other and Sue felt betrayed by people she thought were her friends. "I was so upset I got to the point that I refused to associate with anyone on the staff. I saw things that were wrong and unethical, things that had to do with basic values that were more important to me than anything else. It was very disturbing to me, but I was getting no support from the staff or the department. I felt alone in it. That was the hardest part."

After two years Sue noticed the signs of burnout. Her response was to work harder. She started teaching one course each quarter at a community college. "I had to get some rewards so I could feel like I was competent in some way. I derived a lot of gratification from my teaching." Teaching involved much time, little money, and no security, but there were intrinsic rewards. "I could see students learning and getting excited. I was teaching things that I enjoyed talking about." She tried to balance these rewards against the stress of her job. But with two jobs she had little time off. "One of the patterns I've always had is that when things are going on that I can't cope with, or don't want to face, I get even busier. I would work the whole day, teach from seven to ten, and get back home at eleven at night too tired and too depressed to sleep."

Living this way increased Sue's burnout. "I didn't want one more person to ask anything of me. Instead of listening to my friends and trying to be helpful I would feel like screaming. It seemed like I cried the whole time. I was really depressed."

In her work Sue tried to avoid contact with her clients.

> Sometimes I would be late for home appointments. I would make stops on my way to home visits and do errands that had nothing to do with my work. I sometimes spaced out during interviews with clients and I started referring people to other agencies or counselors. I would have a negative attitude before I even went in; I would be very curt, with no warmth at all. In retrospect I think that I was fighting to create this distance so the clients wouldn't like me. I thought that if I wasn't helpful and I wasn't sympathetic, when I asked if they wanted another appointment, they would say no.

One of the ways Sue dealt with her burnout was humor. "I felt that if I couldn't at least laugh at myself and my work, I was really in trouble. So I did a lot of it. I would make fun of the clients, not maliciously, but as a kind of catharsis. This constantly got me into trouble."

Sue felt she could not take any more, and after four years with the police department she quit her job. She had to sort out what she wanted to do with her life. She knew she was burned out as a public servant. "I don't have any more to give to needy, dependent, victimized people. I have done my stint as a 'do-gooder.' I have really paid my dues." Sue wanted to use her teaching and analytical skills. She wanted to work in pleasant surroundings with people who enjoyed their work. She looked for work in a company that encouraged creativity and was both supportive and challenging. After a long search, she found such a job.

Sue's case presents many of the elements that characterize burnout of professionals in the human services. She chose social welfare because she wanted to help people in need and make the world a better place to live in. She thought that this kind of work would give her life a sense of meaning. As is typical, she did not receive any formal preparation for the inevitable job stresses. Sue burned out on her first job after three years and on her second job after two years. This time period before burnout has been reported by many of the human service professionals with whom we have worked.

The causes of Sue's burnout are common. In her first job burnout was mainly a result of the futility of working with needy and chronically ill people and seeing little change or improvement; in other words, doing work that has no impact, no significance. In the second job it resulted from the hopeless situations she encountered daily and the interpersonal conflicts on the job. Both of these are frequent causes of burnout, because they deprive the professional of a sense of meaning in the work itself and in the interactions with other professionals who can otherwise be a social support network. Sue's responses to the experience of burnout are typical: the initial flight to "workaholism" ("Maybe it is my fault, because I'm not working hard enough. Maybe if I work harder I'll get from the work what I'm not getting from it now.") and the subsequent exhaustion, emotional attrition, anger at co-workers, and resentment toward clients. She felt she had paid her dues as a "do-gooder." This is also common among many formerly idealistic human service professionals. Often they turn to teaching as a way to replenish themselves; the rewards of facilitating change and growth seem more accessible in a teaching career, and thus more likely to provide the professional with a sense of meaning. We stress the typicality of Sue's experience to emphasize that it was primarily the emotional demands imposed by her work, and not personal idiosyncracies, that caused her burnout.

Common Causes of Burnout
in the Human Services

In modern industrial societies professional organizations perform many of the functions traditionally met by the extended family or the community. This is particularly true in the treatment of personal and interpersonal problems. The result is a large number of medical, educational, social, and psychological services. These human services are performed by millions of professionals who share three basic characteristics: (1) they perform emotionally taxing work; (2) they share certain personality characteristics that made them choose human service as a career; and (3) they share a "client-centered" orientation. These three characteristics are the classic antecedents of burnout.

In the human service professions, people work with others in emotionally demanding situations over long periods of time. The professionals are exposed to their clients' psychological, social, and physical problems and are expected to be both skilled and personally concerned.

A job in which a person helps others involves a certain degree of stress. The specific degree and kind of stress depend on the particular demands of that job and on the resources available to the professional. Each occupation has its unique pressures, anxieties, and conflicts inherent to the work itself and to the context in which the work is done.

Medical personnel encounter some intensely emotional situations. These can be especially difficult among physicians. According to Harold Lief and Renee Fox, who studied the psychological basis of medical practice, these emotion-laden experiences include "exploring, examining, and cutting into the human body; dealing with fears, anger, sense of helplessness, and despair of patients; meeting emergency situations; accepting the limitations of medical science in dealing with chronic or incurable disease; being confronted with death itself."[1] Another source of stress for medical professionals is the knowledge that they are going to fail to conquer death and disease. Other stresses shared by doctors and nurses include the fear of contracting disease by contact with contagious patients, talking to patients about marital and sexual problems, and carrying out physical examinations.

As Dr. Daniel Federman, the chairman of Stanford's Department of Medicine, described it: "Within a few minutes you are granted physical access to the patient with an intimacy and a potential for embarrassment unique in human relationships. The patient offers you vulnerability, accepting medication from you, physical abuse, even the ultimate subservience, the unconsciousness of general anesthesia, and physical alteration of the body through surgery."[2]

Dr. Donald Oken, Chairman of Psychiatry at the State University of New York, noted that providing medical services requires the professional to be regularly exposed to the most forbidden aspects of human functioning, including the sight, sound, and touch of all parts of the nude body and its products, even in private or unpleasant states. Doctors and nurses are also exposed to the most personal intimacies and conflicts and are frequently the focus of intense, primitive transference reactions, both affectionate and hostile, to which they dare not respond in kind.[3]

Teachers burn out at all levels of the educational system, from kindergarten to college. One of the causes of burnout shared by many educators is the assumption that if students do not learn it is because the teacher did not teach. This assumption is frequently false and is the basis of unrealistic expectations that educators share with students, parents, administrators, and the public. These expectations are a source of frustration, guilt, and a sense of failure.

A second stress for many teachers is maintaining discipline in the classroom. Nationwide studies show that since the 1970s classroom murders have increased by 18 percent, rapes by 40 percent, robberies by 37 percent, and physical assaults on teachers by 77 percent.[4] In 1975 a Senate subcommittee on juvenile delinquency reported that vandalism and violence in school were continuing to increase, annual destruction of school properties exceeded $600 million, and 70,000 classroom teachers reported serious injuries from physical assault by students. The result for teachers in inner-city schools, where the problem of classroom violence is most prevalent, may be "teacher's combat neurosis."[5]

Teachers may also have to deal with psychological and emotional stress. At all levels of the education system teachers face uninterested, unmotivated students. The teachers may feel alone in their struggle to maintain discipline and minimal standards of education without the support of parents or administration. These problems are particularly painful for those idealistic teachers who see their major role as that of educators but find themselves instead policing, testing, and physically managing their students.

In many social service occupations the danger of burnout and emotional exhaustion results from the constant demand to give emotionally on the job. As Alfred Kadushin, a leading social work scholar, noted, the flow of emotional supplies goes only one way— from the workers to the client—and may lead to the emotional depletion in the workers. The most important tool for professionals providing psychological help is the professionals themselves. Workers may feel that failure with a client reflects both on their competence as technicians and on their competence as people.[6]

Jobs that are closely allied to life may make the separation of work from other areas of life exceptionally difficult. The interpenetration of life and work, according to Kadushin, is one of the most significant occupational problems faced by the worker dealing with emotionally evocative experiences. Exposure to others' intense feelings is a stress peculiar to the task of extending psychological help.[7] It is, in a sense, an occupational hazard.[8] When the emotional stresses inherent in providing social and psychological help are not acknowledged and dealt with, they often lead to burnout.

All work with people involves some degree of stress. Certain categories of human services, such as medical, educational, and social-psychological services, share particular kinds of emotional stresses. Specific occupations within each of these categories have their unique stresses.

For Sue, whom we met at the beginning of this chapter, the main emotional pressure in her job as a family counselor resulted from witnessing domestic violence. This pressure was compounded by the fact that she could not change the destructive living conditions of the families she saw.

Nurses who work in children's leukemia wards experience great emotional stress in dealing daily with the pain of their young patients. They feel helpless against the unfairness of the childrens' inevitable death. Nurses who work with chronic patients talked about the emotional stress of the right-to-die issue. One nurse told of hurrying with emergency equipment to fight for the life of an 87–year-old woman who had previously begged to be allowed to die. Dialysis workers discussed the difficulty of accepting patients' decisions to give up on life. A teacher of blind, deaf, and retarded children talked about the drain involved in working with youngsters who show little progress. "After months of teaching Sandy to tie her shoe laces, she had an epileptic seizure and forgot everything," recounted the teacher. A priest who had survived a tornado told of having to explain God's will to the mourners in his parish, when he himself felt he could not understand it. A policeman talked about his helpless rage after visiting the home of an abused child. He said he knew he was leaving the child in danger, but there was nothing he could do legally to prevent it.

In each of these jobs the emotional stress is inherent because the work is with people. Yet each "people profession" has its own unique stresses that contribute to burnout.

Another source of stress stems from the special characteristics of the professionals themselves. Most times those who choose to help others as a profession are individuals who are particularly sensitive toward the needs of others. If emotional arousal is a taxing experience for any human being, it is particularly disruptive to people who choose such work expecting it to give meaning to their lives. These people tend to have especially great empathy to the suffering of others.

Occupational identity can be enhanced by the homogeneity of people selecting an occupation. The nature of the occupational task acts as a screening device, attracting people with particular kinds of personality attributes. Most human service professionals (as we saw in the discussion of the Jungian types in the previous chapter) are feeling types and are essentially humanitarian. Their dominant approach is to help people in trouble. They tend to be oriented more toward people than toward things.[9] Social workers, for instance, tend to value themselves most as sympathetic, understanding, unselfish, and helpful to others.[10] In almost every encounter we had with human service professional, we asked participants to list their reasons for choosing their profession. With almost no exception, whatever their occupation, their lists included such items as "I like people," "I am a people's kind of person," "All my life I wanted to work with people."

People who enter human service careers have other traits that make them vulnerable to the emotional stresses inherent to their professions. For example, a high degree of empathy can hamper people who choose to work with children and the elderly. Aides in homes for the elderly must deal with the thought, "This could be my mother" or "What if this happens to me?" Professionals working with children often report the emotional pain associated with the thought, "That could have been my child." They also must face their limitations in helping suffering or dying children. Some professionals who work with child abuse have had personal experiences that motivated their choice of career. Similarly people working with alcoholics are sometimes themselves recovered alcoholics or had an alcoholic parent. This personal history serves to intensify both their empathy and their pain.

A third cause of burnout is the "client-centered" orientation that characterizes human service professions almost exclusively.

In a client-centered orientation, the focus is on the people receiving service. The professionals' role of helping, understanding, and support is defined by the clients' needs. The professionals' presence is justified only as long as they continue to serve. Feelings are legitimate only when expressed by the clients.

Most human relationships are symmetrical, but the therapeutic relationship (like parenthood) is not; it is complementary: the professionals give and the clients receive. Kadushin sees social service workers responding to a "dedicatory ethic" that elevates service motives.[11] In many of these professions, work is seen not as a job but as a calling, and the reward is supposed to be inherent in giving.

In scientific literature and course material relevant to human service fields, little attention is given to the emotional stresses experienced by the professionals. Instead the focus is almost exclusively on the recipients of services and their problems. Thus, in training, the students learn the implicit lesson that it is illegitimate for them to have needs while in the professional role. In her book *Reality Shock*, Marlene Kramer, a nursing professor, writes about the devastating impact work has on unprepared novice nurses.[12] The reality shock often results in an induction crisis, and turnover is particularly high in the first few months on the job.[13]

Training schools deal almost exclusively with theoretical material, and traditionally no attention has been given to developing skills for dealing with people or with the stresses experienced by the professionals. More recently, as a result of widespread information about burnout, there has been a trend to provide practitioners with more concrete skills and practical training.[14] And yet there is still not enough attention given to the stresses the workers should expect and how to deal with them. Even in modern, more enlightened, training manuals in which the professionals are asked to engage in role-taking activities (taking the role of the client as a way of building empathy), these training exercises are almost never directed toward building empathy for the plight of the professionals who are forever giving and never receiving.

The absurdity of an orientation that is exclusively client centered was dramatically demonstrated in a case reported by Martin Lipp in his book *The Wounded Healer*.[15] It was the case of a psychiatrist who committed suicide, which, statistically, is not that unusual. But it was a shock to all his friends and especially to his colleagues who, despite their expertise in recognizing depression, did not notice anything unusual about his behavior prior to the suicide. He was young, at the prime of his life. Even though he had been through a painful divorce, he seemed to be doing well. He was very successful professionally, and a brilliant future lay ahead of him. No one suspected he was as depressed as his suicide note indicated. The only people who seemed to have any indication of what he was going through were his patients. One patient said she had noticed that he was upset and sensed that something was very wrong. When she asked him about it, his response was to smile at her gently and say that her job was to look after herself, not after him. Even at his most desperate hour he could not break the client-doctor relationship and take the hand that was offered to rescue him.

A client-centered orientation defines an asymmetry in the therapeutic relationship and can become stressful for the professional providing help. Its effects are doubled when combined with the emotional intensity characterizing most human service work and with the selective sample of people who choose to work in the human services. And since all three elements are present in nearly all human service work, they make the process of burnout almost inevitable.

The Goal: Detached Concern

Human service professionals struggle to obtain "detached concern." Harold Lief and Renee Fox coined this term for a stance in which "the empathic physician is sufficiently detached or objective in his attitudes toward the patient to exercise sound medical judgment and keep his equanimity, yet he also has enough concern for the patient to give him sensitive understanding care." In this way "the patient, rather than just his liver, heart or even psyche, is the concern of the physician."[16]

Professions differ in the ideal balance between detachment and concern. Most people agree that it would be inappropriate for a bank teller to inquire what people intend to do with the money they withdraw from their accounts, but many people become distressed when a physician treats them primarily as their disease.

Detached concern is a balance that is hard to achieve and hard to maintain. There is the danger of becoming overly involved, losing objectivity, and therefore the ability to help. "Once you are in the shoes of your patient, you cannot possibly be of any help," said one clinical psychologist, "because he has been in his shoes all along, and obviously not done too well. In order to help you have to be able to see more and understand more than the person who seeks your help." At the same time, the opposite danger of complete detachment is always present and with it the loss of concern and the dehumanizing attitudes that characterize burnout. With excessive detachment there is not enough involvement to motivate successful help. Research has shown that the clients themselves also demand a certain balance between personal support and understanding on the one hand, and expertise, guidance, and decisiveness on the other.[17]

Within the same organization some professionals need to detach themselves more than others. For example, in one mental hospital, psychologists and social workers were burning out on the locked ward because relationships with patients were so difficult and rewards so minimal. One physician, however, loved working there. He said that the psychotic patients in their drugged state were easier for him to work with than his regular patients. "Usually I have to small-talk with patients and be careful about their feelings, which I hate. With these guys I didn't have to talk or be concerned about their feelings. I could concentrate on their sick organs which is really why I was there to begin with."

In our experience the most idealistic and highly committed "social servants" are the ones who have the greatest difficulty detaching themselves and as a result tend to burn out relatively soon. They end up detaching too much as a defense against the power of their own emotions. Psychologist Bruno Bettelheim describes that process:

> One becomes worried about being drawn into the maelstrom of the patient's anger, anxiety, despair; fear for one's own sanity emerges; one may even begin to question which of their delusions are delusions, and which may be reasonable. The most "natural" defense against this is a near automatic response of buttressing one's defenses to avoid the impact of such experiences; and of closing one's heart, if not one's mind, to those who apparently threaten to overwhelm us with the power of their emotions.[18]

Human service professionals may attempt to achieve the ideal balance of detached concern in many different ways. Some try physical withdrawal, some try emotional withdrawal, and some try mental withdrawal. Often people use elements of all three. Unfortunately, as the following examples show, the mode of detachment a professional uses for self-protection is frequently felt as dehumanizing by the recipients.

Physical Withdrawal

Some of the most difficult jobs are those in which professionals cannot distance themselves even after working hours. For many physicians and psychiatrists one of the drawbacks of private practice is that the distinction between job and private life cannot be maintained because they are always on call. One physician told us, "Everytime you hear the telephone ring at night, you think, 'Oh, no, I hope it's not a patient.' At times it seems like you can never even get away from your patient's problems for some peace and quiet for yourself." Some psychiatrists who could have made more money in private practice chose to work in a hospital setting because "at the end of the day I can close the door behind me and know that somebody else will take care of the emergency cases." Counselors and educators who live on the job tend to have unusually high rates of burnout. At residential treatment centers the turnover rate is typically very high. Often the centers are run democratically, and both staff and patients are involved in the therapeutic process day and night. Counselors cannot tolerate the emotional intensity and the lack of the time off, and burnout leads them to quit, often within one or two years.

Physical distancing also shows up during work hours. For example, a psychiatrist noticed that as he was burning out in his private practice, he used his desk as a barrier between himself and his clients. Many administrators who start a job with an "open-door" policy begin to close their doors when they feel imposed on; they develop a need to get away from everyone, to be alone and work. When they reach that stage they are more comfortable communicating with their staff in writing than in person, and try to do even that as infrequently as possible.

Another example of how people may avoid human interaction in their work is the professor who remained on campus during his sabbatical year to finish writing a book. To avoid disturbances he put a card on his office door bearing the name of a nonexistent person. It worked: no one knocked. Three years after his sabbatical the phony name is still on his door! Office hours by appointment only, a secretary to scrutinize visitors, and distance-creating furniture arrangements are a few of the techniques used by professionals to minimize physical involvement in stressful interactions.

Other professionals simply spend less time with their service recipients. Many cut to a minimum the time they spend in direct contact. For example, one pediatrician took as long as possible getting from her office to her first appointment in the morning. Because she was late for the first appointment she could justify cutting short any stressful encounter she had during the day. In a college counseling office counselors found every excuse to look into the students' files because the files were housed in an adjacent building and the walk was a welcome relief from encounters with students.

Two independent studies found that workers experiencing physical, emotional, and mental exhaustion tended to be consistently late for work, to take extended work breaks, and to have a high frequency of unexplained absences from work.[19] In mental health settings it was found that the longer workers have been in the field of mental health, the less they liked working with patients and the more custodial rather than humanistic their attitudes became.[20] Those who worked with schizophrenics in the past tried to avoid, as much as possible, direct contact with them. In one hospital, nurses who were burning out gradually spent more time socializing with other staff members and less time with patients. They became almost hostile when a patient approached them, seeing it as an intrusion into "their" time. A child-care worker told us she used her sick leave to get away from people in general and "knee-high people who talk in single syllables" in particular. Clerks in health and welfare departments started "cutting corners" in their interaction with clients by taking increasingly long lunch breaks. Taking longer breaks, spending more time on paperwork, leaving work early, or being absent are all examples of withdrawal by means of spending less time with clients.

Professionals also distance themselves physically from their clients by standing far away, avoiding eye contact, or keeping a hand on the doorknob. They communicate with clients in impersonal ways, such as superficial generalities and form letters.

Finally, a less common distancing technique was described by a consultant who said that when sitting in boring meetings with particularly difficult clients, she would develop "telescopic visions." She saw her clients as very small and far away, so far that it became impossible to hear what they said.

Emotional Withdrawal

When physical distancing is impossible, people who are burning out use emotional withdrawal. Lief and Fox found that during the first two years of medical school the primary problem for students is that of acquiring greater emotional detachment.[21] "To protect myself from my own emotions I feel like I am putting on emotional armor every time I walk into the emergency room," said a young intern. Other professionals who encounter clients' pain use similar modes of emotional detachment. In the case presented earlier, Sue distanced herself by "turning off" her compassion, empathy, and warmth, and by "spacing out" during interviews with clients.

A welfare department worker described her growing emotional detachment:

> When I started I was deeply involved in every aspect of the sixty families I had. I really cared and was supportive of everything that went on. But if you continue at this level of involvement you get to be crazy very soon. So I started to withdraw a bit and see things as the client's problem. I went from total involvement to a kind of standing back. In the end I developed a callousness towards the people I was working with. I was so emotionally detached that I might as well not have been there. I was earning money, but I didn't feel the work was part of my life.

In order to protect themselves from the emotional stresses of their work, some professionals make sharp distinctions between their jobs and their personal lives. One prison psychologist said that when he meets new people socially he refuses to tell them what his job is. In response to questions he only says, "I am a civil servant" or "I work for the state." A policeman said that he made an explicit agreement with his wife and friends not to "talk shop." He encounters crime and filth all day and wants none of that, not even talk, at home. Such emotional compartmentalization enables professionals to limit their occupational stress to the time and place of their work.

Although professionals detach themselves in self-defense to avoid overinvolvement, this emotional withdrawal may escalate and result in total detachment and the loss of concern for the recipients of their services. It is also difficult to turn on and off one's emotions at will, and as a result the detachment often spreads into relationships outside of work as well.

Mental Withdrawal

Mental withdrawal is a set of attitudes that protects service providers from overinvolvement and justifies detachment from the recipients of their services. In different ways these attitudes help the professional to see the other person as less human, to view the relationship with the other person in objective and analytic terms, and to reduce the intensity and scope of emotional arousal. One such attitude includes reliance on rules to define relationships with service recipients. For example, a parole officer, who was asked to co-sign a loan for a parolee as an indication of trust, found to her relief that there was a rule against it. That made it easier for her to say, "No, but it's nothing personal. It's the rule." A formerly enthusiastic teaching assistant in a large course said he burned out when the 313th student came to him after an exam asking for a change of grade. This student explained that his mother was seriously ill and that's why he had been upset and confused at the time of the test. He misunderstood the question, and really needed the extra three points, otherwise he would flunk the course and be kicked out of the university. Hearing this, the teaching assistant adopted a brusque manner said, "Sorry, but I can't change your grade. It's a university rule. . . . " He reduced his own emotional overload by making his response to the request impersonal and rule-governed.

The medical profession provides numerous examples of this mental detachment. Physicians, in order to deal with their feelings, tend to use intellectualization and place a premium on "pure rationality." A patient may become an interesting diagnostic problem rather than a human being in pain. Nurses who burn out become more technical and custodial; their primary concern may become the disease, not the patients.

Marcia Millman, a sociologist who studied the work of physicians, described medical work as demanding exceptional emotional risks because mistakes in the line of duty may cost human life.[22] To protect themselves, those in the medical profession have developed group techniques for justifying their errors and minimizing the appearance of injury to the patient. One of the best places to observe this collective rationalization, according to Millman, is the mortality conference, where patient deaths may be reviewed in such a way as to justify retrospectively decisions that physicians had made. Physicians may excuse their errors by blaming the patient: if a patient can be discredited as crazy, alcoholic, uncooperative, or otherwise undeserving, the responsibility for the medical error may be shifted off the physician. Collective rationalization and blaming the victim can be seen as protective devices used by physicians to defend themselves from the emotional stress of guilt about medical mistakes.

Mental withdrawal also shows up in the use of terminology. Generalizations enable professionals to detach themselves from individuals with whom they empathize; people they know individually become "deprived masses" and "sick and needy victims of society." Other terminology is more derogatory: one teacher called her students "monsters," a drug rehabilitation worker referred to her clients as "junkies" and a prison guard talked about the "animals" behind the locked gates of the prison. Another way of achieving distance from people's pain is to identify them by their problems rather than their names, such as the "root canal case" or "the kidney in room 202." Terminology enables professionals to deny the humanity of the recipients of their services and thus to minimize their emotional involvement.

Another way professionals defend themselves against emotional stress is humor. One example is the "sick" humor of medical students in particularly stressful situations such as the anatomy lab. According to Lief and Fox, medical students anxious about cadaver dissection generally give the cadaver on which they work, an amusing name such as "Elbow" or "Bones." This helps the students reduce the seriousness of "cutting into" or "taking apart" a human body.[23]

Many employees collect funny stories to tell about their clients. A woman who works in a boutique told how she and the other employees privately mock difficult customers. The two of us, after a demanding three-day workshop, found relief in hysterical laughter about ourselves, the participants, and the situation as a whole. Being able to joke and laugh about a stressful event reduces the tension and anxiety that the professional feels. It also serves to make the situation less serious and less overwhelming.

All the modes of detachment described above—physical, emotional, and mental—are used by professionals working with people to reduce the intensity of the emotional arousal inherent in their work. The detachment techniques are most useful when they aid the professional in achieving the ideal balance of detached concern. They become dysfunctional when used to an extreme and when they produce the dehumanizing attitudes associated with burnout. Unfortunately, even when detachment is useful as a self-protective device, it can make professionals less helpful to their clients. The *ideal* balance is not only desirable for the professional but is also preferred by the clients. Some balance can be attempted by situational mechanisms. For example, the professional who creates a very formal situation can afford to become emotional on occasion.[24] In Part Three we will introduce coping strategies that help professionals achieve relief from burnout in ways that do not diminish the quality of the service they provide for their clients. These coping strategies enable the professionals to replenish themselves emotionally by accepting their own needs as legitimate. Ultimately, it is effectiveness on the job that prevents burnout best.

People often turn to "trait" theories to explain the ills of society. They believe that antisocial behaviors are committed by people who are basically "bad." For example, a professional's indifferent, rude, or dehumanizing behavior may be attributed to such internal traits as coldness or cruelty. This interpretation is frequently erroneous. As we noted earlier, social psychological research has helped bring a more accurate and useful perspective to these problems by emphasizing situational attributes.[25] Rather than attributing behavior to a deficiency in character, we argue again that it is often more helpful to focus on environmental factors, both social and physical, that cause people to act in particular ways. Such an approach does not deny the importance of individual traits. Rather, it suggests that antisocial behavior may also have a strong situational component. Thus, although a person who behaves rudely may simply be a "rude person," it is more likely that he is an average person currently under pressure. If we view him as a rude person we can do little except to despair, avoid him, or get angry at him. If we think of him as a well-meaning person working under pressure, perhaps we can alleviate the pressure. Burnout is not a function of bad people who are cold and uncaring. It is a function of bad situations in which once-idealistic people must operate. It is then the situations that must be modified so that they promote, rather than destroy, human values.[26]

FIVE

Burnout in Bureaucratic Organizations

WORK for most people is central to life. For many in our secular society it is also a primary path for finding meaning in life. One-third of our waking lives is spent in work. Vocational roles define lifestyles, social networks, self-image, and general health and happiness. Albert Camus said, "Without work all life goes rotten. But when work is soulless, life stifles and dies." There is a growing awareness in this country of the enormous cost of workers' dissatisfaction both for the individual and the organization. A great proportion of this dissatisfaction is found in bureaucratic organizations.

"Bureaucracy" stems from the French *bureau,* which has come to mean a department or a subdivision of a department, usually of government. Bureaucratic organizations are gaining control over vocational life in most industrial societies. Their impact on workers is of great theoretical and practical importance. The study of bureaucracies has been greatly influenced by the pioneering work of the German scholar Max Weber who first described a model of "ideal bureaucracy": a social institution of professionals organized in a hierarchy and applying uniform norms to the handling of individual cases. Weber believed that bureaucracies had a "rational character, with rules, means-end calculus, and matter of factness predominating."[1] He perceived bureaucracies as a means of translating social actions—relationships between individuals that were sufficient to guide simple societies—into rational relationships, a form of activity necessary in complex societies.

Recently this positive view of bureaucracies has undergone dramatic changes. In their size and complexity bureaucratic organizations are slow and unresponsive. Usually they are considered equipped to solve problems that existed two years earlier. They are blamed for being self-serving instead of public-serving. Work in these bureaucracies can be frustrating and burnout-causing, especially for energetic and ambitious people who want to see quick changes.

The first chapter of this book presented case studies of people. This chapter presents a case study of an organization because the organization is the "patient." We chose a welfare department because it demonstrates the impact of working both within a bureaucracy *and* with people.

The Welfare Department

In the Welfare Department, approximately 381,000 employees interact with over 23,241,000 welfare recipients. Employees are required to work with large numbers of people in situations that can be very demanding. In addition, they contend with paper work, changing regulations, and a downward channel of communication. Welfare programs include aid to families with dependent children, food stamps, medical aid, general assistance, and supplemental security income for the aged, blind, and disabled.

As a social service organization, the Welfare Department imposes two kinds of stress on its employees: stress inherent in its bureaucratic nature and stress inherent in the services it provides.

An investigation of the Welfare Department described it as "an entrenched bureaucracy so complex and so inefficient that it seems to invite cheating and other abuses." Excessive red tape, inept management, poorly trained frontline personnel, and careless investigative policies in such organizations cost taxpayers billions of dollars every year.[2] The picture painted is one of "chaos, confusion and conflict in the management of welfare, particularly in big urban areas." "The degree of administrative morass within welfare departments in large cities is almost beyond description," Robert Reed, director of Michigan's Legal Services, told a Senate subcommittee.

Identifying "The Boss" is difficult in any large bureaurcracy, and in a government agency it can be nearly impossible. The source of welfare policy can be the federal government, the state government, the courts, or the agency itself. This unclear responsibility keeps workers from effectively stating and correcting their grievances. There are many levels of administrators and many employees in the system. Caseworkers are monitored by supervisors who are in turn monitored by other supervisors. At the top are administrators who often are not familiar with the problems of the workers seven steps below. As a result, although there are many supervisors, caseworkers often complain that direction is inadequate.

Workers are often bewildered about how to do their jobs. Old programs are frequently altered and new programs are added, creating constant confusion. "Just keeping abreast of policies that are forever being revised by Congress, HEW, state legislatures, and state and local administrators can be a full time job. By the time you understand one regulation, another is coming down the pike," said Patricia Johnson, head of Georgia's Division of Family and Children Services. Some rules are vague; others are set forth in minute detail: to implement one program that began as a four-page law, HEW drafted seventy pages of regulations followed by a 1,200-page instruction manual.

The welfare bureaucracy generates so much paperwork that caseworkers say they are shuffling paper instead of investigating clients. New York State processes three billion pieces of social service paperwork annually. Certain states may require up to sixty forms for a single welfare application. The Commission on Federal Paper Work examined the welfare application process and found it "needlessly complex, unduly burdensome, inefficient, inequitable and unnecessarily costly."[3]

Caseworkers in the Welfare Department screen applications, determine eligibility and benefit levels, and decide when a person no longer needs public aid. "In many parts of the country workers are overburdened by trying to manage loads double or triple the 60-case limit once prescribed by the Department of Health, Education and Welfare. Many labor under pressure in offices that tend to be tense, crowded and rundown, and that may lack even the basic equipment needed to keep track of the work."[4]

Despite such conditions, caseworkers are expected to offer informed assistance to people who require their services. Urged to show compassion, they are also responsible for guarding the public interest by accurately appraising aid applications and staying alert for mistakes and fraud. Employees must answer to their own supervisors, to their clients, and to state and federal governments.

Such work demands skill and training, but in twenty-seven states only a high school education is required to become a caseworker. Most eligibility workers are young, two out of three are women, and relatively few have an education beyond the college level. Inexperienced caseworkers with minimal training are the ones most likely to be fooled by people out to defraud the system. Instead of receiving formal training from supervisors, many caseworkers are trained by fellow workers. It takes new workers about six months to learn their jobs, but many do not stay in the department that long.

Compounding the abundance of negative features in welfare work is a dramatic lack of positive features. The pay is always inadequate for such demanding work. In New York in 1978, the starting salary for an interviewer ranged from $9,600 to $13,000, less than the income of some welfare families.[5] Promotions are not a source of satisfaction because local policies often require officials to promote everyone whenever a vacancy occurs, without concern for individual performance. Official concern for forms and routines also creates problems for welfare workers who feel they have become clerks instead of social servants.

When these pressures are not dealt with they can lead to the physical, emotional, and mental exhaustion of burnout. Consequently in some welfare offices turnover exceeds 40 percent a year. Many employees quit when they realize that they cannot handle the bureaucratic pressures combined with the job demands. A few change careers after being threatened or physically assaulted by welfare clients. Often caseworkers say they are driven out by the frustration of trying to make an inert system responsive to clients' needs. They know they can continue working with minimal effort even after they burn out, but some feel that when they burn out it is time to leave.

Workers' burnout can be traumatic for the individual, unpleasant for the service recipients, and disruptive and costly for the organization. In the Welfare Department at least $4 billion are paid out "erroneously" every year. Bureaucratic error, as opposed to outright fraud by aid recipients and others, is responsible for more than half the errors.[6] The welfare bureaucracy begins to falter at the level of the caseworkers. They are supposed to be the first line of defense against welfare abuse, but burnout weakens their resistance and alertness. Inadequately trained, overburdened, underpaid, many quit the field.

Three Causes of Burnout
in Bureaucratic Organizations

In his classic book, *Democracy in America*, Alexis de Tocqueville discussed the steady erosion that might develop as a result of a bureaucratic government that "covers the whole of social life with a network of petty, complicated rules that are both minute and uniform"—a situation that, according to de Tocqueville, does not break the human will but rather "softens, bends and guides it."[7]

In one research project,[8] organizational structure was described as a major determinant of job performance, satisfaction, and burnout. Large agencies that are formal, centralized in decision making, and hierarchical were found to have high turnover, low job satisfaction, and rapid burnout.

Consistent with this description is our own work with a large bureaucratic organization in which we found high levels of employee burnout.[9] As burnout increased, many job satisfaction measures decreased, and as burnout increased, so did employees' desires to leave their jobs.[10]

Training schools rarely teach students how to be "good bureaucrats," although most of their graduates end up working for large organizations. Thus people who work in bureaucracies are generally unprepared for dealing with the stress these organizations generate. This is especially true in the human services where people often choose their careers for altruistic reasons but find themselves filling out forms rather than working with people. Bureaucratic organizations in general can promote three causes of burnout: (1) overload, (2) lack of autonomy, and (3) lack of rewards. All three are tied to the failure of work to provide a sense of meaning to life. They exist in other work settings as well, but they are especially prevalent in bureaucratic organizations.

One characteristic of work in high-burnout organizations is overload. John R. D. French and Robert D. Caplan, studying occupational stress at the University of Michigan's Institute of Social Research, have done extensive research on the effects of the organizational work environment on psychological and physiological health.[11] They describe role overload as a key variable in job stress. Overload is often built into the work definition of bureaucracies.

French and Caplan distinguish between objective and subjective as well as quantitative and qualitative overload. Objective overload is the actual volume of information that individuals are expected to process per unit of time. The number of telephone calls to answer, letters to write, office visits to receive, or patients to examine in a day are quantifiable indicators of objective overload. Subjective overload, in contrast, refers to people's feelings that they have too much work to do or that the work is too hard for them. Quantitative overload implies that they have more work than they can do in a given time period. Qualitative overload implies that the job requires skills and knowledge exceeding those of the workers. Individuals experience quantitative overload when they have the skills to perform the tasks but do not have the time to get them done. They have qualitative overload when, no matter how much time they are given, they do not have the skills to perform the tasks at acceptable levels.

Both quantitative and qualitative overload are correlated with psychological and physiological indices of stress. Overloaded workers show increased heart rate and serum cholesterol levels; they smoke more, have more job dissatisfaction and tension, and show lower self-esteem.[12]

J. G. Miller, a pioneer in the work on information-input overload, has developed an apparatus to study the psychological response to overload.[13] He described several mechanisms of adjustment to information overload, including omission of information, error in processing information, delaying responses during heavy load periods and catching up during lull periods, filtering some items of information, giving an imprecise response, and escape either by leaving the situation or by cutting off the information input. Miller suggested that excessive information overload can cause cognitive and behavioral disorganization.

Many studies have documented the prevalence of overload among people working in large bureaucratic organizations. In a national survey, 44 percent of the male white-collar employees reported some degree of overload. A study of university professors showed that many of them suffer from a quantitative overload that is mostly self-induced and related to their achievement orientation.[14] In one of our own studies, 724 human service workers were asked to identify the most stressful aspects of their work. Over 50 percent of the stresses mentioned pertained to overload.[15]

The specific job components that contribute to overload differ for different professions. Robert L. Kahn, director of the Survey Research Center at the University of Michigan, found overload to be one of the most frequent forms of role conflict in bureaucratic organizations. He summarized the response of people he studied as, "We don't object to the things we're asked to do, and we don't find them inappropriate or unreasonable, but we can't meet all the demands simultaneously within the constraints of time and resources."[16] In police work, qualitative overload may occur as a result of unrealistic expectations placed on police by society. "Society demands too much of its policemen. Not only are they expected to enforce the law, they must also be curbside psychiatrists, marriage counselors, social workers—even ministers and doctors. A good street officer combines in his daily work splinters of each one of these complex professions, and many more."[17] Among those "many more" we would add the role of a skilled bureaucrat who can manage a large, complex, and inefficient bureaucratic system. An informal survey found that over 70 percent of police officers feel that they are under the stress of overload.[18]

In a study of one social service bureaucracy, we asked 52 employees to identify the msot stressful aspects of their jobs.[19] Their most frequent responses were: "There is a heavy work load"; "There is not enough time in the day or enough people to handle the work load so service to the public is not as positive as it could be"; "Folders pile up and clients have to wait excessive lengths of time and I don't see an end to it." Such overload was found to be highly correlated with burnout.[20]

Similarly, studies of child-care workers and mental health workers found that the larger the ratio of children or patients to staff, the less staff members liked their jobs and the more frequently they reported cognitive, emotional, and sensory overload. As the ratio decreased, the quality of care improved.[21]

The experience of overload can be aggravated for people in social service bureaucracies by the imposition of tasks that have high priority for the organization but low priority for the service recipients. Paper work and red tape are more difficult to deal with when there are people waiting for help. We have heard social workers, counselors, policemen, and probation officers say that it is not the contact with clients that is most stressful for them but "writing a report in six copies that I know for sure no one will ever look at." A survey of over 4,500 police officers found that they consider "too much paperwork" their major job-related problem.[22] Our studies also found excessive paperwork and red tape to be highly correlated with burnout;[23] the more paperwork and red tape, the more burnout.

Why does overload cause burnout? Because overload puts people in situations in which failure is built in. If they comply with the bureaucratic demand for quantity (see a new patient every 20 minutes), they fail the demand for quality service. If they spend the time needed to do the work the way it should be done (which in some cases may mean seeing a patient for 40 minutes), they are sure to fail the demand for quantity. This failure is particularly devastating for people who care deeply about their work, and for whom success at work is a prerequisite for finding meaning in life. (Such people, as we know, can be found both in management levels in general and in the helping professions—the subjects of our two previous chapters.)

Lack of control over one's environment is a highly stressful experience (as you may recall from our previous mention of the subject during the discussion of hardiness). Martin Seligman suggested that when people repeatedly undergo negative experiences over which they have no control, the result is "learned helplessness" and depression.[24] The exposure to uncontrollable events leads to motivational and effective debilitation. People who develop "learned helplessness" do not believe that success is the result of their performance but attribute failure to themselves. They develop low self-esteem and become passive and sad. Learned helplessness can explain some of the symptoms of burnout experienced by employees of bureaucratic organizations as a result of lack of autonomy.

Social psychologists have found that people can stand more pain when they have control over its duration and intensity than when they do not.[25] It has also been reported that the mortality rate in old age homes is higher among those residents who had no choice in the decision to be there than among those who made that choice themselves.[26] A study of homemakers found that housewives who chose this career tended to be healthy, happy, and comfortable in their role.[27] They did not want to work, took pride in what they did, felt in control, and were satisfied with their lives. Homemakers who wanted to work away from home, but did not, exhibited the "bitter housewife" syndrome: they were dissatisfied with their lives, had low self-esteem, and often masked their loneliness and worry with drugs.

The need for autonomy is so great that people will even blame themselves for accidents in order to maintain their sense of control. The underlying reasoning in such self-blame is: "If it was my fault that it happened, then it is within my control to make sure it doesn't happen again." Frustration resulting from the lack of autonomy is a particularly common cause of burnout in bureaucratic organizations.[28] In our work with such bureaucratic organizations we found that burnout increased as autonomy, sense of control, and discretionary time decreased. In a study of one social service organization, for example, two of the most frequently mentioned sources of stress were the frequent changes in rules and the poorly planned changes with little advance notice.[29] In another study we asked people to indicate if they did professional and personal activities mainly because they wanted to or because they had to. Those who answered "have to" showed far more burnout than those who answered "want to."[30]

Lack of autonomy in bureaucracies is especially apparent in administrative pressures on the individual worker, unnecessary rules, and lack of voice in decisions that affect one's job and life. William Kroes, a psychologist who worked extensively with police officers, wrote about the stress inherent in situations in which patrolmen were transferred from one partner, assignment, or district to another without advance notice.[31] Police officers generally have no say in their assignment to direct traffic, write parking citations, or investigate such petty complaints as too many weeds growing in a property owner's lawn.

Brian Sarata, a professor of psychology at the University of Nebraska, notes that the feasibility of providing most staff in large bureaucratic health service organizations with a significant degree of autonomy is limited by at least two considerations: first, many decisions are made only by professional staff; second, providing good care requires that the efforts of all disciplines be well coordinated and that treatment plans be implemented in a consistent manner. This necessarily limits the autonomy of the individual staff members' involvement in the process.

Lack of autonomy can be aggravated by a communication gap between those at the top and those at the bottom of the bureaucratic hierarchy. This gap may be due to the inherent inefficiencies of communication in large organizations or to the different perspectives available to management. The lack of personal control is more clear and stressful in the lower ranks of the organization. As a result, employees often feel a loss of individuality, "like little insignificant wheels in a gigantic machine." Characteristics of bureaucratic organizations such as circumscribed authority, downward channels of command, specialization, formal accountability and hierarchy, and broad-base participation all contribute to feelings of helplessness and lack of autonomy and control, and thus to burnout.

Bureaucratic organizations are inefficient distributors of rewards, appreciation, and recognition. This contributes to discouragement and demoralization and eventually to burnout. In some bureaucratic organizations, we found employees were able to withstand great work stress when they felt appreciated and adequately rewarded. Unfortunately, that was rarely the case.

In the Welfare Department, employees developed burnout both because of the negative features in their work and because of the lack of positive features. Their pay was inadequate for the work they were expected to do, thy received little positive feedback from supervisors, and promotions were given for political considerations rather than as an acknowledgment of special effort or superior performance. In the study of a bureaucratic social service organization we mentioned earlier, the lack of rewards, such as pay, benefits, and promotion, was a significant contributor to burnout.[32]

But it turns out that appreciation on the job is more important than dollars for most people. Indeed it seems to be the case that phenomenologically the ideal income tends to remain 10 to 20 percent above a person's current income, even at the very highest socioeconomic status. For example, hospital physicians we interviewed were as likely to complain about financial strain as were social workers and clerks. People who received appreciation, satisfaction, and a sense of significance from their work were more likely to be content with their income, no matter how low it was. And burnout was more highly correlated with lack of a sense of success and significance than it was with salary. Burnout was also more highly correlated with poor physical health and lack of self-actualization than it was with salary.[33]

The cause of burnout in bureaucratic organizations is therefore the subjective sense of inadequate reward rather than the reward itself. Burnout comes in part when people feel that they are working hard, beyond the requirements of the job, and yet their efforts are not appreciated. One employee expressed this sense of frustration by saying, "You never hear a good word from management, no matter how consistently excellent your performance is. The only thing you will ever get from them is a cold memo when something goes wrong." The lack of recognition and appreciation is a major cause of burnout in bureaucratic organizations, because it deprives people of a sense that their contribution is significant. Bureaucracies can only benefit by providing positive feedback to employees.

How to Avoid Burnout
by Being a "Good Bureaucrat"

Despite the increasing number of large bureaucratic organizations, most people who work in them never learn how to be "good bureaucrats." For many the phrase "good bureaucrat" is a contradiction in terms. In popular speech, a "bureaucrat" is identified with all that is antihuman. Furthermore, the role of a bureaucrat has been almost totally ignored by educators, practitioners, and researchers. But Robert Pruger, a professor of social welfare at the University of California, contends that achieving one's professional goals in a complex organization requires great competence. He recommends that workers develop the skills needed to cope with a bureaucracy rather than try to escape the organization. As bureaucrats, workers are required to negotiate the stresses, opportunities, and constraints that permeate organizational life. Competent bureaucrats have identified the following skills that enable them to avoid the three major causes of burnout we just discussed.[34]

Avoiding Overload by Getting to Know
the Organization and Acquiring Skills

Overload is built into the size and complexity of bureaucratic organizations. Some overload will dissipate when people learn the work routines and the organizational structure. This requires staying on the job long enough to master the initial stresses.

Employees in bureaucratic social service organizations reported an overwhelming overload during their first six months at work. The information to be learned in that period was enormous and the training inadequate. This initial overload was associated with feelings of inadequacy, guilt, and failure which for some employees never disappeared.

Adequate training for employees is necessary to reduce this initial overload. Effective training programs and supportive supervision are two methods for skill acquisition and improvement that reduce overload and, consequently, burnout. Again, this requires the employee to remain in the organization long enough to learn whatever skills are needed to be efficient. These may include general skills increasingly required by bureaucratic organizations but for which formal training is frequently unavailable, such as proposal writing, budgeting, or problem analysis. They may also include specific abilities such as clerical, computer, or communication skills.

Bureaucratic organizations can reduce employee overload by defining their priorities for employees. A priority list includes both internal organizational goals and more general goals such as service to the public and a good image for the organization. A priority list for work activities can also ease overload. This job analysis includes all the activities to be performed and identifies which ones are causes of overload. These activities can be divided into necessary activities that create overload and activities that create self-imposed overload. The necessary activities need to be accepted as such and time should be organized accordingly: more time to the more important activities and less time to the less important ones. Priorities need to be established among the self-imposed activities also. Those deemed important are alloted time, and the others are minimized or eliminated.

These techniques do reduce overload but they rarely eliminate it. The basic strategy is to help people live with overload, set priorities, and reduce the stress caused by worry or guilt. When overload is accepted as a necessary evil, and is not accompanied by worry and strain, it is easier to cope with.

Exercising Autonomy
and Remembering Goals

In bureaucratic organizations, processes of decision and action move forward at a measured pace. One characteristic of a good bureaucrat, according to Robert Pruger, is staying in power. "Whatever ideas, changes, projects, or other professional aspirations the worker may have, he will not be able to realize them unless he stays in the organization and keeps working for his goals over a sufficient period of time. But it is not enough merely to survive as a physical presence. The good bureaucrat must maintain his vitality of action and independence of thought. He must continue to be led by some progressive vision of what the organization might accomplish and nurture the scope and consciousness of discretionary behavior."[35] Individual employees can almost always preserve and enlarge the discretionary scope of their activities and, by extension, their sense of autonomy and control. Research shows that when staff authority is decentralized and workers at all levels are involved in decision making, there is a significant improvement in performance as well as staff morale.[36]

To achieve these objectives the good bureaucrat is attentive to authority and avoids behavior that earns dismissal. To the astute bureaucrat, things are always more flexible than they seem at first glance. Because authority is most commonly expressed in rules, job descriptions, and work schedules, such statements are general in character and employees can interpret them to their advantage. That built-in degree of generality requires the exercise of discretion. In this sense, skillful bureaucrats have more control over the content of their jobs than does the organization.

Burnout is associated with feelings of helplessness and lack of control. Many people in bureaucracies believe and act as if nothing can be done about anything around them; they feel they must perform their duties with little or no autonomy. These are the "dead wood," the "paper-pushers," the "yes men," or the "bureaucrats" in the colloquial meaning of the word. As mentioned previously, people like that, when in supervisory positions, can cause burnout in new employees by discouraging them and by derogating their enthusiasm. Managers' tactics of discouraging idealistic employees are frequently motivated by their need to insure that subordinates will burn out, thus justifying their own burnout. Other people, usually recently hired, are overly optimistic about the possibilities of change in the organization. These people often end up angry, frustrated, and despairing.

To avoid the pitfalls of overoptimism and overpessimism, employees can evaluate each aspect of the job for its possibilities for change. Those changes that seem impossible after close scrutiny are written off. Energy is then usefully directed toward those elements of the job and the organization that can be changed. Focusing attention on what is possible increases one's sense of power and control.

The need for control and autonomy is the other side of the need for security. As we have seen, employees who are attracted to bureaucratic organizations (and especially government bureaucracies) are often motivated by needs for security and retirement benefits. For this reason they remain on their jobs despite high levels of burnout.

Employees of a bureaucracy can use their sense of autonomy and control as a buffer against burnout. They can maximize their discretionary ability to define their roles and establish their priorities at work. We draw a distinction between what serves the organizational purpose and what merely serves the organization. The good bureaucrat does not yield unnecessarily to the requirements of administrative convenience. As a result, the good bureaucrat is less likely to experience burnout. The good bureaucrat, says Pruger, also knows that the most useful skill against inflexibility, officiousness, and the other frustrations of organizational life is a sense of humor.[37]

Not Expecting Rewards Only from Above

Employees of a bureaucratic organization can make their work more satisfying by refusing to rely exclusively on their supervisors for praise. This will increase their own freedom to take the initiative and to develop innovations that may keep the individual and the organization alive. Employees who expect to gain their sense of achievement from management's praise alone will most likely be disappointed. Superiors will rarely comment on an employee's work except when things go wrong. They do so not out of ill will, but because they themselves are busy on the one hand with impressing their own supervisors, and on the other hand with protecting themselves from the possible consequences of errors made by their employees. Instead of expecting recognition only from above, workers can look for alternative sources. They can give and receive it from co-workers and clients and can achieve a sense of success from the work itself.

Management can help relieve burnout by recognizing rewards and appreciation as powerful buffers against burnout. Understanding employees' needs for rewards and appreciation, and understanding their impact when coming from a superior, can give managers great power to alleviate burnout in bureaucratic organizations.

Managers can also increase the staff's sense of power by decentralizing authority and involving people in all levels of the organizational structure in decision making.[38]

Organizational development experts are trying to intervene and affect the reality of bureaucratic life on the organizational level and report success in their efforts.[39] Employees who find themselves working in such an enlightened organization are lucky and most probably feel less burned out.

Obviously, some organizations are better than others on the dimensions of overload, power structure, and rewards. To the extent that an organization is structured in ways that increase such positive features as communication and autonomy, there will be a general reduction in burnout. At the same time, even the most enlightened organizations cannot solve this problem for all of their employees. Individuals require sensible and useful coping strategies. These are discussed at some length in part three of this volume.

SIX

Burnout in Women

Rose was 29, sensitive, and exceptionally bright. She graduated first in her high school class and Phi Beta Kappa from college. She met her husband while working toward her Ph.D., which she received with highest honors. Throughout her education she was supported by the most prestigious grants, fellowships, and scholarships. In addition to her graduate school career, Rose pursued interests in sports and music. She ran several miles every day and played competitive tennis. She also played the violin and appeared with local amateur orchestras.

When her husband took a position with a law firm on the East Coast, Rose moved with him. Because they both wanted a child she became pregnant as soon as they settled in their new community. A few months after her child was born, Rose received a job offer from a prestigious university that was located sixty miles away. It was a great compliment and an ideal job for her, but now there was a baby with whom she wanted to spend her time. Rose was torn. When she stayed with her child, she felt she was disappointing the people who believed in her and who helped her get the job offer. When she worked on a manuscript she was preparing for publication, she felt guilty about leaving her baby at home. Her conscience tormented her: "Why did I have a child if I was going to leave her with strangers? She is changing every day now, and I am missing it. Why did I take advantage of all these scholarships when I am never going to publish the research anyway? How can I even talk to my professor again if I turn the offer down?"

The conflict drained Rose of her mental and emotional energy. As her conflict increased she was less able to separate the issues involved. Her sleep was disrupted and she was frequently upset and nervous. Occasionally she lost her temper and screamed at her child or her husband and then was tormented by guilt and despair. She felt alienated from her family and sometimes cried for hours. She knew she could not stand the situation much longer.

Rose finally turned down the job offer. Two years later she had another baby and took a part-time teaching position at a community college. She received great satisfaction from students' enthusiastic responses to her classes but she devoted so much time to preparation for her lectures that there was little left for sports, music, or her own research. She remained torn between her roles as a professional and a mother, and her role conflict continued as a source of great emotional strain. Yet she felt that at least life provided her with a compromise that many women did not have, and she was grateful for that.

Role conflict is a major stress shared by most women who are combining the careers of homemaker and professional. For some women this conflict is the main cause of burnout. Since these women are trying to get a sense of meaning both from their domestic roles and their careers, the conflict between the two gives them the feeling that they have failed in both. We will address women's role conflict after discussing separately the stress of the homemaker and the stress of the professional woman.

Homemakers' Work Stress

More individuals contribute goods and services as homemakers than as any other single occupation. Although these goods and services are not accounted for in the gross national product, they are a necessary part of our economy.[1] But although the role of the housewife and mother may be important for society, for some women it holds little opportunity for a sense of significance and success.

Until recently the role of homemakers was not the subject of much research. In recent years the growing interest in women's issues has prompted a review of the homemaker's role, and social scientists have begun to study it as they study other jobs. According to industrial psychologist Richard Arvey, there are important distinctions between the homemaker's jobs and jobs outside the home. One difference is that the homemaker receives no pay for the goods produced or services rendered. Another distinction is that the homemaker has little, if any, separation between her employment role and her other roles. The roles of housewife, mother, and wife are closely intertwined, perhaps inextricably so.[2]

Myra Marx Ferree, a sociologist at the University of Connecticut,[3] described the American housewife as "besieged." On one side stand the traditionalists who tell her that her greatest pleasures come from satisfying the needs of others: making a home for her family, raising healthy children, and pleasing her husband. On the other side stand the egalitarians who tell her that her own needs are important too. Marx Ferree, who interviewed 135 women, found that almost twice as many housewives as employed wives said they were dissatisfied with their lives. More housewives also claimed that they had not had a fair opportunity in life and wanted their daughters to be "mostly different from themselves."

The reasons for the housewives' dissatisfaction were found in the nature of their work:

> A housewife's day is never done and her tasks often bring neither tangible rewards nor social connections. Husbands and wives alike have an uncertain idea of how much housework is work. Housewives expend great effort but don't get recognition for it: their husbands accuse them of "doing nothing all day" and in the next breath remind them that their duty is to stay home and keep house. As a result many housewives have an uncertain idea of what their occupation requires, and how well or poorly they are doing it.[4]

Not long ago, writes Marx Ferree, housewives shared a social network. They were likely to live near their mothers, relatives, and friends and to establish close-knit groups. Within these groups there was no doubt whether someone was or was not a good homemaker. In recent decades, however, a rise in mobility and in the number of working women has made housewife networks less common and more difficult to maintain. With husbands at work and children in school, wives may become isolated. Women who were interviewed by Marx Ferree felt they were going crazy staying home, "not seeing anyone but four walls all day." "Staying home all day," said one woman, "is like being in jail."[5]

Many portraits of the housewife in the literature describe her as neurotic, bored, depressed, and anxious. They depict her work as the essence of boredom and triviality, work that is degrading, unpleasant, and self-negating. Housework has been described as consisting mainly of drudgery, with no formal wages, no social support, and no recognition, resulting in dissatisfaction among homemakers. In Jessie Bernard's words, "being a housewife makes women sick."[6]

Ann Oakley, who conducted in-depth interviews of British homemakers,[7] found that 70 percent of the women she interviewed were dissatisfied with their homemakers' role. In other studies, Richard Arvey reported much lower percentages of dissatisfaction than did Oakley.[8] Psychologist Linda Fidel and sociologist Jane Prather suggested that the new stereotype of the neurotic housewife may be just as distorted as the old stereotype of the happy homemaker.[9] Fidel and Prather distinguished between those homemakers who do not want to work outside the home and those who want to but do not do so because of family responsibilities, lack of child care, a limited job market, or illness. The latter are the ones who fit the "unhappy housewife" stereotype. They are dissatisfied with their lives, have low self-esteem, feel trapped by circumstances, and mask their loneliness and worry with drugs. In contrast, the housewives who do not want to work outside the home are happy, healthy, and comfortable in their role. When their husbands have high incomes they do not need a salaried job and they fill their days with tasks related to their home and family as well as hobbies and visits with friends. They also have time for themselves. They have happy marriages, feel in control of their lives, and have very good physical and mental health.

In working with homemakers[10] we found, as did Fidel and Prather, that they were concentrated in two groups in terms of their burnout. Those exhibiting the "neurotic housewife syndrome" ranked very high in burnout. They were chronically exhausted and emotionally drained. They felt that spending their days with chil-

dren was making their minds "shrink." They felt trapped and depressed and considered their lives empty and meaningless. Many of
them had burned out in their roles as wives and mothers. Those
women who ranked low in burnout took pride in their roles as wives
and mothers, were creative about their homemaking tasks, and were
involved in adult education classes and community politics. They
felt that their lives were full and had meaning. Terry and Sara are
two women who exemplify these extremes.

Terry had a bachelor's degree in English. She was married and
had one child. For years she tried to get a job but failed because
there were simply none available for an English teacher. She became frustrated and bitter, feeling that life was passing her by. She
felt that her household chores were wasting her skills and education.
"How much creativity can you put into dusting?" she asked. When
she compared herself to her husband she felt cheated and trapped.
When asked what she did for a living, her apologetic, embarrassed
response was, "I am just a housewife and a mother."

Terry dreaded the empty hours of her day. She took "uppers"
to fight off depression and smoked, drank, and watched television
to pass the time. She did not have sufficient energy to read a book
or call a friend. She found it difficult to communicate with her son;
she often lost her temper and became afraid that she would hurt
him. She began to have fantasies of suicide. "If that's all that life
is," she said, "it's not worth it."

Sara, in contrast, was happy with her life. She came from a very
poor background, and was one of nine children. She had worked for
a number of years as a nurse but was very happy to leave her profession when she married. She always wanted to be a mother, a wife,
and a homemaker in a beautiful house. Sara took care to be properly
dressed and groomed. She spent time every day in exercise and
beauty care. She took as much pride in her house and garden as she
took in her appearance. Sara liked to spend time with her children
and was involved with their school and after-school activities. The
children liked to bring their friends home, and her house was always
filled with people.

Sara had many friends who were housewives like herself. They
provided a supportive social system for each other. She was active
in a charity organization and in the PTA and worked in ceramics
with great success. She perceived her life as meaningful and fulfilling. It was a dream come true.

There are some objective differences between Sara and Terry.

Sara's husband had a higher income; her house was more luxurious; she could afford clothes, beauty salons, tennis lessons, and help with the house and the children. She could take time for herself. Sara appreciated the material benefits of her marriage because she had none of them when she was growing up. Terry felt disappointed with what life had done to her great potential. Sara had low expectations and a luxurious environment. Terry had high expectations and a stressful, disappointing environment. The results of the interaction between expectations and environment made Sara reach her own peak performance, but made Terry burn out.

Other differences between the two are more subjective and cannot be explained by economic realities or by fulfilled or failed aspirations. Sara was involved in a support system of other women like herself, but Terry felt isolated and lonely. Sara felt in control of her life, and her housework gave her variety and a sense of success and significance. Terry, however, felt very much out of control of her life. She was ashamed of her role as a housewife and derived neither meaning nor satisfaction from it.

Two decades ago most American women worked only at home. Primary occupational roles were those of wife, mother, and homemaker. Occupational success was measured by cleanliness of the home, well-behaved children, and contented husbands. Like Sara, many women who chose to stay home felt very lucky, luckier than men in their freedom from work. They could do what they wanted while fulfilling their ambition: raising a happy family. They did not resent, as Terry did, being called "Mrs. John Watkins" or "David's mother." They were proud and secure in their roles.

Women's work in the United States has evolved since then. Most women in the paid labor force no longer work only to supplement the family income. Today more women work outside the home, choosing demanding professions in which they excel. But American culture still expects that the working woman will make marriage and motherhood her primary vocation. These expectations result in external situational stress and in internal emotional stress, both affecting the working woman's self-perception as a competent human being. Both kinds of stress deprive women of a sense of meaning in life and lead to burnout.

Individuals can change their attitudes—with effort. Women who know they are going to be homemakers for several years can make the most out of this period by taking interest in the tasks homemaking entails. Getting involved in adult education classes, community work, or a hobby can also make this time more satisfying. Taking a day off is very important when a housewife feels under particular pressure: she can stay home while the family is away, or have lunch with a friend or tour the city. Most important, she can arrange a support system of other homemakers who are dealing with similar issues. The availability of such a group can determine a homemaker's success in coping with burnout.

Working Women's Work Stress

Sex-role stereotyping of occupations exists at all levels of the labor force. Women are believed to prefer, or to be best suited to, work such as teaching, counseling, and nursing. Such careers represent an extension of their domestic roles and involve helping, nurturing, and socializing activities. Employment figures in industrial countries bear out this stereotyping of occupations: the bulk of women workers are in teaching and nursing.[11]

In research investigating people's perceptions of professional women,[12] we found that being "feminine" was highly correlated with being "sex-appropriate" and "better adjusted" and with being less "aggressive" and "active" and more "sensitive," "warm," and "kind." The attributes that make women seek work in the human services and may make them more qualified for that work may be the same attributes that make them more vulnerable to the dangers of burnout.

The homemaker who is a service professional has the added stress of a job at home. She is expected to spend both her professional and personal life being empathic, understanding, and sensitive to the needs of others. In Chapter 4 we mentioned three causes of burnout: (1) working with people, (2) a self-selective sample, and (3) a client-centered orientation. These causes of burnout are particularly powerful for women, especially those who are carrying the double burden of a family and a profession:

1. Women are often drawn to occupations in which they work with people, especially in a helping role. Women are disproportionately represented in teaching, nursing, counseling, social work, and social welfare. These are professions that require contact with people in intense, painful, or emotionally demanding situations; women also are expected to provide this nurturance at home.

2. Sex-role stereotypes describe women as affectionate, caring, empathic, sensitive to the needs of others. If this is true for women in general it may be more true for women in the human services. Of the self-selected helpers, women are the most predetermined.

3. The professions that many women choose are often client-centered, and similarly the role of mother is child-oriented. Being child-oriented is an endless process: there is always more a "good" mother could do, and this societal norm is a source of guilt for many women.

If a woman is sensitive, the professional struggles can be more frustrating than if she is not. If she is empathic, the suffering and helplessness she sees are more painful. If she knew herself as a caring human being, the realization that she has become numb to others' needs is more devastating. Thus the problem of burnout has special relevance for professional women in the human services.

A study involving 424 women in three generations explored similarities and differences in burnout and its causes.[13] The first generation consisted of preprofessional female students whose average age was 21, the second generation was professional women whose average age was 34, and the third generation was postprofessional retired women whose average age was 66. The women were questioned about their burnout, daily activities, attitudes toward women's issues, and life and work satisfaction. The results of those surveys are summarized here.

Those career women/housewives-mothers who were the ones supposed to be the most overburdened by two full-time jobs were found to project the most positive picture of the three groups. Though they worked more than the others they had more satisfaction from their work, found their professional role more enjoyable and rewarding, and held more liberal attitudes toward working women and working women's issues. They felt they had more variety, more autonomy, and more complexity in their lives. Although they had less time for themselves, they were in better health and had more positive life attitudes than the younger and older women. In short, they revealed a very positive attitude toward both family and work, and felt that both gave meaning to their lives.

The student group reported the most burnout and the least satisfaction in their work and life. They felt overextended in commitments and social obligations and were conflicted about their school work and social life. They frequently reported being disturbed while studying by thoughts about romantic involvements, but while with their dates, they were distressed by guilt and anxiety about neglecting their school work and the effect this neglect would have on their future. These women felt they had less autonomy than the two other groups and they enjoyed their professional role less. They spent more time than the other women in study and reading but they enjoyed these activities less. They had poorer relationships with people at school, probably as a result of academic competition.

The younger women, in summary, were experiencing more burnout than their dual-career counterparts. One possible explanation for these unexpected results is a process of selection: those young women who are most distressed as students may drop out before they begin a professional career or shortly afterward. Another possible explanation for the positive picture of the career woman is self-rationalization: it is easier for some people, like the students, to acknowledge distress before choosing a career. Once the decision has been made and has been costly in training and the effect on marriage and home, it may be harder to admit difficulties.

The postprofessional women had the worst health, felt the least overextended, and had the fewest distractions and conflicts. They spent more time than the other groups watching television and in hobbies and community work; they also spent more time in housework and shopping, the traditional homemaker's activities. Although these women had been professionals at a time when careers were unusual for women, they agreed more than the younger women with statements such as "raising a child can keep most women satisfied," "children of working mothers tend to be maladjusted," and "the spouse's career is more important" than their own. These women spent the least time talking to friends and relatives and, though they rated highly their relationships with friends, they felt they had the least unconditional support when they needed it.

In summary, the main findings in three generations of professional women were the stressful environment of college for the preprofessionals and the isolation and the traditional attitudes of the postprofessionals. The mid-career professionals had liberal attitudes toward women's issues, more satisfaction from their lives, and more satisfaction from their work. Although they carried the dual burden of home and career, they did not have more role conflict and did not report higher levels of burnout.

In the case study of Rose, presented at the beginning of this chapter, we described role conflict as one of the major causes of stress for professional women. Yet it appears from the data presented above that dual-career women experienced less role conflict than did preprofessional college students. This contradiction is resolved when one considers that the mid-career women were compared not to men or to professional women without families but to students and retired women. The contradiction is further clarified when one looks at the mid-career women's perceived autonomy and variety. The professional women felt more in control of their lives than the other two samples and perceived their dual roles not as conflicting but as sources of greater variety. There may also be a cohort effect operating: active career women today came of age and chose their careers on the crest of the feminist movement's endorsement of "doing it all." Before and since, women—and society in general—have expressed more ambivalence about the desirability or feasibility of combining career and family.

Professional Women and Men: A Comparison

The study of burnout among three generations of professional women found that women in mid-career who carry a double load of a job and a family had the most satisfaction from their lives and their work. Although they worked more and had less time for themselves, they had more variety, autonomy, and sense of significance. However, the picture of professional women changes when they are compared to professional men rather than to professional women at other times in their careers. In a study of burnout and its causes and consequences in men and women, we found that women were at a disadvantage, especially in their work conditions.[14]

Professional women had slightly higher levels of burnout than professional men but had four times more of its most extreme level; they felt they had less freedom, autonomy, and influence in their work as well as less variety, less challange, and a less positive work environment. They reported having fewer opportunities for self-expression and self-actualization and felt less adequately rewarded for their work. These women also had more of such negative features as environmental pressures and overextension caused by the demands of other people. These findings, plus research that showed how women suffer from discrimination and harassment in male-dominated professions, can explain the findings of greater burnout among women.

One reason for the burnout-causing work environment of women is the occupations and roles most women choose. Another reason, according to Margaret Henning and Anne Jardim, is sex-role differences in work attitudes.[15] Henning and Jardim, who interviewed more than 100 women working as executives in business and industry, claim that women see a career as a source of personal growth and self-fulfillment and they seek in it the satisfaction of doing what they want to do. These perceptions may cause women to have higher expectations of their careers than men. When these expectations are not met, women burn out. In our study we found that the more self-actualized women were, and the more opportunities for self-expression they had, the less burned out they were. This was less true for men.[16]

Men may see a career as an upward progression of jobs with recognition and rewards, whereas women may be less concerned with advancement, seeing their work as a series of jobs rather than a life career. In our study, low position and inadequate financial rewards were correlated with burnout for men but not for women. Although men look upon a particular job as part of a career, women usually separate the two. For them, a job involves the present and a career is in the future. Men concentrate on achieving long-range goals; women focus primarily on short-term planning with less concern for long-term implications.

Men, claim Henning and Jardim, find it difficult to separate personal goals from career goals. They see each as dependent on the other and try to negotiate between them when they conflict. Women, however, try to keep their lives separate from their careers. In our study we found that the conflict between life and work was very stressful for both men and women, but women saw their life outside work as more important than men did.

Women reported to have more stressful work environments with significantly fewer positive features than men. In the sphere that women felt was most important, their homes, they had little variety. They worked at home more than men, felt more frequently overextended emotionally, and had more guilt and anxiety about not fulfilling their duties as completely as they wanted. As a result of their stressful work environment and the added emotional burden of their dual roles, women have more extreme levels of burnout than men.

In a study done by Dalia Etzion, 29 women and 29 men holding middle-management positions were compared regarding their job burnout, life and work satisfaction, and various other life and work features. The men and women were matched in age, seniority, and managerial level. As in all previous studies, results indicated that the women were more burned out than the men. It was also found that with the same level of education a man was likely to climb to a higher managerial position. For women, burnout increased with education, for men it decreased. Apparently, the higher expectations associated with getting a higher education were more easily achieved by men, and at a lower price.[17]

Women also paid a higher personal price for their careers in terms of family life. Thirty-one percent of the women in this group remained unmarried, yet not even one of the men was single. In addition, the more successful a woman manager was in her career, the less successful she felt about her home life. For men, success at work was not related to either success or failure at home.

In personal interviews, women managers talked with great pain about the personal sacrifices they had to make for the sake of their careers; many times they doubted whether it was all worth it. A public relations director in a large governmental agency said:

> Now that I am getting close to my fiftieth birthday, I spend a lot of time thinking about my life, evaluating things, wondering. . . . If a young woman would come to me today and ask whether I recommend this life to her I would have to say "no". The price you pay is just too high. Look at me. I may be the head of the department, but I am home alone at night. My marriage just couldn't sustain the pressure of my career. And it wasn't even that the household chores were not taken care of, because they were. I always made sure that the house was clean and food was on the table on time. What got to my husband was the fact that I was more successful than he was. At parties people knew who I was and knew him only as my husband. He just couldn't take it. My marriage was literally the price I paid for my success, and now I am no longer sure it was worth it. . . .

Women's values may make ambition and competition secondary to good work relationships and good personal relationships at home. Good personal relationships were very highly correlated with burnout for women[18] (the better the relationship the less burnout); this was less true for men. Burnout was found to be lower for employees, especially women, who were involved in social networks and support systems. Women seem to have a higher sensitivity than men to the social aspects of their life and work; they have better personal relationships, more emotional assistance from their family, friends, and co-workers, and more unconditional support in times of stress than men. And social support is more important to women than it is to men.

Men's and Women's Perceptions
of a Professional Woman

At the beginning of this chapter we demonstrated the effect of role conflict in the case of Rose. Every career woman who wants to have a family faces Rose's dilemma. A critical issue for many career women is other people's perceptions of their double role. In one study we examined these perceptions.[19] The woman who served as the example in our study was Rose herself, who wanted to examine people's perceptions of her as one way to sort the issues. We asked her to separate her two roles onto two videotapes. Both tapes started with the same interview in which she talked about her history, educational background, and interests. The tapes had two different endings in which she talked about her plans for the future. In one tape she presented only her career plans, saying she wanted to accept a university position, teach, and publish scientific articles. In the second tape she presented only her family plans, saying she intended to stay home with her child while he was young and work in the house and garden.

College students were shown only one of the two tapes and asked for their perceptions of the woman in it. All the students saw the initial interview that established her abilities. Yet, after viewing the career tape, students described her with more adjectives traditionally ascribed to career-oriented males: aggressive, dominant, independent. In addition, she was perceived as more success-oriented and ambitious, attributes that are associated with the pursuit of a career. By contrast, in the family tape she was seen as less independent, less active, less aggressive, less ambitious, less dominant, less success-oriented, and less able to withstand pressure. A woman's choice to have a family seems automatically to decrease her perceived competence.

There was a difference in response between men and women who saw the tapes. The women perceived Rose as more competent and attributed more positive characteristics to her when she described her career goals than when she described her family goals. For many of them her conflict was not an intellectual exercise but a real issue they had to face themselves. It seemed that Rose was perceived more favorably by women when espousing career goals because of the role-conflict identification and because of the social desirability of women's movement ideas among college students.

In contrast, men had a more favorable impression of Rose in the family tape. They found her to be more feminine, open-minded, sincere, intelligent, kind, well adjusted, sensitive, warm, and determined. They also liked her more in the family tape and said they would want to spend more time with her. There are several tentative explanations for these findings. It may be that career women are somewhat threatening for men, especially women as competent and successful as this one. It may also be that Rose was perceived as potentially less able to provide for men because of her commitment to a career and thus was seen as less feminine and less desirable. A woman who decides to give up a career and stay at home is more understandable, better fitting the usual sex-role stereotypes, and possibly less threatening. Thus, Rose was perceived by men both as a stereotyped woman (warm, sensitive, and kind) and as more open-minded, well adjusted, and similar to themselves.

One result seemed evident. Even for students, most of whom have been schooled in the negative effects of sex-role stereotypes and who are considered open-minded, the professional woman is still in a bind in which she is "doomed if she does and doomed if she does not." If she chooses a career she will be seen, especially by men, as less feminine, less likable, and less desirable. If she chooses a family she will be seen as less competent.

The Double Bind of Professional Women as a Cause of Burnout

With the changing roles of women and the growing influence of the women's movement, more women are choosing careers as an integral part of their life. This change is evident in the growing proportion of women who are entering the job market: the percentage of women in the United States labor force increased from 20 percent to 40 percent between 1920 and 1978, and has been increasing steadily.[20]

There is also a qualitative change in women's participation in the labor force. More women are choosing professional careers over occupations.[21] Occupations offer primarily financial gains and relatively few challenges. Careers involve continual learning and require high degrees of commitment. This change in work orientation has important consequences for women who regard their work as essential and central to their lives as a result of their increased commitment.

When they decide to have a family, many of these women feel conflicted about their two roles. Because of the career commitment, their roles at home and at work take on a new meaning. Sometimes this results in changed priorities, in which equal priority for home and work roles replaces the traditional preference for the home role. The changed priorities reflect a change at a far deeper level. For these career women the home role is no longer enough to achieve self-fulfillment. To feel that their lives have meaning they need to feel successful both in their homes and in their work roles. This is why role conflict leads dual career women to burnout,[22] and, in extreme cases, to emotional breakdown and suicide; among professional groups such as physicians and psychologists, for example, women have higher suicide rates than men, though the reverse is true for the general population.

In order to avoid this role conflict, increasing numbers of women are choosing not to have a family at all. Others resolve this dilemma by giving the family precedence over the career when they conflict. Other options, such as part-time positions and job sharing, are becoming more common and are making the choice of having both family and career more manageable.

Some professional women deal with their conflict by overadhering to sex-role stereotypes at home. These women do not see their jobs as a justification for doing less at home, as most men do. They therefore have high expectations of themselves that, when frustrated, cause them to feel guilt and anxiety about not fulfilling all of their responsibilities. These women believe that in addition to being "superprofessionals" they have to be "supermothers" and "superhomemakers."

It is the unfortunate reality that the woman still carries the burden of the conflict between career and family and she may pay the ultimate price of her choice—burnout.

In addition to the occupational stress that they have in common with men, working women may have stresses that result from their womanhood. These stresses can stem from external or internal social mores such as the belief that a woman can be either feminine (desirable) or competent and successful (unfeminine, undesirable). Thus the professional woman often finds little support from most of society in dealing with this dilemma.

Stress can be the result for women who combine a career and a home. A woman who takes a job outside the home is taking on two full-time jobs: she has the duties of the job as well as the major responsibilities for housework and child care.[23] As a result, employed wives have the least time to spend on themselves. The career woman/housewife-mother has been described as frantically performing all her duties simultaneously.[24] She may be the first one up in the morning to prepare breakfast for the family. During lunch she takes care of the family's errands. She shops for groceries on the way home and often, while her husband and children relax, she prepares dinner. In the evenings and on weekends she cleans the house, does the laundry, and takes care of the emotional needs of her husband and children.

Women's daily routines also contain a higher proportion of domestic interruptions than do those of men.[25] It is usually the mother who takes the children to the doctor and stays home with them when they are sick. It is usually the mother who goes to "conference day" with the teacher and is called when there is a problem at school. She may have no choice but to do these tasks at the expense of her job.

Most of the difficulties professional women encounter are the result of social barriers to women's abilities to implement their personal skills in a career.[26] Some of these barriers are sex-related role and occupational stereotypes that lead to the career/home conflict. In research on women, we found that role conflict and the distractions at home and at work were highly correlated with burnout: the more conflict and the more distractions, the more burnout.[27] The mother employed in a full-time job is more likely to be the one who is overburdened, harassed, and guilt-ridden. She is someone who cannot afford to get sick, take time for herself, or even collapse. She is also more likely than the professional man/father to be chronically exhausted and therefore is a likely candidate for burnout.

Shared Causes of Burnout
for Professional Women
and How to Cope with Them

In the study of three generations of professional women, the women showed similarities in their life satisfaction, their enjoyment of their roles as women, and the quality of their family relations. All of these are negatively correlated with burnout: the more satisfied a woman is with her life—the better her family relations and the more she enjoys her role as a woman—the less likely she is to burnout.

For all three groups we found that burnout increased as a result of being overextended in social obligations, having conflict between work and life outside of work, being distracted at work by thoughts about home problems, and being distracted at home by occupational obligations. These are sources of stress and thus causes of burnout for all professional women.

In the scientific literature, role conflict is perceived as a major source of stress, and not only for women. Role conflict exists when any individual in a particular role is torn by conflicting demands. Most commonly this occurs when a person is caught between two or more groups who demand different behaviors. Role conflict has serious consequences for one's subjective experience of stress as well as for one's performance.[28] Previous research found that those who suffered more role conflict had lower job satisfaction and higher job-related tension.[29] It was also found that the greater the authority of the people "sending" the conflicting role messages, the more job dissatisfaction produced by the role conflict and the more physiological strain. Role conflict also tended to make women more likely to work less effectively and to leave the organization.[30] And we found, as expected, that burnout increased as role conflict increased.[31]

In our research, we found that home pressures contributed as much to role conflict and stress of professional women as out-of-home pressures.[32] Other research has shown that the marriage role and the motherhood role are most likely, and the work role least likely, to be perceived as conflictual.[33] In another of our studies overlap between life and work stresses was found to be highly correlated with burnout.[34]

One recommendation for professional women is to separate home and work as much as possible, especially in regard to problems: when at work concentrate on the job and avoid thinking about home and home problems; try not to bring work home and avoid the intrusion of work problems into the home time. This is, of course, easier said than done. One way of implementing this strategy is to make a period of relaxation and "decompression" between work and home, allowing time to unwind from one set of stresses before facing another. One woman we interviewed said she went window shopping for decompression. Another just sat at the bus stop watching buses pass by. Others mentioned walking, jogging, listening to music, and meditating. Compartmentalization can help keep stresses limited in time and place and thus reduce conflict and burnout.

Although role conflict is a very important cause of burnout, the number of roles does not necessarily mean more conflict and more burnout. Various roles may be different routes to a women's self-actualization and self-expression and thus add to her life satisfaction rather than cause distress. Our recommendation is to use home and work activities as alternate sources of success and satisfaction. On days when you feel incompetent as a mother and a homemaker you can use your job to boost your self-esteem and sense of success. When things don't go well at work, your home can serve as an excuse. (This recommendation can also be applied by men who try to keep a balance between their work involvement and their involvement at home.) The happiest women are those who feel competent and successful in both roles. They derive a sense of meaning and achievement from the different activities in their multiple roles. In each role they express a different part of their personality and their abilities. As a result they are likely to be busy but they may live a full and exciting life. Sylvia is an example of a dual-career woman who coped successfully with the demands of her home and work.

Sylvia was a social worker in a perinatal unit of a children's hospital. Instead of being overburdened by the emotional stress of working with premature babies and their mothers, she found in her work a daily reminder of the value of life and health and her own good fortune. She knew she could not handle a full-time career while her child was young, so she worked only part-time. When at work she was involved totally, but when she left her work she avoided thinking about the tragedies her clients were dealing with. After working as a caseworker for two years, she decided to participate in a research project as a way to obtain some distance from her work. She needed to intellectualize several of the issues her clients were presenting because she felt too close to them. She was learning about research and felt she was growing professionally. Sylvia loved her work and felt successful in it. She also felt good about herself as a mother and a wife. The balance between her work and her role as a parent gave her life a sense of meaning. She was very aware of the dangers of burnout in both her work and parenthood and was very careful to avoid them both.

There are burned-out homemakers and happy homemakers. There are overburdened and harassed career women, and there are fulfilled and self-actualized career women. These are just two of the many contradictions of modern women. The ancient Hebrew scholars said that, although everything is a given, one still had the final choice. The choice that women have is their greatest advantage, an advantage many of them never realize.

A woman can choose to have or not to have a family. She can also choose to have or not to have a professional career. It is crucial for these decisions to be made in full awareness of their possible consequences. Each decision should be based on the woman's needs, desires, and abilities and be minimally influenced by social pressures. Each decision has almost irreversible consequences. It is difficult for a career woman to decide at age 45 that she would like to have four children. It is equally hard for a homemaker to decide at age 45 to venture into a brilliant scientific career. These far-reaching consequences make the initial choice complex and difficult.

Thus this decision must be made in full awareness and, once made, must be accepted without daily regrets. With either decision a woman may face powerful social pressures, and she must weigh her ability to withstand or accommodate such stress. She must be aware that she will face daily struggles for priorities of her time and energy. The home/career woman must define her goals in each of her different roles and distribute her mental, physical, and emotional energy accordingly. A decision to combine family and career means making compromises. The woman herself must decide how these compromises will be made, both between and within her roles.

The conscious and continual allocation of resources among a woman's various roles will reduce conflict and stress. This allocation may go beyond preventing burnout to bring about personal growth, if it takes into account the woman's own needs.

PART THREE

Cures

SEVEN

Intrapersonal Coping Strategies

COPING with burnout can (and should) happen on three levels: the level of the individual, the work team, and the organization. We will devote this chapter to the first level—coping within the person—and then proceed to the next two levels.

People experience life differently, and these differences have an effect on their likelihood to burn out. All of us know the eternally anxious person who expects a major disaster to be lurking around the corner at every moment of his waking hours. The disasters seem to follow this person around, and justify his world view. If a few days pass without a disaster, he will manufacture one to explain his feelings and behaviors. Even minor events take on the significance of a major catastrophe.

On the other hand, all of us also know the eternally relaxed person, whose peace of mind nothing in the world can shake. An event that is making you slightly hysterical produces only an understanding smile and a "Don't worry, it will work out." "How will it work out?" you demand to know, ready to tear out your hair and pound your fist against the wall. But her peace of mind is unshaken, as she calmly maintains that "everything will be all right." And somehow, against all laws of probability, for people like this things often do work out all right. It stands to reason that two such people will respond very differently to stresses imposed on them by their work, and consequently will have very different likelihoods of burning out.

What happens to *you* when you wake up in the morning, and realize that the alarm clock did not go off, and you are already late for an important meeting? Do you curse? Kick the dog? Punch something? Or do you take a deep breath and think calmly about what to do? Personality differences such as these mediate between the stresses of the external world and the experience of burnout. In some people this internal mediator buffers against burnout, in others it enhances its likelihood.

One type of behavior that increases the stress experienced by an individual and thus increases the likelihood of burnout, is the "Type A behavior."[1] You may recall that a Type A individual identifies too much with his work, sees in competition a threat, and responds to it with anxiety, hostility, and aggression. Hostility is the defining core of the Type A personality, and explains both its negative health outcomes and its relationship to burnout. Type A people see the world as adversary, interpret the intentions of others negatively, and adopt a self-protective and aggressive stance towards others. If such a person is also ambitious and has high expectations for self-actualization and success, the result is chronic frustrations, struggles with everyone around, and—with time—burnout.

Drs. Friedman and Rosenman believe that "Type A behavior can be altered and altered drastically; and it is a terribly dangerous delusion to believe otherwise."[1a] But since Type A's don't easily admit—even to themselves—the existence of any defect or stigma, most of them underplay the intensity of the syndrome.

In order to help Type A's free themselves from the thralldom of the syndrome, Friedman and Rosenman first attack their belief that their behavior was directly responsible for whatever success they achieved. They argue, instead, that Type A behavior actually impeded their progress in life:

> First, review your successes. How often were they really due to impatience? Were you ever promoted or did you achieve success in your job, position, business, or profession because you did things *faster*

than anyone else? Or because you easily became hostile or belliger-
ent? (pp. 211–12)

    ... If you have been successful, it is not *because* of your Type A
Behavior Pattern but *despite* it. (p. 213)

They go on to discuss a long list of coping strategies, out of
which we will mention only some of those that are also relevant for
coping with burnout:

- Submit your basic capacities and qualities to a rigorous self-
  appraisal. (p. 217)
- Try to retrieve your total personality by developing interest in the
  broader satisfactions of life and human culture. (p. 221)
- Establish life goals for your work and for your private life. These
  goals should serve to give purpose and meaning to your life.
  (p. 223)
- Don't devote as much energy and attention to trifling tasks as to
  truly major problems. (p. 228)
- Let your means justify your end. (p. 229)
- Accept the fact that your life must be structured upon and maintained by uncompleted processes, tasks, events. (p. 232)

All these suggestions can help the Type A person find a sense
of significance in things other than completing work in a hurry. This
is why they are also effective in preventing burnout.

    Another personality dimension related to burnout is "nonhar-
diness," characterized by alienation, helplessness, and indifference.
The three elements are obstacles for effective coping. With their
"help" nonhardy people make stressful events more stressful, and
thus increase their chance to burn out.[2]

    In Chapter 3 we argued that it is more helpful to look at hardi-
ness as a set of attitudes that can be learned and unlearned than to
see it as an innate personality structure (in other words, "once a
hardy person, always a hardy person").

    Of course traits such as curiosity, the tendency to find experi-
ences interesting and meaningful, a belief in one's power to influence one's environment, and a strong desire for variety are not limited to hardy people. We can look at curiosity, involvement, and
variety as universal human needs that are fully expressed in some
people and are stifled in others. Hardy individuals do not need to
be reintroduced to those elements. They only need to be reminded

of their rewarding power, or possibly assisted in transferring these traits from some other sphere of life—in which they are being expressed—to the sphere of work.

Curiosity, involvement, and variety promote tendencies in the individual that work against burnout. They remind people of those things in their work or outside of work that can give their life a sense of meaning.

Learning and understanding are basic motivators for human action. Human beings are born with a quest for learning and exploration that is sometimes called "curiosity." Curiosity is almost universal among children, but is unfortunately stifled in many of them on their way to adulthood. Those adults that allow themselves the luxury of indulging their curiosity tend to be more self-actualized and less burned out.

Albert Einstein once commented, "My scientific work is motivated by an irresistible longing to understand the secrets of nature and by no other feelings." Yet most of us somehow become immersed in the trivia of everyday living and do not allow ourselves to exercise our curiosity, thereby neglecting our own learning and development.

Some organizations provide opportunities for the expansion of learning and awareness by continuing education, conventions, or in-service classes. Unfortunately, not all organizations provide this and, even where it is available, many employees do not take advantage of the opportunities available to them. Interviews with professionals showed that people's use of available resources for growth at work and outside of work can affect their level of burnout. A learning environment can be somewhat subjective. Even in the same environment, different people can see different opportunities for learning. For example, we encountered two people who held the same job in a bookstore in a small university town. One of them developed burnout. "My job is so boring that I can't take it anymore. All I do is sell books or help people find them, which I can't do efficiently since I don't know where most of the books are anyway. Sometimes there are no people in the store and all I do is sit and wait for the day to end." The other person presented a different picture: "I make it a point to know about most of the new books that come into the store. I read their covers, try to read some of them at home or at the store when there are no customers. I feel that I'm constantly learning about books and about people. I sometimes exchange opinions with customers and like to note what kinds of books each person buys. I am busy all the time and I don't have one moment of boredom."

These two people shared an external environment but their internal environment differed markedly: one made himself open to new experiences and the other did not. People vary in their need for learning and the chances they take for its enhancement. Those for whom the need is most important tend to seek environments that facilitate it and to use every opportunity for intellectual development.

The point we want to make should be obvious by this time. Learning and development need not involve formal institutions; openness to new experience leads to constant acquisition of information. For people who are interested in other people, every train ride, museum visit, or stroll can be exciting. Those who are interested in natural phenomena or technological developments can also be exposed to new ideas almost incessantly. When we decide to be more open to learning, and when we make ourselves aware of the fact that the world is full of new experiences, we all become less likely candidates for burnout.

Curiosity motivates inquiries that lead to learning. It requires openness to new experiences and is often manifested in a high degree of involvement.

Involvement is primarily an active engagement with or in one's activities and environment. The opposite of involvement, according to Salvador Maddi, is "existential neurosis," a sad state that has some of the elements of burnout. More specifically, burnout is a failure in the existential quest for meaning.

Maddi describes existential neurosis as the belief that one's life is meaningless. Its primary characteristics (differentiating it from burnout) are apathy, boredom, and alienation from self and from society.[3] Maddi's example of an existential neurotic is Meursault in Albert Camus' *The Stranger*. Meursault believes that his life is meaningless and arbitrary, and he feels bored and apathetic. The major event of the novel is Meursault's murder of an Arab while walking on the beach. One would expect the commission of such an act of violence on the part of a middle-class bureaucrat like Meursault to be a major emotional trauma. And yet what is so strange about this murder is that it is committed in an apathetic, almost matter of fact, manner. Meursault murders without provocation or reaction, as part of his random behavior. His life is a psychological death, a state of nonbeing. The novel ends with Meursault, on his way to his execution, uttering that "nothing matters."

As we know, people can develop burnout because of the lack of meaning in their life or work. The need for meaning may be especially acute in those jobs where the employee does not have a sense of completion or effectiveness. This is a problem for professionals who deal with a client for brief periods of time without being able to follow through or for people who produce a small part of some product and do not see the product in its completed form.[4]

Certain activities are inherently more meaningful than others. For example, working as a brain surgeon is almost certainly more meaningful than working as a salesman of used cars. And yet it is possible for some brain surgeons to become apathetic, believing that their work is meaningless, while some car salesmen do derive a sense of meaning from their work. Like the two salesmen in the bookstore, we can either introduce meaning into our work activities or turn our backs on the inherent meaning in those activities. Even though there is no universal list of significant life and work values and even though meaningful things differ for different people, the way to change burnout to passion for life is to become involved.

The most intense experiences of involvement are probably the "flow experiences." It is customary to think that people who are involved in creative work experience less burnout than others. In a recent book, Mikaly Csikszentmikalyi describes such people: people who have "peak experiences," who are internally motivated, and who are involved in play as well as in work activities including chess players, rock climbers, dancers, surgeons, composers, and basketball players.[5] He looked for similarities in their experiences, motivation, and in the situations that produced enjoyment in them. What he found was that these people engage, more than others, in activities that are performed for their own sake and not for the purpose of receiving tangible rewards. These activities explore the limits of one's abilities and attempt to expand them. Most people studied described these experiences as involving creative exploration; they are experiences that lie at the optimal place between boredom and anxiety. The feeling during these activities was described as a "flow experience," a complete involvement with little distinction between the self and the environment and between past, present, and future.

Such "flow" is found most readily in activities such as chess and sports. It can also be found in art, in sciences, and in religious activities. Csikszentmikalyi reported that these various experiences have in common an inner flow where the activity is all, a state so enjoyable that people are willing to foresake a comfortable life for its sake. In his opinion, the clearest sign of "flow" is the merging of action and awareness; the person is aware of the action but not of the awareness. The awareness is centered around the activity and not around performance.

Another characteristic of the flow experience is the centering of attention on the activity alone, ignoring other stimuli in the environment. Nikolai Krogius, the Russian chess grandmaster, reported an incident that occurred during a chess tournament: a water jug fell to the floor with a resounding crash; almost everybody looked up except the English master Burn, who continued gazing at the chess board and later reported not hearing anything.[6] Other characteristics of flow are the loss of ego or self-forgetfulness, without losing touch with one's own physical reality; the control of actions without an active awareness of control and without worry about lack of control; coherent, noncontradictory demands for action with clear feedback on the actions; and no need for external goals or rewards.

Flow experiences constitute some of the happiest moments in people's lives, and remembrance of these experiences can be a major determinant in people's perceived happiness. "The peaks decide the meaningfulness of life, and a single moment can retroactively flood an entire life with meaning. Let us ask a mountain climber who has beheld the Alpine sunset and is so moved by the splendor of nature that he feels cold shudders running down his spine—let us ask him whether after such an experience his life can ever again seem wholly meaningless."[7]

The experience of flow seems to be the opposite of burnout. And, indeed, data indicate that people who are involved in activities to the point of "flow" report less burnout.[8] All of us can identify flow experiences in our own lives. We can determine their frequency and consciously attempt to increase it. This seems easier said than done, and yet we can make a start by exploring the conditions required to have such experiences and arranging to produce those conditions both at work and outside of work. As Csikszentmikalyi has indicated, certain kinds of activities are more likely to yield flow experiences than others. If such an activity is part of your vocation, you are indeed fortunate. If it is not, there are two things you can try to do: one is to try to make them part of your avocation (e.g., you could think about the kinds of things that you do, such as hiking, dancing, or painting, that produce a "flowlike" feeling and try to increase the frequency of these activities). Since, like most people, you probably spend almost half of your waking hours at work, it is important for you to find some aspect of your job that lends itself to a flow experience—that is to say, while very few people play chess or paint as an occupation, it is also the case that very few occupations are so barren as not to include some possibility for the creative individual to find a way to flow, at least some of the time, on the job.

Most people spend part of their time performing routine activities; most routine activities, repetitive and brief, are sources of stress when performed exclusively for long periods of time. But people may prefer them to nonroutine activities when they break long periods of overload. The same police officer or nurse who developed overload during the day can feel underload on a tranquil night shift. Routine, however, results from both the number of activities performed, and the types of activities. If you perform a large number of repetitive activities, you may suffer both from boredom and from overload.

Our studies have shown that people who perform monotonous activities tend to experience burnout; people who perform a variety of activities that enable them to use their capabilities rarely experience it.[9] This was true for both work and nonwork situations. For many people, boredom with their daily routines is a part of life. But these routines can be used to add variety to life. You can enjoy a creative, stimulating activity and then relax in a routine activity. The sense of variety and interest is not necessarily a matter of outside stimulation; rather, it can originate from within the person who can seek it or try to avoid it.

Several theoretical frameworks may account for the effects of variety on behavior and happiness. One of these involves the physiological activation or arousal system.[10] People function at their best at an optimal activation level. Extremely high activation levels create anxiety and strain and extremely low levels create boredom and anger. Studies of sensory deprivation, in which people were put in situations where visual, auditory, and tactile stimulation were severely restricted, documented reduced cognitive and motor capabilities, irritation, emotional regression, and even hallucinations.[11] After eighteen months in solitary confinement as a suspected spy in France, Christopher Burney wrote, "I soon learned that variety is not the spice; it is the very stuff of life."[12]

The variety of stimulation, as well as the level of stimulation, affect people's reactions. There seems to be a certain level of stimulation needed to satisfy the psychological complexity level of the organism.[13] When this level is not met, either because of overstimulation or understimulation, the individual tends to react negatively. When stimulation is too novel and variable, the individual will attempt either to narrow attention or to integrate it in large units of processing. When the amount of novelty and variety is too low, individuals will either become bored or will attempt to change their environment by seeking new events in their physical environment, their social environment, or their own thoughts.

No matter how initially exciting work may be, over time, boredom with the task and the monotony of the problems can wear anyone down. One way of circumventing these debilitating reactions is to change tasks periodically. Rather than simply repeating what you are good at, you can give yourself permission to be less than perfect as you experiment with new ideas, abilities, and approaches.

There are jobs in which there is little room for innovation; here, the people themselves can provide increased interest because people, in their uniqueness, can be a great source of variety. This can be a positive rather than negative characteristic of work, particularly for individuals in the human services who tend to choose their profession in order to work with people. Recall that one of the recommendations we made to dentists (see Chapter 1) was to spend more time getting to know their patients: dentists can get bored drilling and filling innumerable teeth. Teeth can be boring. But dentists are working primarily with people—not teeth. When they begin to recognize that every person they deal with is different and needs a different kind of reassurance, treatment, and conversation, then each appointment can become a unique experience. Our interest and sense of variety can be continually freshened by humanizing each situation, differentiating each person, and offering each a different part of ourselves.

One alternative available for increasing variety in certain settings is lateral job change. Another solution is more drastic job change—i.e., getting out of the profession. Before making a radical change, you should be certain that you are using all the resources for variety and lateral change that are available on the job. When radical job change is unavoidable, it is most productive to go "toward" new challenges rather than "away from" problems. Such positive career changes at mid-life, described as "starting over in midstream," were the subject of a study by Sol Landau, a Miami rabbi.[14] Landau interviewed individuals who switched to a new career during their middle years, ages 35 to 54. His interviewees represented a wide educational and socioeconomic background, but all of them were financially successful in their first careers. "I wanted to interview people who were making midlife changes because of their internal needs," he said, "not because they had been unsuccessful in their first career." Landau found most of the participants in his study "secure" and "self-reliant." "They are not habitual or compulsive changers," he learned. Theirs was a "quest for self-renewal," an escape from the dull routine that their day-to-day work had become. Landau found that among those he interviewed the most satisfying second careers were those most dissimilar to the first ones. Such switches included a mattress distributor who became a stockbroker, a military pilot turned physician, an executive who became a hypnotist-counselor, and a photographer who became a sociologist.

Expressing a range of interests and skills is a crucial factor in allieviating burnout. In the words of Bertrand Russell, "The secret of happiness is this: Let your interests be as wide as possible, and let your reactions to the things and persons that interest you be as far as possible friendly rather than hostile."[15]

Perhaps the best way to sum up what we have been saying in the last several pages is by focusing our attention on the young bookstore employees. You will recall that, although they were working at the same job, one of them found it full of opportunities for learning, while the other found it boring and stagnating. It would be tempting to explain the differences in their experiences in terms of their personalities: Sam is a more curious, sunny person; Harry is closed and sullen. Needless to say, people do differ from one another; at the same time it would be a grievous error to assume that vast differences in behavior are solely the result of rigid and unchangeable traits. In our work we have learned time and time again that individuals can change their own behavior and orientation to the world without the necessity of long-term psychotherapy or deep-seated personality change. What people need is the opportunity to become aware of the causes of their own stress, the drive to take some responsibility for change, the opportunity to gain cognitive clarity over what aspects of their environment (including the internal environment) can be changed, and the development of certain basic skills.

Thus, with some effort, Harry could learn to treat the bookstore as a place where he could be involved and learn a lot, and could also see his occupation as one that is meaningful. For example, working in a bookstore can be envisioned as providing people with a service and instilling in them an excitement about books, some of which might change their lives. Similarly, both Sam and Harry, with the proper orientation, would be able to make proper use of whatever success they were able to achieve. As we indicated earlier, even success can be a cause of burnout, if it is simply viewed as a step on a never-ending ladder toward some mythical goal or as a means of comparison to someone who is apparently more successful. With a little thought and care Harry could learn to take the time to enjoy and appreciate his own accomplishments before moving on to the next challenge. We have already indicated that Sam saw the bookstore as a place of infinite variety: different kinds of books, different kinds of customers, and so forth. There is no reason why Harry could not become aware of the same aspects of the bookstore with a little bit of effort and a little bit of trying. By the same token, while we would not presume to tell Sam, Harry, or those who read this book precisely what activities in their life would produce flow experiences or would help them actualize more of their potential, we do believe that the active examination of their day-to-day life, and the search for ways to increase these experiences, are reasonable first steps toward coping with burnout.

What to Do about Burnout

In the overview to this book (Chapter 1) we presented four major strategies for dealing with burnout: (1) being aware of the problem, (2) taking responsibility for doing something about it, (3) achieving some degree of cognitive clarity, and (4) developing new tools for coping and improving the range and quality of old tools. In subsequent chapters we recommended that managers try to increase their autonomy, commitment, and love of challenge; that people who work in the human services change their client-centered orientation to a more balanced relationship between themselves and their clients; we specifically recommended developing and maintaining a "detached concern." For people in bureaucratic organizations, we recommended learning how to become "good bureaucrats." We have suggested to professional women that some of their conflicts are a result of a social-psychological double bind and recommended that they make their life choices without succumbing to pressures from the outside, without guilt and without regrets. To move beyond burnout we suggested in the present chapter that individuals attempt to increase involvement, learning, and variety at work.

Although we can make generalized recommendations about strategies for coping with burnout, people obviously vary in their individual coping styles, and those coping styles differ in their effectiveness. Coping refers to *efforts* to master conditions of harm, threat, or challenge when an automatic response is not readily available.[16] Coping in itself does not imply *success* but *effort*. It is the link between stress and adaptation. This formal definition of coping was used in stress research and in our own studies. Stress studies focused mainly on coping at times of severe stress, such as injuries, the death of a child, imminent death, natural disaster, and job loss. Despite the clinical and theoretical importance of coping with everyday life, there was until very recently little research on this topic. Thus, our own work focused on coping with chronic stresses inherent in everyday life, rather than with dramatic life events.[17] We believe that it is the chronic nature of the stresses and their mundane meaningless character that makes them so difficult to endure.

Richard Lazarus, a leader in the field of stress research, suggested two general types of coping: (1) direct action, in which the person tries to master the stressful transaction with the environment and (2) palliation, in which the person attempts to reduce the disturbances when unable to manage the environment or when action is too costly for the individual.[18] Direct coping, or direct action, is a strategy applied externally to the environmental source of stress, and indirect coping, or palliation, is a strategy applied internally to one's behaviors and emotions. In our own work, in addition to the direct/indirect dimensions of coping, we found an inactive/active dimension.[19] Active ("approach") coping strategy involves confronting or attempting to change the source of stress or oneself, while inactive ("avoidance" or "withdrawal") coping strategy involves avoidance or denial of the stress by cognitive or physical means. These two dimensions, direct/indirect and active/inactive, generate four types of coping strategies, each of them represented by three actions (see Figure 7–1).

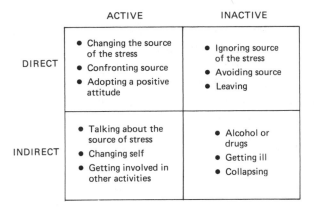

Figure 7-1   *Coping Grid*

1. Direct-active: changing the source of stress, confronting the source of stress, finding positive aspects in the situation
2. Direct-inactive: ignoring the source of stress, avoiding the source of stress, leaving the stressful situation
3. Indirect-active: talking about the stress, changing oneself to adapt to the source of stress, getting involved in other activities
4. Indirect-inactive: drinking or using drugs, getting ill, collapsing

In one study involving 147 subjects, we asked what their major life and work stresses were, and then asked them to describe how they coped with these stresses. Twenty percent of the respondents reported that they confronted the source of their stress as a coping technique. Twenty percent indicated that they avoided the sources of stress (18 percent) or did nothing about them (2 percent). Forty-nine percent used a variety of indirect-active techniques: talking about the stress (20 percent), thinking about it (12 percent), studying (9 percent), getting involved in other activities (7 percent), physical activities, religious activities, and relaxation (1 percent); 11 percent reported a variety of indirect-inactive coping styles: worrying and crying (4 percent), drinking, eating, and smoking (1 percent), accepting the situation (4 percent), doing nothing (2 percent).

In a second study involving eighty-four subjects, we provided a list of the four categories of coping strategies and asked them to indicate how often they used each coping strategy and how successful they subjectively perceived the coping to be. The results of this study indicated that active strategies were used most often to cope with burnout and were reported the most successful. Inactive strategies were used less frequently and were reported least successful: the more frequent the use of active strategies, the less burnout; the more frequent the use of inactive strategies, the more burnout. An exception to this pattern was the direct-inactive action of ignoring the source; this action was found more similar to the active strategies than to the passive ones. It is important to make the distinction between ignoring and avoidance on the one hand and denial on the other hand. Ignoring the stress is a conscious decision that an individual makes about the problem. In effect the individual says "This is a difficult, unpleasant set of circumstances that I choose not to deal with right now; but I know it's there, and I know I'll have to deal with it sooner or later." In contrast, the individual in denial convinces himself that there *is* no problem, that everything is just fine. But, unlike the avoided problem, the problem that is denied will eventually grow without the individual's awareness, and will ultimately cause greater distress when least expected. Moreover, since individuals require considerable effort to continue denying, in the face of mounting evidence to the contrary, individuals in denial are typically experiencing emotional exhaustion. Indirect-inactive strategies seem to be symptoms of high levels of burnout. Individuals who use them frequently also report high levels of burnout. It is not clear whether burnout causes an individual to drink, smoke, or take medication to excess or whether these excesses make one burn out, but clearly there is a relationship between them.[20] Indirect-inactive strategies are at best ineffective, inasmuch as they do not reduce stress but ultimately weaken individuals so that they become less capable of functioning adequately. In fact, it might be argued that drinking alcohol to excess, depending upon sleeping pills, and so forth are not coping strategies at all but simply ways of attaining very temporary relief from anxiety.

People who use active strategies successfully find they alleviate burnout because active strategies are likely to change the source of stress. Professionals who attack the source of their stress directly, for example, by confronting their boss; professionals who avoid the stress, for example, by ignoring the outburst of a client; and professionals who deal with stress indirectly, for example, by talking about it with a friend are all going to experience less burnout than the professionals who drink to forget the stress.

Even though people are aware of the coping strategy they

tend to use most commonly, it is important that they do not label themselves as such copers exclusively, i.e., "I am a direct-active coper." A comparison between men and women, for instance, revealed that women tended to use indirect methods of coping more frequently, such as talking about the stress, getting ill, and collapsing. Men tended to use the direct strategies of changing the source of stress and ignoring the source of stress more often. More women than men also said that talking about the stress was a more successful coping strategy and ignoring it was less successful. Even if one strategy is used successfully in certain situations, that does not mean it has to be used exclusively. We encountered men who labeled themselves direct-active copers and who found themselves paralyzed when they had to be in a situation where a direct-active approach would be dysfunctional. For example, suppose the major source of stress for someone is the gruff and threatening behavior of his supervisor, and he knows that if he confronts him directly on the issue the supervisor will respond in a gruff and threatening manner. If he has labeled himself a "direct-active" person, and if somehow that is tied up with his self-image as a "man," what he has succeeded in doing is paralyzing himself—that is, if by his own definition it would be "unmanly" to try to cope indirectly with the stress, and since he is convinced that the "manly" approach would be a disaster in this situation, he has doomed himself to live with that stress. The best coper is a person who is capable of mastering conditions of harm, threat, and challenge in a variety of ways, and who uses in each situation the best, most effective strategy for that particular situation.

Under what circumstances is each coping category (or response cluster) appropriate or likely to be effective? Dov Eden, a business administration scholar at Tel-Aviv University, attempted to answer this question.[21] According to Professor Eden, stressful situations can be classified according to two independent dimensions, which combine to make the different responses to stress more or less feasible or effective. The first dimension is mutability. The situation may be immutable, such as a hazard built into the task itself which threatens the individual's well-being. For example, a test pilot can't remove potential dangers from his job; one of his tasks is to reveal these dangers by exposing himself to them before they have been discovered. The situation may be mutable, as in the case of a subordinate caught between the conflicting demands of two superiors. By informing them of the conflict, or by meeting with both together, or by using the good services of a third party, the stressful conflict can be in principle, and often is in practice, reduced or eliminated. So the first step in diagnosing a stressful situation is to determine its degree of mutability.

The second dimension is continuousness or intermittency. Some stresses are continuous, that is, they constantly pose a threat to the individual. Others are intermittent. Intermittent stresses have different periodicities. Tax consultants have a period of stressful overload building up gradually for several months and peaking in April. Stress periodicity is predictable for many jobs, such as urban taxi drivers (rush hour), school teachers (beginning and end of school year), and preventive maintenance crews (during scheduled shutdowns). Periodicity may be variable and unpredictable, such as emergency crews, hospital emergency room staffs, military units in wartime, negotiations during wildcat strikes, and fire-fighting crews. The combination of dichotomized mutability and intermittency produces four categories of stress situations.

The best coping with a mutable and continuous situational stress is direct-active coping. Mutable stress can be changed, and, since it is continuous, it is probably worth investing the effort to alter the source. When the source is mutable but the stress is intermittent, direct-active coping is still possible, but, depending on periodicity, how severe the stress is, and how much effort is required to change the source of stress, the individual might prefer to leave or ignore it.

When the source is immutable and the stress is intermittent, people cannot use direct-active coping. They can seek relief—temporary (catharsis or diversion) or permanent (change self)—and thus adjust to an unalterable situation. The suggestion here is that people need intermittent relief from intermittent stress. They do not need to adjust when the stress is "off" but do when it is "on." Adjustment can aid them in getting through peak periods of stress.

Immutable stress that is continuous causes the most difficulty for individuals. They cannot cope because it is immutable. The situation offers no relief, for the stress is continuous. If the individuals can use indirect-active coping, they will generate their own relief. If, however, they cannot change themselves enough to narrow the gap between the environmental demands and their own capacity, or if the temporary relief achieved through catharsis and diversion is insufficient to enable them to continue functioning in the situation, their only alternative to burnout may be to escape stress by leaving the situation.

The general strategies for dealing with burnout that were presented in the previous chapters, and the classes of responses to stress presented in the previous paragraphs, can be viewed as general approaches that can be effective against burnout. The rest of this chapter will be devoted to more specific and concrete recommendations for coping on the level of the individual. Some of them have been mentioned earlier but we feel that they should be emphasized even at the risk of redundancy.

Keeping a log of daily stresses, coping strategies, and success or failure in coping can be a first step in becoming aware and in reducing burnout. At the end of each day (for a period of one week to one month) you can list and describe the day's stresses and joys. People who have kept such a log claim that it is important to start with the list of joys, since starting with stresses can be so depressing that by the time you are finished you may not remember any joyous experiences at all. Each stress and joy can be evaluated on the following intensity scale:

1	2	3	4	5	6	7
not at all intense			moderately intense			extremely intense

Each stress should be described in terms of the coping effort it generated. For example, if the stress was a nasty comment by your supervisor, what was your response? Did you confront your supervisor actively and directly and tell her how her comments made you feel (direct-active)? Did you avoid her for the rest of the afternoon (direct-inactive)? Did you call up your best friend and cry on his shoulder (indirect-active)? Or did you sneak out of the office to get a drink at a nearby bar (indirect-inactive)? For each one of these responses you should also indicate how successful it was, from 1 (not at all) to 7 (extremely). At the end of a week or a month you can go over your log and try to identify patterns in your stresses and in your attempts to master them. Some people find their stress generated primarily by work, others by their home life, still others by certain people or activities. Some people also identify in such a log patterns of coping behavior that they find effective. Others realize that they are locked into very ineffective coping strategies. Most people find that they use a rather limited vocabulary of coping strategies and that they should try to broaden their response repertory.

The stresses that are likely to be the hardest to cope with are those generated by frustrated hopes. All of us remember why we chose our line of work; periodically we can explore to what extent our original hopes and expectations are being fulfilled. Burnout is usually associated with the lost awareness of hopes and ambitions. It is not clear whether losing the awareness of goals is the cause or the result of burnout, but their coexistence implies a recommendation: It is very important for you to continually reappraise both your long-term and short-term goals. These goals and hopes must be realistic both for yourself and for those with whom you deal. For example, it may be worthwhile for therapists to develop their diagnostic skills so they know what to expect realistically of themselves and of their clients. In this regard we mention a self-destructive experience shared by many such professionals: when starting a career, professionals attempt to do things simply because they do not know that these things are impossible. They may devote themselves to a case and perform a "miracle." But forever after these professionals feel guilty doing less than that first effort, knowing they once were capable of that maximum. Such goals are unrealistic and self-destructive.

Before setting goals it is important to clarify priorities. One way of doing this that we have used successfully in our workshops is fantasizing stripping off roles. When you think about the roles you play in your life, what is important in those roles, and what is their relative importance? In evaluating each role, you should try to get in touch with the feeling of what life would be like without that role: what it would be like without being a "loving father," a "beloved wive," a "sexy woman," or a "successful professional." In order to do that you can imagine peeling off these roles as you peel off layers of clothing. Getting in touch with the feeling of what it is like to peel off each one of these roles forces reconsideration and a rewriting of priorities in a way that simply thinking about priorities doesn't.

Focusing on reevaluation and reassessment enables consideration of what changes you may want to make in the way you live your day-to-day life, and exactly how much power and how many options you have in making these changes. Some changes may be extraordinarily difficult to make; others may be easier than you think.

When setting and clarifying goals, it is important to distinguish between problems that can and cannot be changed. The two most common mistakes are giving up too early and hanging on too long. You can both see how to solve a problem and distinguish the problems that can be solved from those that cannot. Some people have a dysfunctional tendency to focus on fifty things that cannot be changed, thereby either frustrating or depressing themselves. You can be most effective by focusing on the few things that can be changed.

It is always easy to put off making changes by convincing yourself that, for one reason or another, "the time isn't right." This occurs primarily because the anticipation of change almost always produces some anxiety. At the same time you should realize that if you have decided that the change is important, it is unlikely that there will be a better time than now. A friend of ours who never went to college projected herself as graduating from college five years in the future. But then she said, "But my God, I am forty-eight years old. If I start college today, I will be fifty-two by the time I am finished." "And how old will you be in four years if you don't go to college?" we asked. It is helpful when planning for the future to project life five years from now in terms of such things as house, car, spouse, job, and so forth. The greater the difference between the future projection and current reality, the sooner the change must start. It is important to recognize time as a precious and limited resource.

There is a limit to everybody's energy. We all must be aware of self-imposed stresses and of danger signs of burnout, and be willing to nurture ourselves. Our emotional, mental, and physical energy supplies are not endless. After a certain point, the longer and the harder we work, the less we are probably accomplishing.

If you are feeling fatigued, resentful, disenchanted, and discouraged, or experiencing even more severe symptoms of burnout, it may be wise for you to take some time off work. Time off can be a long weekend, a week, a couple of weeks, a month, or even more if possible. During this "time off" you can analyze what is happening and why it is happening. Such analysis will probably also suggest better coping strategies.

People should not wait for a crisis to take time off. They must limit the number of hours on a given job and regularly take time off on evenings, weekends, and vacations. This is especially important if they work and live in the same place; if they do (residential counselors are a case in point), then it is best if they can work four weeks and take the fifth week off, work three months and take the fourth month off, and so on. All people must have an outside life that is separate from the work sphere, have some space of their own even in a live-in situation. This is true for homemakers as well as for professionals. It is essential to beware of workaholism, of working overtime regularly and letting work get introduced into your home. When the job becomes overwhelming, the worker must stop and examine priorities.

It is important to keep a balance between energy invested in the work sphere and the energy invested in life outside of work. It is also important to compartmentalize life and work, being at work completely, and then leaving completely. This compartmentalization enables people to be involved in each one of the roles they play and yet to limit the stresses inherent in those roles to their time and place. Overlap between life and work stresses was found to be highly correlated with burnout. It is important, for example, not to bring work problems home. Discussing a work crisis with friends or spouse will recreate the traumatic experience; presenting one's own side of the situation is not likely to provide any new understanding or any new resources for coping. The best people to talk with about work problems (as we will see in the next chapter) are co-workers who know the situation and may be able to provide new perspectives, insights, and resources.

It is useful to have a period of "decompression" after work, time to be quiet, meditate, exercise, or relax. Such a period of decompression will help one get away from the problem at work and make homecoming less stressful, especially for dual-career women. In our work we found a variety of decompression techniques people use, including listening to operas on the long drive home, sitting at a bus stop and watching the buses pass by, sitting in a jacuzzi, jogging, swimming, sleeping, and window shopping.

Committed workers tend to burn out because they take on too much for too long and too intensely. They need to develop safeguards that will help them cope more effectively. The safeguards include being aware of work stresses, recognizing the danger signs of burnout, acknowledging vulnerabilities, putting reasonable limits on their work, and setting realistic goals. Most important for people in the human services is to be willing to provide for themselves as well as for their clients by changing the client-centered orientation to a more balanced client-provider relationship. They can learn to treat themselves as if they were their own client. They should make time to do the things they love but do not do often enough and acknowledge themselves as people who have legitimate needs. In order to be of help to others people must have a nourishing life of their own. Overinvolvement at work—a problem not only for people in the human services but for managers and corporate executives as well—can be a sign that workers have given up trying to find meaningful outside activities and relationships. Executives can become so immersed in the organization that they have no time left for themselves and their own lives. Since only one thing gives them a sense of meaning in life, in the long run such overinvolvement increases their likelihood of burnout.

One technique to avoid overinvolvement is to list the three things you enjoy but seldom do and the three things you hate but do too often. A need to reorder priorities may be apparent. For example, if your work life is primarily cerebral, verbal, future-oriented, (as is the case with corporate executives) or emotionally demanding, (as is the case with human service professionals) you may need to add more physical things that are nonverbal and are present-oriented. One of the most consistent findings in our studies is the high correlation between burnout and poor physical health.[22] Being in good physical shape enables you to withstand better whatever stresses you encounter. You can provide your own reinforcements. This means building your self-esteem so that if people at work have difficulty appreciating your skill, you can provide that appreciation and that respect for yourself. Specifically, at the end of each day, or at least at the end of each week, you can ask yourself what you did this day or week that was good. You can allow yourself the luxury of real appreciation for the skill and hard work that go into your day-to-day life. You can be your own best audience. This is easier if you set your own short-term goals and are willing to acknowledge achieving them.

Burnout is the result of a social-psychological interaction between a person and an environment. We need to learn to see ourselves in situational rather than dispositional terms. For example, it is not helpful for us to think of ourselves as "shy" people.[23] It is much more useful for us to cut through the labeling and examine the situations that induce us to pull back and not assert ourselves and thereby fail to get what we want. Once we examine this it may become clear that with a little extra effort we can behave in ways that are more productive and personally satisfying.

Some things that look serious at the time they happen can appear funny a week or a month later. If we can learn to laugh at ourselves thirty minutes later rather than a month later, we can ease our stress. We can rank difficult experiences on a 1 to 10 stress scale, remembering to save the extreme negative end of the scale for the real tragedies of life and bringing our ranking of everyday stresses down the scale *when* they are happening. We *must* keep a sense of humor! Although as professionals we have to take our work seriously, we don't have to take ourselves seriously all the time. We must be prepared to laugh at our own foibles and at some of the difficult but often hilarious things that happen in our work and life.

These intrapersonal coping strategies are not all-inclusive. They represent the best of our knowledge about buffers against burnout and about those experiences that can transcend prevention to enhance personal growth.

In the struggle to go beyond burnout, having faith that we can do something often provides its own verification. In some instances the belief that a task can be accomplished helps get it accomplished. But even when the task does not get finished, or does not get done well, having faith in our ability makes performing the task more interesting, more exciting, more fun. Reality demands a certain degree of compromise, but the concessions made should not be too large. A belief in the power to shape our life and a merging of reality and imagination are important for happiness. It is important to believe in the congruence between actions and needs, lifestyle and wills, dreams and daily living.

Achieving this congruence is not simple. Past paths promise the security of the known; new avenues provoke the anxiety of the uncertain and the risk of failure and regret. But this anxiety is an integral part of life that involves change and growth. Choosing new paths requires courage and the recognition of our power over our life. It also requires a sense of control over our actions in selecting among existing alternatives and generating new ones. If we want to go beyond preventing burnout, if we want to achieve congruence between dreams and reality, if we want to get a sense of significance from our work, we have continually to seek alternatives for actions and to create new options.

Although burnout can be a traumatic and depressing experience, it can also be the beginning of greater understanding and increased awareness. Such growth can be likened to the martial arts in which one uses the momentum of the opponent to defeat him or her. So it can be with burnout. If people are provided with adequate tools for coping with stress, they often emerge wiser, stronger, and more insightful than if they had not burned out in the first place.

EIGHT

Social Support Systems

"No man is an island, entire of itself; every man is a piece of the continent," said John Donne, the sixteenth-century poet. Poets as well as psychologists have recognized for a long time that human beings are social animals, that their need for intimacy and their interdependence on one another are a vital aspect of being human. We all know that the human infant could not survive for very long without being cared for and nurtured by that part of a social system known as the family. What is equally true is that adults as well are dependent on membership in an elaborate social system without which survival as a human being would be extremely unlikely. Social factors play a primary role as both causes and cures of burnout.

Kurt Lewin, one of the founding fathers of social psychology, emphasized the importance of social factors such as group membership for almost every type of behavior: the goals that people set for themselves are influenced by the social standards of the groups to which they belong and wish to belong.[1] The individual is usually a member of many overlapping groups. One might be a member of a professional group, a political party, and a hobby club. Different groups influence an individual's behavior to different degrees. For one person business may be more important than politics; for another, the political party may be the most influential. The influence of different groups varies at different times; at home, for example, the influence of one's family is generally greater than when one is at work. The group to which a person belongs is one of the most important constituents of the "ground on which he stands": "The speed and determination with which a person proceeds, his determination to fight or to submit, and other important characteristics of his behavior, depend upon the firmness of the ground on which he stands."[2]

Marc Pilisuk, the University of California scholar, wrote that "for most of the history of humankind, the particular web in which an individual was enmeshed consisted of a group of perhaps 15 to 150 individuals, spanning the life cycle."[3]

Most people belong to one family in which they are children and to another family in which they are spouses and parents. People also belong to extended families in which they are grandchildren, grandparents, in-laws, aunts, uncles, nieces, and nephews. During their lives, people develop networks of friends. Some maintain very special relationships with childhood friends throughout their adult lives. Others change friends frequently and develop relationships with people they live near to or with whom they share interests. Some neighbors and group members become intimate friends; others remain at the level of acquaintances. In addition to the social systems of family, friends, and community, people belong to social systems at work. These social systems include supervisors, subordinates, co-workers, and clients. They also include colleagues in other settings and professional groups.

Each of the systems we belong to involves demands that are built into the role we play in that system. For example, there are certain things expected of a "father," a "wife," or a "business partner." If we violate these demands we can be ridiculed or criticized. In extreme cases of role violations we may be divorced, fired, or punished by law. Each one of the systems involves some common and some unique stresses and rewards.

Given the fundamental importance of this elaborate network of social systems with their concomitant benefits and demands, it should not be surprising to learn that conflictual demands from various systems, or the ambiguity of such demands, are a major source of burnout, and that the efficient and creative use of a social support system is among the most effective ways of coping with burnout.

We have found it to be very valuable for individuals to clarify the extent to which various social systems place demands on their time. In our workshops we ask participants to make a list of the social systems that are most salient to them (such as nuclear family, extended family, and work) and under each heading to make a list of the demands that each of these systems places on the individual. For example, Philip teaches biology at the university. He is 34 years old and has three young children. For Phil, the most demanding aspect of his life is his job. His list of demands includes:

1. Doing a lot of individual research
2. Publishing that research
3. Training graduate students to do research
4. Being a stimulating and entertaining lecturer in a large undergraduate class
5. Advising dozens of students about courses, careers, etc.
6. Being a helpful resource to his colleagues
7. Serving on a great number of university committees (and impressing the other committee members with his brilliance)
8. Being the "life of the party" at social gatherings organized by the chairman of his department
9. "Casually" dropping references to poetry and literature during conversation with his older colleagues as a way of letting them know that he is not "narrow"

When we list demands in this manner and then examine the list, we are in a better position to ascertain the extent to which the demands are essential, current, legitimate, and reasonable. For example, Philip feels that all of these things are important and that he must exert a great deal of energy meeting these demands if he is to be promoted to tenure in his department, which is his paramount concern.

Compared to this, the demands imposed by his family are extremely light. Naturally he must earn a living to support his wife and young children; he also stays home and babysits one afternoon a week so that his wife can take a pottery course. And he helps discipline the children, occasionally tells them bedtime stories, occasionally takes them on a weekend outing, and so forth.

Interestingly enough, Philip felt more resentment at the relatively small demands placed on him by his family than he did at the huge list of demands that he saw as emanating from his job. Moreover, he considered his family much more important to him than his job. What Philip learned from making this list was that he was shortchanging his family. In addition, by scrutinizing his list in a careful and honest manner, he came to realize that many of the demands he listed as emanating from his university job were more self-imposed than system-imposed. In other words, under close inspection he gained insight into the fact that he was making demands on *himself* as a teacher, researcher, and colleague far in excess of what his university expected of him, and these demands were usurping time and energy that could perhaps be spent more productively in other systems that, according to his own values, were more important to him.

We would recommend that you make your own lists and do your own scrutinizing. As we noted, it is of great importance to clarify any ambiguity that exists between a real demand imposed by a particular system and your own self-demand. For example, Susan's mother might like her to call home occasionally, but Susan puts the demand on herself to call three times a week. After a while she may act as if the "three times a week" dictum emanated from her mother, but under close examination she will realize that this was her own. We must separate actual requirements from our interpretation of them and from the requirements we impose on ourselves. Occasionally we can even test this—thus Philip could take on fewer advisees and serve on fewer committees, Susan could cut back to one phone call a week and see if there were any serious repercussions.

In addition to making demands, social systems are a source of some of our most important rewards. One of the main rewards provided by people, and a major function of a social system, is support.

Social support was defined by Sidney Cobb, M.D., of Brown University, as *information* leading subjects to believe that they are cared for and loved, esteemed, and valued, and that they belong to a network of communication and mutual obligation.[4] Dr. Cobb reviewed an extensive body of literature documenting that supportive interactions among people protect them against many of the health consequences of life stress from low birth weight to death, from arthritis through tuberculosis to depression, alcoholism, and social breakdown. Furthermore, social support may reduce the amount of medication required and accelerate recovery. Strong evidence over a variety of transitions in the life cycle from birth to death documents that social support is protective.

Social support systems have been defined by Gerald Caplan, who studied them extensively, as *enduring interpersonal ties* to groups of people who can be relied upon to provide emotional sustenance, assistance, and resources in times of need, who provide feedback, and who share standards and values.[5] The practical definition of a support system is the people who support an individual through crises and calm and with whom feelings can be shared without fear of condemnation. By providing emotional sustenance, supportive others help individuals master their own emotional problems by mobilizing their psychological resources. Additionally, by providing these people with tangible aid, resources, information, and guidance, the supporters further enhance the individuals' ability to cope with stressful situations. Ideally, according to Caplan, one belongs to several supportive groups at home and at work, in church and in recreational or avocational sites. Social support systems serve as buffers for the individual; they help maintain the psychological and physical well-being of the individual over time.

In our work we have found that the creative use of social support systems provides an effective prevention mechanism against burnout. We have also found that most people do not make adequate use of potential social support systems; rather, they squander this valuable resource out of a lack of understanding of the importance of social support systems, their various functions, and how best to utilize them.

The Functions
of a Social Support System

Social support systems serve a multitude of functions. We have found it useful to organize these various functions into six basic categories: listening, technical support, technical challenge, emotional support, emotional challenge, and the providing of social reality. When individuals encounter people in their environment who fulfill all these functions they are well protected against burnout and go a long way toward reducing stress in life and work.

It is extremely important for individuals to learn to discriminate among the different social support functions. People in a situation that tends to produce a great deal of burnout often have the vague feeling that they are not getting enough social support. This often results in a general feeling of disappointment that those people who are closest to them (e.g., a wife or a husband) are not providing enough support *even when the specific support needed is far beyond the scope of their usual role.* To be disappointed in a person for not supplying the kind of support that could not reasonably be expected from him or her is, of course, terribly unfair. The nature of this unfairness will be clear in a moment, when we describe the various functions of a social support system. For now, let it suffice to say that our listing six functions is not simply an academic exercise. It has immediate, practical application because individuals must learn to discriminate among these functions, so that they can be aware of which functions are being fulfilled and which are not. Moreover, once individuals have learned to discriminate among the various functions, they can make a realistic assessment of which individuals in the environment would be most appropriate to fulfill those functions that have been left uncovered.

Everyone has occasions when they need one or more people who will *actively listen* to them, without giving advice or making judgments. They need someone with whom they can share the joys of success as well as the pain and frustration of failure. They need someone with whom they can share conflicts as well as trivial everyday incidents. People working in a stressful occupation occasionally need to let off steam. A good active listener is understanding and sympathetic. A poor listener can blunder in several different ways. For example, suppose a ninth grade teacher working in a very difficult ghetto school has just had a difficult time with a student and comes into the teachers' lounge complaining about the intractability and aggressiveness of that student. What the teacher needs is someone who will pay attention and who will indicate interest, understanding, and perhaps even sympathy for the situation. What the teacher *doesn't* need is someone who will immediately give free advice or someone who will play "Can you top this?" (i.e., who will say, "You think *that's* bad, let me tell you about one of *my* students"). Another thing the teacher *doesn't* need is someone who seems insensitive to the fact that the teacher is simply letting off steam and who will decide the teacher doesn't really care about or understand students. It should be clear that finding a good active listener (and being one for other people) is not as easy as it seems; indeed most people in our environment are quick to give advice or make judgments rather than simply listen. And giving advice, making judgments, or playing "Can you top this?" usually increases burnout.

All individuals also need *technical appreciation* for the work they do; when they do a good piece of work, they need to have it acknowledged. In order to provide individuals with technical appreciation and affirmation of competence, people must meet two important criteria: they must be expert in their field and their honesty and integrity must be trusted. In other words, these people must understand the complexities of the job they do and be courageous enough to provide honest feedback. If those requirements are met, individuals can accept support as genuine. A moment's reflection should reveal that, for most people, their mother is not an ideal person to fulfill this function: most people's mothers are not technical experts; moreover, their mothers are not objective enough to provide them with "trustworthy" positive statements. Mothers, spouses, or nonexpert friends *can* provide general encouragement, but it may not be as meaningful as if it came from someone who can appreciate the technical intricacies of the job situation. The ability to provide technical appreciation is especially powerful and useful when it comes from knowledgeable supervisors.

It can be comforting to be in an environment where you are the expert and no one challenges that expertise. This comfort might be especially useful and welcome when under stress. Unfortunately, too much comfort of this sort can produce burnout; that is, if we are not challenged we run the long-term risk of stagnation and boredom. A comedian may go from nightclub to nightclub telling exactly the same jokes. As long as the audience changes at each nightclub he can get away with doing the same routine. Chances are that within a year he will begin to burn out. If the comedian has a weekly television show, he is forced to change his act, because the audience is the same from week to week. While this is more difficult, it prevents him from stagnating. Television presents him with a *technical challenge* that forces him to develop new routines continually, and the challenge produces growth.

Contact with colleagues who know as much or more about the job keeps workers from stale or superficial efforts. Critical colleagues can challenge workers' ways of thinking, stretch them, encourage them to attain greater heights, and lead them to greater creativity, excitement, and involvement in the job. People who fill this role of challenger must have two characteristics: they must be good enough at the job to be able to identify what could be improved and they must be trustworthy—that is, workers must know that the colleagues' criticism is not intended as humiliation or to enhance their own egos at the worker's expense. The best of colleagues can trust each other both in appreciation and in challenge functions.

An important function of an effective support system is *emotional support* or appreciation. By emotional support we mean that people are willing to be on an individual's side in a difficult situation even if they are not in total agreement with what the person is doing. Most individuals need someone who is willing to provide unconditional support at least occasionally. This can be vital in a stressful job. It is enough to have one person who is in your corner; it is marvelous to have this kind of support from *four* or *five* people. If this is not present or possible at work, it is essential to have it at home. Unlike technical support and technical challenge, for which the supporter must be an expert in the individual's field, emotional support is something that people at home—parents, spouse, and friends—can do. Emotional support does not require any kind of technical expertise; what it does require is someone who cares more about the individual as a human being than about the particular position the person is espousing at the moment, the particular piece of work just completed (which may not be among his or her best), or even about the bad mood the person might be in at the moment. Especially when under stress, individuals appreciate the people at work and at home who support them win or lose.

People can delude themselves into thinking they are doing their best when they are not. It is comforting for them to convince themselves that all avenues have been explored when they have not. Occasionally it is easy to blame someone else rather than take responsibility for problems or crises. These defense mechanisms occasionally are useful because they keep people from putting excessive emotional pressures on themselves, but their continual use can block emotional growth and impede the most efficient employment of their energies. At that point friends can help by questioning their excuses.

To serve in this stretching function, friends can challenge the individuals, questioning if they are really doing their best to fulfill their goals and overcome the obstacles. *Emotional challenge* is different from technical challenge. Friends do not have to be expert in a particular area of expertise in order to offer the opportunity to grow emotionally. Friends merely have to say, "Are you sure you are doing enough?" But trust is still a prerequisite for this function.

In other cases individuals may be so emotionally caught up in a situation that they cannot think rationally or logically, and yet they have a problem that needs a rational solution. The rational solution may be right in front of them, but their emotionality prevents them from seeing it. An emotional challenge in this situation does not require specific expertise but rather requires the use of logic as a way of helping the individuals cut through their own emotionality in order to arrive at a rational solution. An example will clarify.

A friend of ours whom we will call Joshua reports an incident where his old college roommate visited him in a state of obvious distress. His roommate was facing a serious crisis in his marriage and needed advice. He was upset and confused and couldn't make up his mind as to whether or not to seek a divorce. Joshua was in a difficult position. While he cared a great deal about his old college roommate, he had seen him only on a few occasions during the past ten years, hardly knew his wife at all, and certainly did not qualify as an expert on his friend's marital situation. Yet he was able to function as an excellent emotional challenger. As he listened to his friend, it became clear that what was most upsetting to the latter was a certain set of behaviors that his wife persisted in performing and that he found unacceptable. Joshua asked two questions: First, is there any likelihood that she will change those behaviors? His friend's answer was a definite no. Second, is there any way that he can learn to tolerate those behaviors? The answer to that question was again no. Joshua paused and looked at his friend. At that moment his course of action became clear to him. Joshua did not have to give him any technical advice. All he had to do is help his friend see the logical conclusion he derived from the basic characteristics of the situation.

The sixth function is that of *social reality testing and sharing*: a social reality touchstone. There are two kinds of reality in the world: physical reality and social reality. An example of physical reality is the rain that makes you use an umbrella or a raincoat. Social reality is vague; a friend can help you interpret this reality and decide on reasonable action. One example of this function can happen when people think they are losing the ability to evaluate what is happening around them. They may be sitting in a meeting and hear someone saying what seems like nonsense. They may believe everyone else is listening intently and may think, "My God, I must be going crazy! I'm the only one who's not fascinated." But if there is one person in that room whose judgment they trust, they need only to meet that person's eye and exchange annoyed looks. Then they can relax, realizing that this speaker is indeed talking nonsense and that although everyone else may agree with that nonsense or may go along with it for reasons of their own, they need not question their own perceptions. All it usually takes is one other person, not a majority of the people present.

In times of stress or confusion when you need sound advice, someone with similar priorities, values, and views can be very helpful. A person with a shared social reality is most likely to give useful advice.

It should be clear that one person can fulfill several of these functions, but it is extraordinarily unlikely that one person can fulfill them all. Different people are needed to fulfill different functions: anyone can fulfill the function of active listening, whether they know the individual and the subject at hand or not. For emotional support and challenge, individuals need someone who knows them and someone they trust, but that person doesn't have to be an expert on the topic of discussion. For the functions of technical support and challenge they need a person who knows the subject matter, but this person doesn't necessarily have to be someone they know intimately. A person needs to have a similar world view and similar values to be a truly effective social reality touchstone.

We have presented the six basic functions of a social support system. There may be variations on these functions, but we believe that these six are essential. As mentioned previously, it is important to discriminate one function from another, to be able to think of social support not in a global sense but as a number of separate functions. Some people in our environment may be able to fulfill some of these functions but not others. Without realizing it, individuals may expect their best friends or their spouses to fulfill all of these functions, and almost no one can do that. Unfortunately, most people, especially when under stress, do not make the effort to avail themselves of the various functions that a social support system can play and are then left feeling that they are not getting what they need. Frequently this sense of disappointment is not verbalized but becomes associated with home life. The atmosphere of regret and disappointment may begin to erode the marriage and family; the result is burnout at home.

It may be useful for you to realize how many of the six functions of support you expect different people to fulfill and to consider which of the functions are appropriate for these people. One way to do this is to list two or three people at home and work who either do or could fulfill one of these functions (see Table 8–1). If someone

TABLE 8–1
Social Support Functions

The following questions are aimed at helping you discriminate among the six functions of a social support system and examine what people in your environment are fulfilling, or may potentially fulfill, those functions for you.

How important are these functions of a support system for you personally? Please use the following scale to rate all six of the functions:

1	2	3	4	5	6	7
not at all important			somewhat important			extremely important

1. Listening _____ 2. Technical support _____ 3. Technical challenge _____
4. Emotional support _____ 5. Emotional challenge _____ 6. Sharing social reality _____

For each function write down who the person is (or the people are) who fulfill(s) it for you. Indicate what your relation is to the person whose name you have written (i.e., wife, friend, colleague), and to what extent the person fulfills that function for you, on the following scale:

1	2	3	4	5	6	7
fulfills minimally			fulfills to a certain degree			fulfills completely

1. Listening:

2. Technical support:

3. Technical challenge:

4. Emotional support:

5. Emotional challenge:

6. Sharing social reality:

could fulfill a function but you are reluctant to form a relationship with that person, note the source of reluctance. For example, a co-worker might be a superb technical critic, but you may be reluctant to approach that person to request critical feedback on his or her ideas. You should be specific about what is preventing you from approaching that person. Only then can you develop ways to overcome these blocks.

To the extent that social support functions are not completely covered, burnout can occur. When hardly any of them are covered, burnout is almost inevitable in a stressful situation. It is primarily important to deal with those areas in which support is lacking.

We have all seen organizations in which the social environment is terribly unsupportive. People aren't listening to each other, they don't express much technical appreciation for each others' work, and rather than offering technical challenge they offer criticisms that are destructive or wounding both in intent and effect. Occasionally we have seen work environments where the social support systems are functioning beautifully, where people listen to each other, where a great deal of *sincere* appreciation for work well done is expressed, and where people challenge each other in useful and productive ways.

How can we turn nonsupportive work environments into supportive ones? Sometimes this can happen only if two or three people take the lead in offering appreciation and challenge to those around them. Since such behavior feels good, it tends to be contagious. Occasionally, however, individuals are deeply in need of appreciation or challenge but are timid to ask for it and are so caught up in their own needs that they are unaware that others in their environment could benefit from praise and challenge they themselves might offer.

When discussing work in bureaucratic organizations, we mentioned the example of an organization where many individuals were experiencing burnout, in part because of a strong need for appreciation from supervising personnel high up in the hierarchy. Such appreciation would have been almost impossible to arrange without a major reorganization. As the reader will recall, our intervention in that organization involved training people to value and respect the technical appreciation and challenge that could be forthcoming from their peers and to train them to offer such appreciation and challenge to one another.

While it would be presumptuous for us to offer advice on details of how to establish a social support system (since we don't know the details of everyone's work and life sphere), what we can do is suggest finding ways to ask for support from relevant colleagues and to give support where it seems appropriate. It is conceivable that anyone may become the one person who is instrumental in changing an unsupportive work environment to a supportive one.

In order to find how important support systems were as buffers against burnout, we asked 80 people (35 males and 45 females) to participate in a study.[6] Participants were interviewed individually for fifteen to thirty minutes about their burnout and availability of social support (using the Burnout Measure which is presented in the Appendix and the Social Support Questionnaire presented in Table 8–1). Often, following the interview, participants wanted to talk further about their particular social network and how it related to their work stress.

Results indicated that all six of the social support functions were rated as very important (the lowest valued function was rated 5.3 on the 7-point scale). The two most highly rated functions were listening ($\bar{x} = 6.2$), and emotional support ($\bar{x} = 6.0$). It is also noteworthy that the range of responses (the standard deviation) was very narrow (from 1.2 to 1.5). With the single exception of technical challenge— which was perceived by some people as criticism of their work—the importance of all the other support functions was positively and significantly correlated with burnout. That is, the more people experienced burnout, the more important the support was for them. The highest correlation was with sharing social reality, indicating that the more burned out people are, the more isolated they feel, and consequently the more important it is to have other people around who share their view of the world. The second highest correlation was with emotional support, demonstrating again the growing sense of isolation of the burned-out person.

The more burned out people felt, the more importance they attributed to all the support functions. Yet, the more burned out they felt, the less social support they had. In other words, the more different functions of support were fulfilled for a person, the less burnout that person was likely to report.

This finding indicates that people who have social support readily available to them are less likely to burn out. Why is that so? We believe, as we have argued throughout this chapter, that the answer is that the various support functions buffer them from the direct impact of the stresses they encounter. Since our participants were reporting the levels of burnout at work, it is not surprising that the most significant correlation was obtained between job burnout and the availability of technical support. The second highest correlation was between burnout and the availability of technical challenge.

It is interesting to note that all the ratings of availability were lower than the ratings of importance. This suggests that people almost never feel that they have all the support they want or need.

The number of people providing the various support functions (with the single exception of listening) was not correlated with burnout. This suggests that it is not the number of people, but rather the quality of support they provide that determines the effectiveness of the protective buffer they provide against burnout.

For men there was a higher positive correlation between burnout and the importance attributed to various support systems than there was for women. It seems that only when men burn out do they begin to see social support as important (especially technical support at work) while for women the various support functions are always important. Indeed, we found that with the single exception of technical challenge, which many women interpreted as criticism, all other support functions were rated as much more important by women than they were by men. Sadly, the discrepancy between the importance and availability of the various support functions was greater for women than it was for men, indicating that, at least in the work sphere, women receive less support than men. Another interesting result was the finding that challenge was a more effective buffer against burnout for men than it was for women. We will return to the difference between the sexes in the use of social support later in the chapter, when we discuss some other studies on the subject.

In another part of the study we asked participants about the main motivating force in their life—was it people or self-fulfillment? Results showed that for people-motivated people, the availability of support was a more effective buffer against burnout than it was for self-motivated people. With almost no exception, people-oriented people viewed the support functions as more important, had more support available, and received that support from more people. For self-motivated people support became important only when they started burning out.

All these findings suggest that while the different support functions are an important buffer against burnout for everyone, people differ in the importance they attribute to social support, the support

available to them, and the effectiveness of that support as protection against burnout. People who attribute more importance to social support (women and people-oriented people) create around
themselves supportive networks. Debi is an example.

Just a few days after she moved into her new apartment, Debi
knew most of the people in her apartment house, and started a
friendship with two of the women there. It was nothing new for her.
She always made friends quickly and easily. From childhood you
could always find her with people. And as an adult she was always
sitting with someone, having coffee, and talking. People liked to
open up to Debi, and she liked them to. "I simply love people," says
Debi. "To me there is no greater pleasure than talking openly to a
warm and friendly person, or listening to an interesting person. No
book, no instrument, no building, no research is more interesting
than people." Since people are important to Debi, there are always
people around her—listening, talking, supporting, helping—just as
she herself listens, supports, and helps.

Even people-oriented people are not always as involved in
social activities as Debi is. For all people there are times when they
need people more and other times when they need them less. Ed
is an example.

Ed is the opposite of Debi as far as people are concerned. Ed
saw his own self-actualization as the most important thing in life.
He wanted to express himself to the fullest extent possible; to actualize his unique contribution to the world. While there were people
he appreciated—great scientists, for example—they were not an important part of his life. "I don't need people," he explains. This
attitude created problems in his marriage since he didn't need his
wife. During their years of marriage he made every effort to convince her that she didn't really need him either. And his efforts
bore fruit—during those years she withdrew from him further and
further, spending her time with friends and in activities that he did
not want to be a part of. After fifteen years she left him. At that
time, Ed went through a major crisis in his life. He worked very
hard in a computer company he started, but his high hopes for the
company did not materialize, and finally he burned out. Only after
he burned out in his work, and his wife burned out in their marriage, did he realize that he needed and wanted social support.

We examined social systems as buffers against burnout in
another study involving 290 students and 241 professionals. These
531 subjects, between 17 and 87 years old, were asked to describe

their social relationships including family, work, friends, co-workers, and acquaintances. Results indicated that all of the social relations were negatively and significantly correlated with burnout: the better the social relationships a person had, the lower the level of burnout. The highest correlations were for co-workers and friends.[7] Subjects were also asked if when having a difficulty at home or work they could confer with someone to get advice and support. The availability of support in times of need was negatively and significantly correlated with burnout (the more support, the less burnout).[8] The respondents were asked, "How often do you feel lonely?" The frequency of loneliness was very highly correlated with burnout, with poor social relations (especially with friends), and with lack of support in times of need.[9]

Social support systems can be seen as mediating variables that act as buffers to individuals in their social environment; these mediating variables reduce the effects of stressful environmental conditions and thus slow the cycle of burnout.

Work Relations

The nature of the relationship with one's boss, subordinates, and colleagues can be a major source of stress at work; good work relations between members of a group are a central factor in individual and organizational health.[10] Social contacts are almost always a key cause of job satisfaction.[11] A trusting and caring environment is important to the functioning of organizations and an effective support system is essential in combating burnout. Yet workers tend to get so caught up in the daily routine of work that they neglect each other. They do not often enough or caringly enough compliment, support, and acknowledge each other's efforts.[12]

Burnout was found in several studies to be reduced for individuals who had effective social networks or support systems at work.[13] When work relations were good, professionals experiencing stress often turned to others for advice, comfort, tension reduction, help in achieving distance from the situation or in intellectualizing it, and a sense of shared responsibility. In our research, burnout was less severe in those institutions that allowed staff to express their feelings, get feedback and support from others, and develop new goals for themselves and their clients than in those institutions that did not allow it.

In one study involving 76 mental health professionals it was found that work relationships were related to staff members' attitudes toward their work, the institutions, and the patients.[14] When relationships between staff members were good, they were more likely to confer with each other when having problems, express positive attitudes toward the institution, enjoy their work, and feel successful in it, than when relationships between staff members were poor. When work relationships were good, staff members reported many "good days" and few "bad days".

The quality of the relationships between staff and patients was also correlated positively with staff members' perceptions of the institution, other staff members, the work, and the patients. When the interaction was good, staff members liked their work, felt successful at it, and found in it self-fulfillment. They appreciated other staff members more and conferred with them more often than when staff-patient relationships were poor. They also rated the institution more highly, described patients positively, and felt involved with both the institution and the patients.

Staff meetings can be effective organizational buffers against burnout if they fulfill several functions. They should provide the staff with opportunities to express themselves and to influence the organization's policies. This would allow staff to exert some control over their work and would give them a greater sense of commitment to the organization. Furthermore, staff meetings should have a balance between time for discussion of the organization's problems and time for staff to confer about their work stress. In this way the meetings can be divided between task focus and emotional support for the staff; when the work-based emotional needs of staff members are fulfilled, staff meetings can become a tool for stopping the cycle of burnout.

But staff meetings are not always helpful. A surprising set of findings in the study of mental health professionals mentioned earlier was that a high frequency of staff meetings was correlated with negative attitudes toward the patients. Staff members who often participated in staff meetings gave more weight to information about a patient that came from the patient's family or the psychiatric interview than they did to information coming directly from the patient. They saw less chance of curing patients and tended to have job-oriented goals in their work, rather than self- or patient-oriented goals. These staff members spent time with their co-workers in order to detach themselves from patients, rather than give each other sup-

port and advice about problems with patients. Such staff socializa-
tion, to avoid contact with patients, was a reliable indication of
burnout. This is not meant to imply that staff meetings *increase*
burnout; rather, individuals who are burning out frequently attend
staff meetings rather than deal more directly with the problem.

In the other health and social service professions, staff meetings
served several important functions.[15] They enabled the staff to socialize informally, to give each other support, to confer about problems, to clarify their goals, and to exert direct influence on the politics of their institution. In those professions, frequency of staff
meetings was negatively correlated with burnout (i.e., the more
meetings, the less burnout). In the psychiatric institutions we studied, on the other hand, the frequency of staff meetings was positively correlated with burnout (i.e., the more meetings, the more
burnout).

We believe that the reason for this outcome was that most staff
meetings centered around case presentations. In these meetings a
staff member would describe a patient in terms of his mental illness,
using professional terminology that identified the patient with a disease and served to distance the staff from the patient. The meetings
very rarely focused on the problems of the staff.

Staff meetings should be a place where workers can discuss staff
problems. Staff complaints are best dealt with when they are eventually stated as positive recommendations. One approach can be
that every complaint must be followed by a recommended solution.
An alternate approach, suggested by industrial psychologist Nor-
man Maier, is to have several steps in the process leading from a
complaint to a recommended solution.[16] In the first step, staff members complain and let off steam in a gripe session; they should be
allowed to express all their feelings of hurt and anger without inhibi-
tion. The second step is the problem definition; this step requires
a different mode of thinking. Every solution should be allowed to
be presented without criticism, judgment, or mockery. The last step
is choosing the best solution among the different alternatives.

Another function of professional support systems that can best
be achieved through staff meetings is power. In these meetings employees can see where they can exercise more autonomy and gain
more control over their organization. A staff meeting can reframe
individual complaints into a staffwide problem and unite all staff
members to solve it; employees can identify areas of stress and develop ways to ease pressure. In organization there is power, control,

and autonomy, and these as we know, are all negative correlates of burnout. Staff meetings are one setting in which staff can attempt to increase them.

Staff meetings can periodically devote time to evaluating staff skills and deficiencies. Skill acquisition and other opportunities for personal and professional growth will increase mutual support in the office and will reduce burnout.

Relationships with supervisors—when growth-enhancing—can also be a buffer against burnout. Supervisors who give direct, specific, and encouraging feedback provide employees with a sense of significance, success, and challenge. Supervisors can reduce the impact of job stress if they are involved with workers on a regular, rather than crisis, basis; communicate concern rather than suspicion; and mediate between the individual and the organization. Supervisors can also make the staff aware of long-term and short-term goals of the organization and can share financial or political problems with the staff. This increases the staff's knowledge of and commitment to the organization and makes them feel that the work they do makes a significant contribution. Such supervisory skills require training, but their benefits to the organization are great enough to warrant the extra expense.

Cary Cherniss, a professor of psychology at the University of Michigan, describes six obstacles to the creation of social support networks within human service organizations.[17]

1. Different theoretical orientations and personal values may cause problems. For example, friction can be created when some staff members in a mental health clinic share a psychoanalytic orientation, while others are committed to a behavioristic approach.

2. Differences in resources, status, and power often contribute to conflict. Competition may exist between older staff members and younger ones, between men and women, black and white, and so forth. The competition can be on who gets the larger office, the approval of the supervisor, or anything else.

3. The role structure itself sometimes hinders the development of support networks. For example, when most of the work is done in the field, and the professional does not see much of the other workers, there are not enough opportunities for social and professional interactions. Another example is overload, which can be an obstacle to social interaction when it is so overwhelming that it forces the workers to work on their own, trying to catch up, both at work and after work hours.

4. Outside interests, involvement in family, friends, politics, and hobbies can limit the time and emotional energy that people are willing to invest in the social aspects of their work, especially when they demand involvement after work hours. (We take an exception with Professor Cherniss on this point, because we recommend the very thing that he sees as an obstacle. We think all professionals should compartmentalize their work and home life and get involved in outside activities and interests as a way to prevent burnout.)

5. Informal norms can limit interaction among various groups in an organization that can potentially become support networks. Such norms can also inhibit serious discussions between professionals that could be challenging and growth-producing.

6. High staff turnover rates, which are a common phenomenon in many human service organizations, prevent the development of cohesion and group feelings. Since everyone seems to be quitting, staff members are reluctant to invest energy in each other.

Awareness of the problems is extremely important for staff members who are interested in creating a social support network in their organization.

As we have indicated throughout this chapter, many people burn out in their work because they give more than they receive: they give more effort and energy than they receive in appreciation. This problem is reduced for people who have effective support systems that provide them with feedback, appreciation, and challenge. The problem is amplified for people in private practice who may not have such a support system.

Dentists, to use the example presented in Chapter 1, usually work in offices without other dentists to provide either technical appreciation or technical challenge. They cannot get significant feedback or appreciation from their patients because patients do not see what they do, are not expert enough to evaluate it, and often are uncomfortable and want to leave the office quickly. Patients usually report to dentists only when something goes wrong; it is expected that they will do things right. This bias toward negative feedback is built into most service professions but is particularly painful for private practitioners and for top-level managers and executives who do not have a group of colleagues with whom to share their feelings of success and failure.

Our recommendation for private practitioners and for top executives is to establish a social support system with other colleagues in similar situations. Some people at the top of organizations may have a romantic notion of self-sufficiency. Although this "lone wolf" image may be attractive, it does not prevent burnout; "if the Lone Ranger were still riding around, heigh-hoing Silver today, he'd be one burned out cowboy. . . . "[18]

For people in private practice, and for heads of organizations, the best resources for a support group are those people who do the same work in a different setting. Motivated by impending burnout, professionals can find out who holds the same position in similar organizations and contact them. Such contact can generate new resources and innovative ideas about ways to grow on the job. A support system of fellow professionals can provide a place to share triumphs and difficulties and to give and receive feedback, solace, appreciation, and understanding.

Men and Women:
Differences in Social Supports

In a study involving 96 professional men and 95 professional women, sex differences in the experience of burnout and its antecedents and correlates were investigated.[19] As in the findings of the study reported earlier, it was found that work relationships, as well as other support systems, were more important influences on burnout for women. For example, women's relationships with supervisors, subordinates, and co-workers were negatively and significantly correlated with burnout (i.e., the better the relationship, the less burnout. For men, the relationship with supervisors and subordinates was not correlated with burnout and the relationship with co-workers, though significant, was much less so than for women. For women the relationships with spouse, family, and friends were also negatively and significantly correlated with burnout, but for men only relationships with friends and spouse were significantly correlated with burnout and, again, less so than for women.

Women's sensitivity to the social aspects of their life and work may account for the finding that women considered "people" a greater source of stress in their work than did men. Another explanation is the disproportionate representation of women in the human service professions, which have more "people" stresses. Women felt more overextended emotionally than men both at work and outside of work. But women also received more support from people; they shared more with others in their work and outside of work and felt they received more unconditional support in times of need. Since women are more "people-motivated," they seem to be both more stressed by people and more rewarded by them. This conclusion, again, confirms the findings of the study mentioned earlier.

In another study that investigated coping strategies, the same sex differences were found.[20] Women reported using social support systems for coping with burnout more than men, and women reported the social strategies to be more effective than did men. Women seemed better able than men to share work stresses by discussing their sources of stress and talking openly about their doubts, problems, and failures.

How to Avoid Sabotaging Your Own Social Support System

As we have said over and over again in this chapter, establishing a viable support system is one of the most effective ways of avoiding or diminishing burnout. Yet few people have an adequate social support system. There are several reasons for this; in the following pages we will discuss two powerful forces that help prevent people from making full use of a social support system.

It seems to be part of human nature to seek the causes of events; that is, virtually every time we see something happen we attribute a cause to it. If we were watching our favorite football team and the tight end dropped a very easy pass in the end zone, we could come up with several explanations. It may be that the player is untalented. Another possibility is that he was out drinking the night before. Or perhaps his child is sick and he is distracted with worry. Yet another possibility is that he bet on the other team and wanted to lose the game intentionally; there are any number of possibilities. How we feel about that person depends on what we attribute his behavior to; that is, we will feel differently about that football player if we attribute his dropping the pass to his concern about his child than if we attribute it to the assumption that he bet on the other team.

There are two categories of attributions, dispositional and situational. We make dispositional attributions when we explain the cause of an event in terms of the personality of the person. We make situational attributions when we attribute the cause to something in the situation. Research done on attributions has shown that people tend to explain their own behavior in situational terms and the behavior of others in dispositional terms. For example,

> when a student who is doing poorly in school discusses his problem with a faculty adviser, there is often a fundamental difference of opinion between the two. The student, in attempting to understand and explain his inadequate performance, is usually able to point to environmental obstacles such as a particularly onerous course load, to temporary emotional stress such as worry about his draft status, or to a transitory confusion about life goals that is now resolved. The faculty adviser may nod and may wish to believe, but in his heart of hearts he usually disagrees. The adviser is convinced that the poor performance is due neither to the student's environment nor to transient emotional states. He believes instead that the failure is due to enduring qualities of the student—to lack of ability, to irremediable laziness, to neurotic ineptitude.[21]

This difference in attributions can have a great effect on interpersonal relations, particularly because there are usually few opportunities to correct wrong attributions once they have been made. For example, an individual may have a colleague who is an expert in her area and has a finely tuned critical ability. She may be reluctant to make use of him, however, because on one or two occasions she saw him behave in an aggressive manner, and she concluded that he was an aggressive person. Once she has attributed the cause of his behavior to his personality, she believes that she has a good reason to avoid him. But suppose that he is not really an "aggressive person"; rather, she happened to see him when he was particularly irritable because of sleeplessness, problems in the family, or budgetary concerns. In short, he is not *really* an aggressive person. He is a person who behaves aggressively when he is under certain kinds of situational stress.

Because of the importance of social support systems, it is essential for all of us to periodically reassess our early judgments of our colleagues and acquaintances in order to avoid erroneously dismissing valuable human resources.

Indeed, interpreting people's behavior in situational rather than dispositional terms has general utility. By making a dispositional attribution, we render ourselves powerless to affect the interaction. A situational attribution, however, offers the possibility of changing the situation. That sense of power is extremely useful in combating burnout even if the options for change are limited. The belief that the environment is malleable is important in itself.

Most individuals have within them the capability of behaving intelligently or stupidly, gracefully or clumsily, gently or harshly. All other things being equal, if those around them treat them as a graceful person, it will bring out more of their graceful behavior than their clumsy behavior. This proposition was demonstrated brilliantly in an experiment by Mark Snyder, a social psychologist at the University of Minnesota.[22]

In one of his studies students participated in what they thought was an investigation of the processes by which people become acquainted with each other. Pairs of unacquainted males and females were told that they would engage in a telephone conversation. All male subjects received a snapshot of what they believed was the female member of their dyad. Actually the snapshots were not of the female subjects but were pictures chosen previously for receiving high or low attractiveness ratings. Male subjects were randomly assigned pictures of very attractive or very unattractive women. Female subjects did not get snapshots and did not know they were being given to the men. Each pair then engaged in ten minutes of unstructured conversation by means of microphones and headphones connected through a tape recorder that recorded each participant's voice on a separate channel of the tape. Raters listened *only* to the track of the tapes containing the women's voices and rated them on dimensions such as animation, enthusiasm, intimacy, and friendliness.

The data revealed that those women who were perceived as attractive came to behave in a friendly and likable manner in comparison with those who spoke with men who thought them to be unattractive.

Similarly in everyday life, if we think a certain person is cold or aloof, we will behave in a way that will bring out that person's coldness and aloofness. The same person can be warm and friendly in another social encounter. It is important to avoid writing people off unless the evidence against them is overwhelming.

In summary, while different people may have different needs for support, and while different people can and should serve different support functions for each other, we cannot err if we conclude that social support is an extremely important buffer against burnout. Fortunately, social support networks are also very cost effective;

they don't depend on complicated bureaucratic structures for their development and maintenance. The cost to establish a support network at work is minimal—all it requires is the decision of a group of co-workers to get together on a regular basis at a particular time and place. In addition to being useful, a support network can be enjoyable. One group we worked with set aside the first Thursday night of every month for a fine dinner at a local French restaurant (at which they received a special group-discount rate). Once the initial effort is made to establish such meetings, very little effort is usually needed to keep them going. Because they serve so many important functions for people, they can—and often do—continue indefinitely.

NINE

Organizational
Coping Strategies

Even organizations that are similar in size, structure, and function can have very different levels of worker burnout, depending on organizational flexibility, emphasis placed on the significance of the work, the degree of autonomy given to the staff, the variety of tasks involved in the work, the manageability of the work load, the availability of social support networks, and the comfort of the work environment. Different levels of burnout are reflected in such things as different rates of turnover, differences in staff morale, and differences in employee theft.

In one of our studies, which involved 724 workers in fourteen mental retardation facilities in eleven states, we found significant differences in burnout levels among the various facilities.[1] In a study involving 137 nurses in six different departments, it was found that even though the departments were all in the same hospital they varied tremendously in terms of their work features as correlates of burnout.[2] For example, variety was a negative correlate of burnout (the more variety, the less burnout) in the heart surgery department but not in the department of internal medicine, while complexity was a significant correlate of burnout in the intensive care unit but not in geriatrics. It is difficult in the absence of detailed observational analysis to know exactly why these different patterns emerge. The main point here is that there is a great deal of variability in the causes and effects of burnout even within different segments of the same organization.

If you work in an organization dominated by bureaucratic inefficiency, paper work, red tape, inertia, organizational inflexibility, and poor communication on all levels, you are probably convinced that changing those negative features, and introducing some of the positive features mentioned earlier into your own work place is an impossible goal. And you may be right, but not necessarily. We studied a work place like that, a child-care center, that at first had a very high level of worker burnout. After a series of organizational changes initiated and carried out by the workers themselves, burnout levels went down and worker satisfaction went up significantly. What the workers did is an example of successful coping on the organizational level.

Our first study on burnout examined precipitants of staff burnout in day-care centers. The study involved eighty-three staff members from twelve child-care facilities.[3] Among our findings were that large child-staff ratios resulted in cognitive, sensory, and emotional overload for staff members; those facilities that required the longest working hours with children produced the most stress and negative attitudes in the staff; loosely structured programs took an emotional toll on the staff members; those facilities that had the lowest rates of burnout and the greatest job satisfaction were those with frequent staff meetings where staff could socialize, provide each other with support and advice, clarify goals, and influence the policies of the center.

Various changes occurred at the day-care centers as a consequence of this research. Staff members were asked to complete a burnout questionnaire in which they were asked about their work characteristics, attitudes, and stresses. After considering these issues, some staff members reevaluated their jobs and changed their approaches to their work with children. In one of the day-care centers the staff organized a series of meetings around the findings of the research and made structural changes in the operation of the center. Six months later we conducted a follow-up evaluation of these changes at that center by observing the daily program and interviewing the staff members.[4] We will present what happened at this particular day-care center as a case study in one organization's practical application of research findings and as a demonstration of what an organization can do to combat burnout.

The center was located in a housing complex for married students and served these students almost exclusively. It had a permissive and nondirective educational philosophy. There was no formal structure to the program. Staff members were available to provide play materials, read stories, organize games, and handle problems but they rarely directed the children's activities.

The center was a parent-cooperative drop-in center; each parent was expected to contribute three hours a week as a teacher-helper; children could be dropped off at the center at any time between 8:00 A.M. and 5:00 P.M. The center accommodated a total of sixty-one children: eight pretoddlers (18 months to 2 years), eighteen toddlers (2 to 3 years), twenty-seven preschoolers (3 to 5 years), and eight kindergarteners (5 to 6 years). However, children arrived at different hours so that the maximum at any one time was forty-five. The center was at full capacity between 10:00 A.M. and 3:00 P.M., with a reduced number of children in the early morning and late afternoon.

The center was housed in a garage-like building with high ceilings that amplified sounds. The building was divided by child-high walls into three rooms for children, a staff lounge, a kitchen, and a large play area. Adjoining the main building was a small indoor gym, a children's bathroom, a changing room, and a nap room. Outside there was a yard with climbing structures, swings, a sandbox, and various outdoor toys. The three children's rooms were designated as a babies' room, a toddlers' room, and a "big-kids" room. Each room had a head teacher with a few other teachers under his or her supervision, for a total of twelve teachers. In spite of this room division, children were free to use any room, and all teachers shared coverage of all parts of the center, no matter how many children were there. In addition to parents and teachers, the center used student volunteers who worked as teacher-helpers in return for university course credits. With the addition of parents and volunteers, the adult-child ratio was 1 to 3.

The day-care center was characterized by a lack of structure, a constant flow of people, and high levels of noise and aggression. On the surface, flexibility may seem advantageous. But there were some serious negative consequences to this loose structure. For example, one result was that there was commotion in the center during all hours of the day. Parents came and went, delivering and retrieving their children as well as giving their "parent hours"; children arrived and departed at different times; student volunteers dropped in during their free time. One teacher calculated that he had to communicate with about one hundred people daily, including all of the children in the center, all of the parents, the volunteers, and the administrators. Because of the great number of people and the irregular schedules of the children, activities had to be flexible and spontaneous. It was difficult for teachers to carry out any regular educational program. Because children were coming and going all day, no one knew whom to expect and when. A teacher planning a project had to be prepared for all or none of the children taking part in it. One teacher might have children from 2 to 6 years old participating in an activity while another teacher might be taking care of only one baby. In addition, because of the mingling of age groups the teachers had to be constantly alert to protect the younger or weaker children. Just as there was no structured program, there was no structured space in the center. In addition to the three main rooms, there was a large, empty area in which children were allowed to run and play aggressively in order to "let out their energy." As a result they felt free to use, and sometimes abuse, other rooms and toys.

Although teachers in this center liked children, were affectionate with them, and were committed to their work in child care, they were exhausted after work and were increasingly negative about children and about their jobs. They frequently took vacations in which they engaged in solitary activities, needing to get away from people, especially children. One teacher, who had wanted to have eight children of her own, decided she was not sure she wanted any children at all. Teachers felt they were subjected to tremendous stresses and were dissatisfied with work.

After taking part in our study and reviewing the research report, the staff of the day-care center decided to institute modifications in their program. The changes centered around two of the factors that were identified as contributing to burnout: the ratio of staff to children and the degree of structure in the program. The finding that emotional exhaustion was correlated with nonstructured programs was especially surprising to this group of teachers. Although they recognized their own physical, mental, and emotional exhaustion, they had not associated it with their center's permissive and nondirective philosophy. Indeed they considered these characteristics to be virtues and they were proud of this arrangement.

The staff decided on and implemented two major changes: a new division of the center's physical space and a division of the staff's teaching responsibilities. The staff apportioned six rooms in the center: one for babies, two for toddlers, two for "big kids," and one for kindergarteners. A team of two teachers was assigned to each room, as was a specific group of children. Each staff member was responsible only for his or her group of children. As a result, the teachers could spend more time with each of their children and could prepare specific activities for the group. This change was augmented by several structural changes in the program. Each child was scheduled for a specific period of time at the center, rather than being allowed to arrive and depart at any time. Similarly, volunteers and parents were assigned to work at specific times and in specific rooms, each with its own staff, children, toys, and play materials.

Six months after these changes were instituted, interviews were conducted with almost all of the teachers who had been working at the center before and after the changes were made. The interviews focused on the teachers' assessment of the effectiveness of the changes for the children and for themselves and on their feelings about their child-care work. The changes in the day-care center had a great impact on the children. Because of the new groupings, the children now knew their own room, teachers, and classmates. Children no longer got "lost in the shuffle" because they now had a place in a particular group. This group identity gave the children a new sense of security and belonging. The children's play was more constructive, which the teachers felt produced a greater sense of personal accomplishment. In the small groups, each child received more attention. Negative behavior, such as bullying or clowning, decreased. The staff agreed that the children seemed happier and more relaxed with each other and with the staff.

The teachers commented that close relationships were developing between children who had never interacted before and that the new groupings reduced the amount of fighting among the children. Separated by age, each group of children had activities that were appropriate to their interests and abilities.

Because the teachers now worked with fewer children, they were able to develop a deeper relationship with them. They now knew the location, activity, and feelings of each child. The teachers therefore felt less distracted, confused, and drained. Many reported feeling that only now were they dealing effectively with the emotional development of each child and only now did they have the time to attend to each child's personal needs.

The interaction between staff and parents also changed for the better. Because each teacher was now working with fewer children, he or she was in contact with fewer parents and could get to know them better, both in parent conferences and during parent service hours. The teachers began to know and understand the children in the framework of their families and they felt more at ease talking about them with the parents.

The teachers agreed that the changes in the center had had an impact on their work and on their feelings about the job. Since each now had a specific group of children and a defined space, the teachers felt a stronger sense of order, security, and belonging. A routine was established with fewer unscheduled interruptions, so teachers could now plan and carry out projects. They felt more responsible for the materials in their rooms and kept better track of toys, books, and games; as a result, less time was wasted cleaning up at the end of the day. Because of these changes many teachers felt more able to realize their potential as teachers. They felt that the work they were doing was important and made a significant contribution to the children's lives.

The teachers also described their relationships with each other as greatly improved. Teams of teachers worked together in planning and carrying out activities. The communication between co-workers was more open; they felt more willing to give each other help, emotional support, and companionship. All the staff members became involved in discussions at staff meetings. The teachers felt that these discussions helped them deal with disagreements, find solutions to problems, plan their educational strategy, and focus attention when necessary on particular children.

An additional reason for the improved staff relationships was that they had been able to share and effectively deal with their feelings of burnout. This participatory experience alone helped develop better communication among staff members and increased their identification as a group. However, the teachers attributed much of the improvement to the changes they made in the teacher-child ratio and program structure because these changes directly altered their interaction with each other.

Although the teachers were enthusiastic about the changes in the day-care center, they did note a few negative consequences. Some of the teachers expressed sorrow at being cut off from the other children with whom they had previously had close relationships. The greater degree of structure also imposed some additional demands on the teachers. Because they were now responsible for the program of their group, they were challenged to make it "work." They had to be clearer about their goals, more organized, and better prepared than before. The most negative consequence of the changes, according to some teachers, was the potential for interstaff rivalry. The division of the day-care center into six independent units could have resulted in conflicts of interest between different teams of teachers.

Several things can be recommended to prevent such staff rivalry from occurring. One of these is to arrange some center-wide activities, such as movies or nature trips. Holidays can also be celebrated as all-center activities. As this center had many foreign children, several international holidays were included for greater fun, camaraderie, and unity. For the staff members, meetings, parties, and continuing education programs were encouraged. Such opportunities for interaction allow staff to emphasize their mutual goals as educators and to discuss any concerns about staff divisiveness. Furthermore, they provide staff members with a broad system of social support and intellectual stimulation.

In summary, the staff's reactions to the changes were very positive. They felt that the organizational changes instituted to combat burnout had greatly improved the center's program and had made their work easier, pleasant, more significant, and more exciting. Although the job still involved some emotional stress, it was considerably reduced. As one teacher put it, "The changes have made an incredible difference. I could not have gone through another year like the last one." Another teacher said "I used to get totally drained, but now I enjoy coming to work. Everything is better, and I feel really optimistic." After the changes had been in effect for some time, the staff members all voted to continue the new system; no one wanted to return to the previous routine.

In terms of coping with burnout, this child-care center demonstrates the impact organizational changes can have on the psychological well-being of staff members. It is significant that the changes were initiated and carried out by the staff. We are convinced that the staff's active participation in the decision-making process increased their sense of autonomy and control and improved communication patterns. Focusing on goals for themselves, for the children, and for the center helped increase the staff's sense of meaning; planning and executing their own educational programs increased their sense of challenge and self-actualization. All these procedures reduce the stress and increase the rewards of any job, thereby reducing the incidence of burnout.

Preventing Burnout in the Organization

Our work pointed to several factors in the work situation that influence whether staff will burn out or will cope successfully with the stresses inherent in their work: the ratio of the staff to clients, the availability of "time out" in periods of stress, the amount of time spent in stressful situations, the severity of the problems presented by clients, organizational flexibility, training, positive work conditions, and work significance. We will discuss each of these factors at some length.

Reducing Staff-Client Ratios

The quality of professional interactions in human service professions is affected by the number of people for whom the professional is providing care. As this number increases so does the cognitive, sensory, and emotional overload of the professional. In the research on child-care centers,[5] twelve centers, which varied in the ratio of staff to children from 1 to 4 to 1 to 12, were studied. The staff from the high-ratio centers worked a greater number of hours in direct contact with children and had fewer breaks during work. One consequence was that staff were more approving of techniques to quiet children, such as compulsory naps and tranquilizers for hyperactive children. They felt little control over what they did on the job and in general liked their jobs less than did the staff in the low-ratio centers.

In our research on mental health settings we looked at institutions that varied in size as well as staff-to-patient ratio.[6] We found that the larger the ratio of patients to staff, the less staff members liked their work and the more they tried to separate it from the rest of their lives. In settings with large patient-to-staff ratios, staff said they would change their jobs if given a chance. They did not seek self-fulfillment or social interaction in their jobs; they felt that the best aspect of their work was the money they received for doing it. In contrast, when the ratio was low, staff members had fewer people to provide care for and could give more attention to each. There was more time to focus on the positive, nonproblematic aspects of the patient's life and less need to concentrate on immediate problems or symptoms.

Unfortunately, in most human service organizations, there is a tendency to assign large numbers of clients to each staff member, as a result of cost/benefit calculations or insufficient staffing. We urge organizations to include the cost of burnout in these calculations. Work overload in general, and large ratios in particular, may save money for the organization in the short run, but they are extremely costly for everyone in the long run.[7]

Making "Times Out" Available

Opportunities to withdraw from a stressful situation are important when individuals are under mental strain; these opportunities are of critical importance with *emotional* strain. The concept of "time out" is relevant for any work that involves high degrees of emotional, mental, or physical stress. "Times out" were repeatedly found to be correlated with low levels of burnout.[8]

"Times out" can be particularly beneficial to people who serve other people. For child-care workers[9] and mental health workers,[10] the opportunity to withdraw from direct contact with children and patients when feeling strained and under pressure was the key factor in preventing burnout. "Times out," which are the most positive form of withdrawal that we observed, are not merely short breaks from work such as rest periods or coffee breaks. Rather, they are opportunities for the staff members to choose some less stressful work while other staff take over their more stressful responsibilities. This alternative work is usually characterized by lack of direct interaction with people, such as paper work, cleaning, or food preparation. Thus, staff on time out are serving the organization and replenishing themselves simultaneously.

In the child-care study, times out were often available in centers that had sufficient staff, shared responsibilities, flexible work policies, and, most important, a variety of tasks for each staff member. In centers where times out were not available, work relations were poorer and the staff reported being impatient, irritable, and psychologically distant. In the mental health study, staff who took times out showed more favorable attitudes toward patients and were more optimistic about their patients' chances to be cured than staff who did not have this option.

This form of withdrawal is more positive than other techniques professionals often use to protect themselves, because good patient care can be maintained while the employee is taking an emotional breather. When times out are not available, professionals are more likely to feel trapped by their responsibility to their clients; they cannot withdraw temporarily without feeling guilty. The withdrawal then is often an escape at the expense of the clients because there is no one else to take over. Thus it is important that institutional policies allow for voluntary times out. Such temporary withdrawals from direct contact when used for noncontact work will not be at the expense of the service recipient if the structure of the organization allows other staff to cover.

Limiting Hours of Stressful Work

The number of hours a person works is likely to be related to that person's sense of fatigue, overload, boredom, and stress. Consequently one might suspect that long working hours would result in a higher incidence of burnout. For human service professionals, longer work hours were found to be correlated with stress and negative feelings.[11] The more hours a day they worked, the less they liked the job, the less responsible they felt for clients, and the less control they felt they had. Yet it is not the number of hours per se that has the most impact on staff but the number of hours in direct contact with service recipients. In the child-care study,[12] longer working hours were associated with more stress and negative attitudes in the staff, primarily when the longer hours involved more work with children. When the longer hours involved administrative work, this negative response and burnout were less likely to occur. Staff members who worked longer hours with children developed more negative attitudes toward children; on vacation they wanted to get away from children and child-related activities; after work they reported feeling less tolerant, less satisfied with their performance, less creative, and more moody than staff who worked shorter hours with children. Both the organization and the individual should be aware of the limit to the number of hours one can work and still be productive. The psychoanalyst Herbert Freudenberger described the common practices of double shifts and frequent overnight work as emotionally suicidal practices that can result in entire organizations burning out.[13]

The negative effect of prolonged direct contact with clients is increased by the severity of the clients' problems. Long hours of direct contact with severely ill or emotionally disturbed children is many times more stressful than contact with healthy, well-adjusted children. In mental health settings, we found that the higher the percentage of schizophrenics in the patient population, the more burned out the staff.[14] These staff members were also less aware of their goals, spent more time in administrative duties, felt less job satisfaction, and were more interested in leaving their jobs. In one social service organization, we found that dealing full-time with difficult clients was the most stressful task associated with the highest levels of burnout.[15] Other studies have shown that crisis intervention and emergency room work are particularly demanding if done exclusively.

Such work can be limited in duration. When workers are assigned to jobs that are known to be stressful, their stay on those jobs could be limited to a certain period of time. Rotation of stressful jobs can prevent the individual's guilt and sense of failure and can reduce the costs of burnout for the organization. For example, priests who worked in certain community-based programs for a maximum of five years were less likely to burn out than those who did not set such a limit for themselves. Rather than succumbing to the stresses of such work, these priests left the programs feeling they had done their best and were ready for a change. Teachers in inner city schools who felt unable to cope but were denied transfers had psychophysiological and psychological complaints that increased until many became disabled.[16] When stressful work is limited in time, employees can devote themselves to it with the knowledge that they will not have to do it forever.[17]

The stressful effect of long hours of direct client contact in the human services is similar to the effect of long hours in peak-stress situations in non-human-service jobs. The recommendations to combat this problem are also similar. The organization must take into account the effects of stressful tasks on the employee and limit the time spent on such tasks. One way to do this is to create shorter work shifts, more breaks, special leaves, or part-time positions. Jobs can balance stressful and nonstressful tasks. Organizations can reduce the number of years that employees are involved in stressful work by job rotation, lateral job changes, and tapered retirement. They can institute shared part-time positions and shared work. Rotation and sharing take some pressure off the individual staff member and make the job more varied, interesting, and stimulating. Research indicates that with more work sharing, jobs are less personally stressful and staff attitudes are more positive.[18]

Increasing Organizational Flexibility

Organizational structures can be made flexible enough to accommodate the individual rather than the individual accommodating the organization. To do this attention must be given to the individual differences among workers. Some workers are interested in policy making, others in community contact, and yet others in serving clients. While there are some costs involved, enabling workers to select tasks they like will reduce burnout and will improve the functioning of the organization and the quality of its services. In one social service department we met a young woman who liked working with cases of incest and was very effective in her interventions, but she disliked working with alcoholics and felt she could not be helpful to them. Organizational flexibility in her department made it possible for her to see all the cases of incest. Within a short time she became an expert on the problem and was invited to give talks and train others. She was also spared the frustration of working with people she felt could be more effectively served by other staff members.

Obviously, not all organizations will accommodate their employees' needs. For example, an anesthesiologist who had difficulty working with babies in the operating room was required by the hospital to continue anesthetizing babies. In her distress she had frequent nightmares and periods of depression following operations on children. She went through a severe crisis of burnout and quit her job for a year. When she returned to work, the rule was still in effect: employees must treat the patients to whom they are assigned. The organization would not change to accommodate her.

These two cases exemplify the impact organizational flexibility or inflexibility can have on the ease or discomfort of the individual's functioning. In terms of cost/benefit to the organization, we feel flexibility is much more beneficial as an organizational policy because it minimizes employee burnout. Above all, organizational flexibility implies awareness and concern about the needs of the individual. It means giving individual workers some freedom to choose their clients or tasks. It also means giving them as much autonomy as possible to work on their own schedules in their own styles. The organization stands to gain by allowing employees to work under their most productive circumstances.

An organization can also be flexible enough to allow growth and change in its workers. If an employee shows signs of burnout on a particular job, he can be given something different to do. In contrast, many organizations ask people who do something well once to do that job "forever." Even if a worker enjoyed his work initially, making it into a routine can result in burnout. Instead of repeatedly assigning the same workers to certain jobs, organizations can rotate functions among different workers. Currently organizations tend to burn out their staff by assigning difficult tasks to the "only" person who can handle them and imposing deadlines on the "only" person, invariably the busiest, who can be trusted to complete tasks on time. Variety in these routines can provide relief from stress.

Some industrial psychologists investigating occupational stress have emphasized the importance of selection as a preventive measure, even though the means of selection for complex jobs are not exact and interviews have not been successful as a selection device.[19] We have often been asked by heads of personnel departments how they can know during their initial interview how likely are different prospective employees to burn out and if we could provide them with some written test that would predict who will burn out and when. The idea, of course, is to select people who will not burn out. Our answer is that even if there were such a test we would recommend against using it. The reason should be clear. As we have emphasized repeatedly, those individuals who are potentially the most valuable resources in an organization because of their idealism and concern are precisely those who are most apt to burn out. Accordingly, such a screening device would deprive the organization of its most valuable potential employees. If we were in charge of an organization we would choose as our employees the most idealistic, caring, and concerned individuals we could find, and then we would work to create an environment that minimizes burnout. An indirect support to this contention is the fact that most of the turnover that is the result of burnout is voluntary (i.e., the employee quitting), while poor selection would result in involuntary turnover (i.e., the employee being fired).[20] Because burnout is largely an inevitable function of system characteristics, it is more practical to focus on organizations than on selecting individuals.

Training

Formal education for a career should include training designed to minimize burnout. For staff members with higher education the original reason for choosing their work is often an existential search for "self-fulfillment." They begin their careers with very high expectations of themselves and their work and within a short time they burn out. Advanced education, especially in the human services, tends to create these high expectations in students, emphasizing the need for significance, self-expression, and authenticity. It also emphasizes the value of the experimental, the new, and the exciting. These great expectations are frustrated when professionals find themselves to be small parts of a bureaucratic machine or in an uneventful career. In training for human service careers we feel it is crucial to prepare students for the stresses that they will encounter in their work and to provide them with a more realistic and balanced view of the professional-client relationship. Students should be able to recognize danger signs of impending burnout in themselves and in people around them and know how to take care of themselves when under stress. It is also important to include training on how to work effectively in a bureaucracy.

Similarly, other professionals need training for handling mental and physical stress. When such training is not included in higher education it becomes the responsibility of the employee's organization. Training for new employees could include familiarization with the job stresses, the danger signs of burnout, and effective coping strategies. In such training the requirements of the job can be made clear so that those who find that they cannot fulfill them will be free to leave.

Continuing education on the job can also be helpful. Staff retreats, conferences, and workshops reduce burnout. Such education provides workers with an opportunity to get away from their work, examine their work pressures, clarify their goals, consider available but unused coping strategies, and develop social support networks.

Staff training can give workers the opportunity to develop skills directly related to their work. These may be clerical skills, computer skills, computer-related skills, or diagnostic and interviewing skills. Effective training programs and supportive supervision are two methods the organization can supply for skill acquisition and improvement.

Improving Work Conditions

Environmental pressures such as noise, uncomfortable work settings, pollution, and extreme temperatures are highly correlated with burnout; the more environmental pressures, the more burnout.[21] Comfortable physical environments that are pleasant and designed to meet workers' tastes, needs, and preferences were found to produce far less burnout than unpleasant environments. Trying to concentrate, interview, and do therapy in inadequate or noisy offices was a source of frustration for many employees. Private, quiet, and tasteful environments were specifically mentioned as positive work features and considered indicative of organizational concern for the psychological well-being of employees. Albert Mehrabian, professor of psychology at the University of California Los Angeles, emphasized that the same kind of environment is not good for everyone.[22] Just as you don't make people wear the same shoe size, you shouldn't make them live and work in the same kind of environment. Working and living spaces should accommodate as much as possible the individual's needs and preferences and be as personalized as possible.

Work conditions also include the degree of bureaucratic interference, such as the extent to which administration interferes with the goal achievement of individual workers, and administrative annoyances, such as paper work, red tape, and communication problems. Both bureaucratic interference and administrative annoyances were found to be highly correlated with burnout.[23] Organizations can attempt to reduce environmental pressures and make the physical work environment as pleasant as possible. This might include partitions to increase privacy and reduce noise, pleasant colors, plants, indirect lighting, or workers' freedom to decorate their own offices. Organizations can also combat burnout by simplifying such bureaucratic hurdles as complex forms, tangled communication channels, and unnecessarily complicated work precedures.

Deriving a sense of significance from our work is the most important reward of working. Often the sense of significance is tied to the completion of the work. When people do not have the opportunity to complete tasks they may not believe they have significant impact. Human service professionals who do only intake interviews are at a disadvantage compared to those who do brief therapy and can see changes in their clients. Industrial workers who put the front fenders on cars are at a disadvantage compared to those who work as a team and put a whole car together. A sense of completion is unfortunately lacking in many industrial assembly-line jobs, as well as in human service jobs involving chronically sick or needy people.

In such jobs it is particularly important for the organization to provide employees with some sense of completion. R. E. Walton, who wrote about innovation in the work place to avoid worker alienation, mentioned innovative and successful management techniques at General Foods in Topeka, Kansas.[24] Autonomous work groups at the plant were given collective responsibility for large segments of the production process, so that workers shared a variety of tasks and enriched their job.

One way to provide a sense of completion is to set clear, achievable organizational objectives and to review periodically individual and organizational success in achieving these objectives. Objectives can include both internal organizational goals and more general goals such as providing the best service to the public and attaining professional excellence.

Feedback is another organizational tool for increasing an employee's sense of significance at work. Feedback and constructive criticism provided by supervisors should be specific and directly related to attainable improvements. Such feedback enables individual workers to improve their performance and enhances their feelings of meaning and success; it also improves the morale of the whole organization.

The rewards provided by the organization can increase a worker's sense of significance. Rewards include pay, extrinsic advantages such as benefits, security, and promotional opportunities, and intrinsic advantages such as appreciation and recognition. Lack of rewards has been found to be a significant correlate of burnout.[25] Organizational psychologists emphasize job enrichment as a tool to increase workers' motivation and sense of significance and to provide them with opportunities for psychological growth.[26]

Organizations must recognize the needs for completion, rewards, appreciation, and meaning. When these needs are satisfied, they serve as powerful buffers against burnout.

Ten

Burnout Workshops

IN our burnout workshops we bring together all of the things we know about burnout, including much of the material presented in the preceding chapters. We present this material to groups of participants in the context of experiential learning—that is, not only do we explain what burnout is, we provide participants with the opportunity to become more aware of the specific stresses in their own occupation, to discuss these stresses with other individuals in similar or identical occupations, and to utilize some of our findings on various coping strategies in a highly personal and individualized manner. One of the great benefits of a workshop is that it enables participants to take time out from their usual activities, focus on serious problems they are experiencing, and arrive at tentative solutions in collaboration with other individuals who are in a similar circumstance. Thus, while we believe that the material contained in this volume can be of great benefit to the reader, we also feel that the benefit is increased by the focus, the individualized guidance, and the social support—the hallmarks of the burnout workshops described below.

There is nothing magical about the actual activities in a burnout workshop. We believe the workshops are effective because they represent a focused and concrete attempt to deal with burnout in a growth-producing way. Thus it is our hope that this chapter, as well as the rest of the book, will encourage readers to try out "workshop-like" activities in their own settings. These activities should be done during "time out" from work, together with other people who share the same stresses and who could potentially become a social support group, and they should focus on concrete, positive ways of coping with burnout.

Since 1976, we have conducted hundreds of burnout workshops throughout the United States and abroad. These workshops ranged in size from 12 to 500 participants, with most including 50 to 100 participants. Some were open enrollment workshops, others were special offerings during professional conferences, and still others were part of in-service training provided by various organizations.

The specific content of the workshops differed according to the composition and needs of the participants.[1]

We conduct two types of burnout workshops. One type of workshop is for employees from different organizations who have similar work roles and work stresses. In these groups participants can discuss the stresses and rewards unique to their position and can establish support systems with people outside of their own organizations. These workshops can be particularly helpful for those management personnel who, because of their position, feel they cannot confer with others or use a support system within their organizations. These occupation-specific workshops can help adjust the unevenness of feedback and rewards in organizations. Many social service employees, for example, expect all their rewards to come from management; they rarely look to their co-workers for feedback and as a result feel unappreciated and demoralized when management does not respond to them. In addition, these expectations create much pressure on management personnel. During a workshop an effort can be made to change this pattern by teaching employees how to be effective support systems for each other.

The second kind of workshop is for people from one organization. These workshops can be especially useful where lack of communication, hostility, and inadequate cooperation are affecting the office's proper functioning. Sometimes participants in such workshops come from different levels of the same organization, but more often only one level of the organization is included.

There are costs and benefits to each approach. If we decide not to include management, the major benefit is a feeling of safety; employees usually feel more comfortable about talking freely—being uninhibited by fear of possible reprisal on the part of a manager who might be upset by criticism. On the other hand, if management is included, employees can benefit if they can offer to management feedback that is well received and results in an immediate change in stress-producing managerial behavior. It has been our experience that including managers and workers in the same workshop almost always results in more useful outcomes. Nevertheless, as you shall see, we often exclude managers from these workshops at the request of workers who are concerned about safety.

Are our burnout workshops effective? We have a good deal of informal evidence from unsolicited letters from participants, usually received several months after a workshop, informing us of the changes they have made in their lives as a direct result of things they learned in our workshops.[2] For the most part, the changes described by the participants are not mere fluff—they are concrete and specific actions that have resulted in concrete and specific outcomes: A social worker might write with enthusiasm about being able to share her frustrations with a support group, and how this has enabled her to be more forceful with recalcitrant clients, to their benefit—"and, oh, by the way, I am now sleeping seven hours a night for the first time in years!" A dentist will write that he is "forcing" himself to spend more time chatting with his clients, getting to know them and *like* them, and "I actually received Christmas cards from some of my clients this year."

While these letters are gratifying, they do not constitute objective, convincing data about the effectiveness of our workshops because they do not constitute a random sample of participants. We worry about those who didn't write to us; did they learn a lot and simply hate writing letters, or did they fail to benefit from the workshop? We will never know for sure.

More convincing are data that come from our own direct observation. On several occasions we have been invited to return to an organization a year or two after our workshop, and have had the opportunity to see the fruits of our labors. On these occasions, almost invariably we see an organization that is running more smoothly, with tangible evidence of increased job satisfaction, energy, and enthusiasm on the part of the employees. This observation is echoed by statements made to us by these employees—our former participants—who, it turns out, were instrumental in bringing us back to the organization either for a more intense follow-up workshop or to perform a workshop that now would include new members of their work team. Let us be clear: We do not see miracles; for example, in a hospital, nurses still experience stress when one of their patients dies and frequently become exhausted and upset by the size of their workload. But most are coping better with these problems, and for a few, even a root of the problem has been modified—by reduction of the workload, for example.

But of course, the most objective data comes from an experiment assessing the effectiveness of a workshop by comparing the behavior of participants with a control group consisting of similar people who did not attend the workshop. In this experiment, we wanted to make it as easy as possible to collect the data. We also wanted to see if we could produce a discernible effect even under minimal conditions. Thus, we chose a workshop with a small number of participants and a short duration. It was also one that did not include managerial personnel, thus excluding the possibility of the kind of dramatic breakthrough, described above, that can occur when workers confront managers. Twenty-three social service employees participated in this one-day workshop[3] that had four major goals:

1. Introduction of the concept of burnout, clarification of its symptoms, and discussion of how people experience and express it. This was done in an attempt to make participants aware of the problem, as the first step in developing adequate coping.

2. Identification of work stresses that commonly cause burnout in social service workers, in an attempt to help participants take responsibility for action directed toward positive change.

3. Development of the ability to distinguish between stressful work features that are under the control of the individual and that can be modified, and those that are an inherent part of the work and must be accepted as such.

4. Development of tools for coping such as the improvement of individual adjustment via more flexible utilization of different coping strategies and the modification of work features that are under the individual's control. A central topic was the development and use of support sys-

tems; other topics included the focus on positive work aspects and the development of positive attitudes as buffers against it.

The day started with a theoretical presentation of the concept of burnout and its danger signs. Participants were able to identify their levels of burnout. They discussed causes and correlates of burnout in their work environment and within specific work activities. We encouraged them to talk about their goals and expectations from their work and their stresses, especially those resulting from their frustrated expectations, as a way of getting in touch with feelings of hopelessness and helplessness and becoming aware of the problem. Through lectures and small-group discussions, employees had the opportunity to increase their understanding of common aspects of their work that could cause burnout and to take responsibility for doing something about them.

We tried especially hard to help participants distinguish between those stresses that were within their control and those that could not be modified. In order to develop new tools for coping and to improve the range and quality of old tools, we introduced a variety of coping resources and coping skills aimed at modifying work features within their control. After participants identified their major cause of stress, we urged them to make concrete plans for changes. In general, we encouraged them to be flexible in coping with stresses; to use a variety of coping strategies *when appropriate:* active-direct coping (e.g., changing the source of stress), active-indirect coping (e.g., talking to friends), and inactive-direct coping (e.g., ignoring or avoiding the source of stress). They were discouraged from using inactive-indirect coping (e.g., drugs and alcohol). Emphasis was put on techniques for recognizing, establishing, and using support systems among colleagues. Recommendations included employee-oriented staff meetings, open communication, active listening, providing of technical support and technical challenge, open discussion of disruptive emotional experiences, looking for positive aspects in the interaction with clients, and work sharing. We also discussed the power of positive attitudes and a sense of humor as buffers against burnout on the individual level. Specific recommendations included acknowledging time as a valuable resource, compartmentalization between work and home, "decompression" at the end of stressful days, awareness of danger signs, acknowledgment of vulnerabilities, and the setting of realistic, achievable goals. The day ended with a summary session in which the relevance of burn-out to one's life as well as work was discussed.

The effects of the workshop were assessed by an immediate feedback questionnaire and by two questionnaires collected one week and six months after the workshop. Responses to the questionnaire given immediately after the workshop indicated that the participants viewed the workshop very favorably and valued especially the introduction of concepts, suggestions for solving problems, and their hopes for future solutions.

The immediate feedback questionnaire also included open-ended questions. To the question, "What was the most important informative aspect of the workshop?" participants emphasized recognizing the shared nature of their work stresses and importance of using support systems on the job. Some of the responses were: "finding out that all of us have basically the same problems," "finding ways of helping one another and getting to know the other person," "stress on co-workers as support system," "don't always rely on management to give you encouragement, get encouragement from each other." Other comments dealt with specific suggestions of the workshop: "controlling work load," "being given positive ways of combating problems and positive ways of looking at problems," "stating you have a problem and a solution." Still others appreciated the opportunity to talk openly, especially without their supervisors present.

The last part of the questionnaire asked for general comments. Responses were of two kinds: evaluation of the workshop and suggestions to management on work improvement. Comments of the first kind included appreciation of the workshop in general, need for a longer, more intensive program, suggestions for specific topics to be covered, and requests for similar workshops for management personnel.

Suggestions to management included ideas about improving work relations: "employees need to talk out their problems without being afraid of management," "management should communicate with all employees," "individuals can withstand many negative aspects of their job when bosses are aware of and appreciate their effort," "be more supportive to employees. It's not sufficient to say it during quarterly discussions and evaluations," "have more 'team work' between management and employees," "have many sessions like today, maybe once a month."

One week after the workshop, its effects were evident in the lower levels of burnout reported by the employees. The workshop participants also reported increased satisfaction from co-workers, supervisors, and contact with the public and their clients.[4] Not surprisingly, the workshop had negligible impact on such work features as variety, autonomy, significance, success, underload, and overload. These features are part of the reality of the job and as such were beyond the control of the individual worker. The workshop had more impact on the social and personal aspects of the work: personal relations, relations with supervisors, and feedback from colleagues were all evaluated more positively after the workshop.

Participants also described themselves as more adequately rewarded after the workshop. Two of the impersonal work features, bureaucratic interference and administrative conflicts, increased after the workshop, but the difference was not statistically significant. These features had been identified in numerous workshop discussions as inherent to the job and unchangeable. As a result they became more salient and could be perceived as more stressful by the workshop participants. The major effect of the burnout workshop was to increase satisfaction.

We also looked at work features and satisfaction as correlates of burnout. Several variables were associated more with burnout following the workshop. These changes suggest that as a result of the workshop the participant became more aware of the relationship between such features as overload, feedback, and especially personal relations with co-workers and the subjective experience of burnout.

This increased awareness, which was the first goal of the workshop, is also evident when we examine the satisfaction measures as correlates of burnout. Although the negative correlation of burnout with general work satisfaction increased for the participants, the correlation between burnout and satisfaction from clients and from the department increased dramatically. The correlation between satisfaction from supervisors and burnout also increased sharply. We interpreted these changes in the correlation between satisfaction and burnout to reflect increased awareness of the concept of burnout.

In summary, the burnout workshop produced three major outcomes: an increased awareness of the relationship between various work features and burnout; a decrease in burnout; and an increase in satisfaction from supervisors, the department, the public, clients, and co-workers.

Six months after the workshop its impact on the social atmosphere was still evident.[5] For the participants, satisfaction from coworkers, clients and the public remained considerably higher six months after the burnout workshop than it was prior to the workshop. The one satisfaction measure that did not show the impact of the workshop after six months was satisfaction from supervisors. This confirmed our general feeling that it is useful to include managers in these workshops.

Despite the limitations of a very small sample, after six months the correlations of burnout with the different variables were consistently higher for the participants in the workshop—this suggests the continuing impact of the workshop on the participants' awareness of the relationships between these variables and burnout.

The material covered in burnout workshops is pretty much the material covered in this book. The difference between the information in the workshop and reading it in a book is that participants aren't simply exposed to information; rather, in a workshop, they have a chance to experience its relevance to their own lives and work circumstances. Let us describe some of the ways that this experimental learning occurs.

When the participants in a workshop get together, whether it is the first hour of a one-day workshop or the first session of a five-day workshop, we take as long a time as necessary to have all of them introduce themselves to the group. In turn, they tell about the work they do, the particular problems in their work that cause them to burn out, and their expectations for the workshop.

We explain to the group members that these introductions have two purposes. First, they give us an idea of the particular needs of the group, so we can direct the workshop as much as possible to fulfill those needs. Second, they give the group members an idea of the human resources available to them in the workshop, in addition to us as the group leaders. We go on to explain that the interaction between the group members is a very important part of the workshop, in which they can practice the skills necessary for developing an effective social support network.

Soon after the first few people tell their story, it becomes apparent that the workshop is a place in which fallacies of uniqueness will be challenged. The statement "I have a very similar problem to the one described by . . . " is repeated in various versions over and over again. Often it is voiced by people who are working in a similar occupation, professional role, or organization. Just as often it is echoed by people who work in very different occupations, or who have very different roles in the organization. In all cases, it becomes clear to all participants that they are not alone—that there are other people who are struggling with similar problems. We suggest that they utilize those people as their support group in the different exercises that will take place during the workshop.

After a brief introduction of the concept of burnout, we introduce an "ice-breaking" experience. Ice-breaking is very important because this is a new and different situation for most people and they don't know what to expect. Understandably, most participants begin the workshop nervous and guarded. To break the ice, we ask them to join in small groups and we suggest topics of conversation that enable them to break out of the usual confines of small talk. Most people in this kind of situation would feel more comfortable if the other participants knew how skillful they are at their jobs or what warm, wonderful human beings they are. But they can't very well announce this; boasting is not socially acceptable. In effect, we give them permission to boast by providing them with a socially acceptable vehicle: We ask them to describe those qualities that their friends and closest colleagues like and admire most about them. Invariably this has the desired effect. Not only does it provide the people in the small group with a lot of information about one another in a short period of time, it also makes participants feel more comfortable.

We end this first session by distributing copies of the Burnout Measure (for self-diagnosis) and a list of several open questions: What were your hopes and expectations when you decided to get into your profession and/or take your current job? What are the three most stressful aspects in your work? How do you usually cope with these stresses? How effective is your coping? When we work with managers we emphasize that they can use the same questions and Burnout Measure (as well as the rest of the exercises and techniques presented in the workshop) with their own employees; that the workshop is directed to them as people, who may themselves suffer from burnout, and not just as managers.

In the next session, we present to the participants the formal definition of burnout. We describe its symptoms and discuss the two paths leading either to burnout or to peak performance (the material presented here in Chapters 1 and 2). Next we ask them to choose from all the people in the room three whom they either know the least (if they come from one organization) or who seem from their earlier presentation of themselves to have similar concerns (if it is a group of strangers). They are asked to describe to these three people what their hopes and expectations were when they decided to enter their profession or take their current job. Each foursome then chooses a hope or an expectation they all share to present to the rest of the group. The shared hopes and expectations are written on the blackboard. (This exercise was described in Chapter 3.)

When the group is of people from one field of work (management, human services) the shared hopes and expectations show the motivation that is the basis for the sense of significance that work provides for them. This motivation also points to the unique profile of the people who chose that work (in the case of managers, a need for control and success; in the case of human service professionals, a need to have contact with people, be helpful and appreciated for the help they provide).

When the group is a random gathering, the shared hopes and expectations point to the universal motivations for work that all people share.

Once their hopes and expectations have been analyzed, the foursomes are asked to present to each other the most stressful aspect of their work, and again decide on one or more stresses that they all share, that they will present to the rest of the group. These shared stresses are also written on the blackboard next to the list of hopes and expectations.

The different stresses are discussed as causes of burnout (corresponding to the material presented in Part Two of this book). When they are analyzed it becomes very obvious that the stresses can be stated, in almost every case, as frustrated hopes and expectations. This realization is used as a lead-in to a discussion on coping. We point out that this is a good way to view stresses, because the focus changes from escaping the stresses to dealing with them in a constructive way (or reevaluating expectations).

We start the session devoted to coping with a discussion of intrapersonal coping strategies (the material presented in Chapter 7). Recall that intrapersonal strategies are those techniques that individuals use to strengthen themselves, relax themselves, and so on, so that they are more able to deal with difficult situations as they arise. In the foursomes people describe their usual ways of coping with stress, and as a group select those that they find particularly useful. We then teach group participants various techniques for improved coping including things they can do alone (such as relaxation exercises, meditation, time management, compartmentalization, decompression) and things they can do with a mate or a co-worker.

When the group is made up of professionals working within one organization, time is devoted to a discussion of organizational coping strategies (the material presented in Chapter 9) and how they can be applied to that particular organization. When there is a problem with a particular person in the organization, role playing is often used to dramatize the problem and explore alternative ways of dealing with it.

We then initiate a thorough discussion of social support systems and their functions (the material presented in Chapter 8). Following the discussion we ask group members to review their own life and work to see which of the support functions are fulfilled for them and which are not. They present their conclusions to the other members of their foursomes (which by now have developed into support systems). They are asked to focus on those support functions that are not adequately fulfilled and to consider all the people they know who might fulfill these functions for them, and how they can ask them for help. The other three people in each foursome are asked to serve as emotional challengers to each individual, forcing the person to examine excuses and make concrete plans.

The final segment of the workshop is devoted to plans for the future. We start by using guided imagery to lead group participants to imagine (in as much detail as possible) a typical day in their lives five years into the future. This provides participants with the opportunity to use what they have learned in the workshop to reconstruct and reprioritize their lives in order to bring their lives and work, in imagery, into line with what they now believe is best for them. Later, based on their projections of the future, we ask them (with the assistance of their support groups) to make a concrete plan that will make the future more likely to unfold in the way that they envision it. The workshop ends with time for final feedback and for leave-taking. By the end of the workshop, the support groups have become close-knit entities. If the workshop consists of people in an intact organization, these groups can continue to function long after we leave. If the participants began as strangers, leave-taking is often an emotional experience.

Eleven

The Spillover
of Burnout
from Work
to Marriage

THOUGH thus far we have focused on occupational burnout, burnout is not merely an occupational hazard. Rather, it can occur in all spheres of life that give people a sense of meaning. It is possible to be a burned-out husband, a burned-out wife, or a burned-out parent. In this chapter we will examine how burnout at work can "spill over" to produce marriage burnout.

If we were to ask you, "What is more important: your work or your marriage?" what would you answer? If you are like the thousands of people we asked, your answer would be: "My marriage." The importance of marriage has been documented in national surveys which show that only a small percentage of people rank work as the central factor in their lives. Family life is consistently described as more important than work on most people's lists.[1]

Yet if we asked you how much of your prime time—time when you are not actually exhausted or preoccupied with something else—you spend at work, and how much of your prime time you spend at home, chances are that work would come out ahead. At work, the people you interact with get the best part of you. To those strangers you are polite and attentive. By the time you come home to the person who is supposedly most important in your life, you have neither the energy nor the patience to be polite and attentive. This is especially true if you are burning out at work. So you dispense with tact and other niceties, and tell yourself that "at least at home I can be myself." Why is it, though, that being yourself almost never implies being your best?

For most of us, once we feel assured of our mate's love and commitment, we tend to start taking this love for granted. We begin to make demands we would not think of making during the early stages of the relationship, demands we would not usually make of other people. The mate becomes the one person who is supposed to understand our work stress. "Who can I expect to be understanding and supportive if not my mate?" we ask self-righteously.

A woman who has been too often on the receiving end of this attitude says:

> When my husband was a student, he said he was under terrible stress because he had to study. I was supposed to understand. When he was a junior faculty member, he said he was under terrible stress being junior faculty. I was supposed to understand. When he became a senior faculty member, he was under terrible stress being a senior faculty member. And I was supposed to understand.
>
> It seems that every period in our fifteen years together has been 'the most difficult period' in his life. And I was expected to be sympathetic, understanding, and never make demands. When I realized that this was the way things were going to be forever, I knew I had to get out of the marriage.

By the time this woman's husband realized his job was destroying their marriage, it was too late. A marriage can survive, or even benefit from, a short dose of crisis at work. In short doses a mate can provide loving support. But when crisis becomes a daily event, it imposes stress that erodes the marriage. Dealing with continuous stress at work has the effect of making work a higher priority than marriage. No relationship can withstand that kind of assault for long.

In a good marriage the job doesn't come first. And such a good marriage can prevent job burnout. That's what we discovered in three studies in which 1187 participants described their work, marriage, and levels of burnout. People who were stressed at work but felt supported by their mates were able to cope with situations that were otherwise intolerable.[2] A young lawyer who was involved in a lengthy and complicated divorce trial describes it:

> I am almost at the end of my rope. The pressures of a court trial are immense, and this one has been dragging on for weeks with no end in sight. I feel very responsible to our client, and I think that the senior lawyer working with me on the case is totally incompetent and irresponsible. Not only that, but the other side is one of the biggest law firms in town. Our team is no match for them under the best of circumstances, and these are definitely *not* the best of circumstances. . . . It is very important for me to know that I can come home at night and be with someone I love who loves and appreciates me. It keeps intolerable things in perspective.

On the other hand, when people are in difficult marriages, the stress involved can have a very negative effect on their work. A computer consultant whose marriage of fifteen years was ending, says:

> I sit in front of the computer and I see blank. Since I am a free-lance consultant, and consequently am never sure about my next project until the contract is actually signed, the pressures of supporting a family have always been very difficult for me to bear. Now that my marriage is on the rocks, the tension is draining all my creative energy. And being creative is essential to my work. It is the essence of what I do, of what I sell to my clients. For weeks now, since the problems between us became intense, I haven't been able to work. I know what needs to be done, but I can't concentrate enough to be able to do it. I am so drained I feel like throwing everything away.

Findings of the three studies comparing job and marriage burnout show that overall burnout was more related to marital problems than to work stress.[3] Apparently, the overall quality of people's lives is more affected by the quality of their marriages than by the quality of their work. This is an important finding considering that most of us concentrate our best energies on our jobs—perhaps in a belief that we have to work at our jobs while our marriages will somehow take care of themselves.

Participants in the three studies described their marriages not only as more important to them, but as more satisfying emotionally, and as less pressured than their work. They had better personal relations at home than at work; they got more emotional rewards, more support, more sharing, more opportunities for self-actualization, and a greater sense of meaning. Work, on the other hand, was a source of bureaucratic and administrative hassles; people felt pressured to make decisions without enough time or information, they had few opportunities for influencing decisions that would have a direct impact on their lives, often they had little respect for the people they worked for and with, and their work environment tended to be more uncomfortable and impersonal than their home lives.

People often ask, "Which is more prevalent: job burnout or marriage burnout?" While estimates of burnout (either in marriage or at work) in the population as a whole are as yet unavailable, we were able to compare the levels of burnout on the job and in marriage in those samples that we studied. In a combined sample of 960 men and women, the average score of marriage burnout was 3.3. This score was identical to the average score of job burnout obtained in a combined sample of 3,916 men and women. Similarly, the average marriage burnout score in a study of 200 Israelis—2.8—was identical to the average job burnout score in a combined sample of 393 Israelis.[4]

From the similarity in people's levels of burnout on the job and in marriage we can assume that there is a similarity not only in the intensity, but also in the subjective experience of both. Indeed, just like job burnout, people experience marriage burnout as a state of physical, emotional, and mental exhaustion caused by long involvement in emotionally demanding situations.

A stressful environment, too much work, too much paperwork, poor communication, being stuck below one's level of competence, not having adequate financial or personnel resources, not feeling appreciated, and feeling like a failure will lead to burnout in marriage as they lead to burnout on the job. Some examples of these stresses in marriage are three kids and a dog in the car in 90 degree weather, too much housework, too many bills, doing laundry, a wife and a husband who can't talk to each other, having to juggle the checkbook, and not feeling appreciated by one another.

People burn out in their marriages for the same underlying reason they burn out on their jobs: their experience doesn't match their ideal. Just as idealistic workers burn out in their careers because they can't achieve what they expected, young lovers fall out of love because married life isn't like the fairy tale they imagined.

Just as job burnout can only happen to idealistic and highly motivated individuals, marriage burnout can only happen to couples in
love who have high expectations for the marriage (see Figure 11-1).

Job and marriage burnout not only parallel each other, they also
affect each other. It is very difficult to isolate the experience of

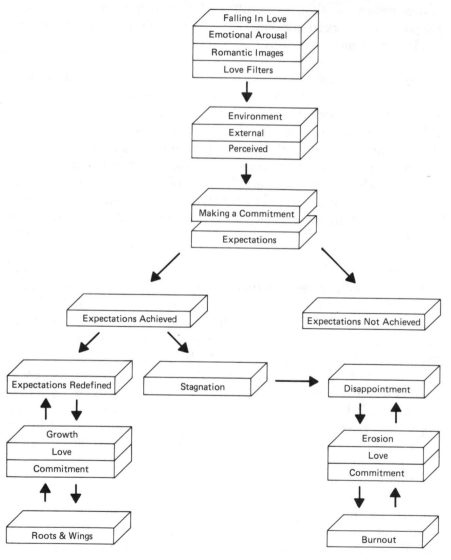

Figure 11-1   *The Love and Burnout Model*

Source: A. Pines, *Keeping the Spark Alive: Preventing Burnout in Marriage* (New York: St. Martin's Press, 1988).

burnout, either at work or in the marriage. When people start burning out on their jobs, typically, they pull back from co-workers and begin to feel isolated. They don't think they are getting enough appreciation for their work, or that the work is challenging enough. Unless they have learned to differentiate among the various aspects of support, all they experience is that something is missing. They simply do not feel supported. And who is the one person in the world who is *supposed* to support them? Their mate, of course. So they start putting increasing demands on their mate for professional appreciation and professional challenge. Such demands are both unfair and unrealistic since the mate is usually not well enough informed or qualified to fulfill them. In addition, instead of focusing on the situational stresses that caused their burnout they focus on their own failings and on the presumed failings of the person closest to them—the spouse. Frequently the atmosphere of disappointment and regret becomes associated with the marriage; it erodes love and commitment between the mates, and contributes to burnout.

Burnout can work the other way as well, spilling over from marriage into work. Most often this happens when people escape marital problems by totally investing themselves in their work. They usually come to work very early, leave very late, and take work home with them, to avoid having to talk to their mates. As long as work gives them a sense of significance, of making a difference, being successful, and belonging, they are able to avoid burnout. But if a problem arises at work, if they experience a crisis or a big failure, they have nothing to fall back on at home. Consequently they start feeling burned out in their work as well as marriage.

When people derive their sense of meaning from both work and love, and they burn out simultaneously in both, their physical, emotional, and mental exhaustion become so all-encompassing that they may become completely immobilized. Things are as bad as they can be, there is no hope of anything ever getting better, and there seems to be nothing worth living for. This is the state that drives people to thoughts of suicide.

Neither the similarity nor the relationship between burnout on the job and in marriage are obvious to the people who experience both of them. Many times after an intensive burnout workshop, participants would confide in us that "If I knew then what I know now, I would still be married." With the hindsight gained during the workshop they realize that they were too quick to blame their spouses for their problems at work, and too quick to give up on their marriage—when the real problems lay elsewhere.

Balancing a Job and a Marriage

Achieving and maintaining a balance between a career you have invested yourself in and a marriage you care deeply about is not easy. Yet it is essential. People who successfully combine a career and a family find a way to achieve that kind of balance between them, and the balance protects them from overinvolvement with either role. When they feel they have failed at one, the other gives meaning to their lives. A professor of chemistry who married another professor in the same department says:

> When I feel like a failure as a wife and mother, I say to myself, "Well, at least I am a decent chemist." When I feel like a failure as a chemist, I say to myself, "At least my husband and children think I am wonderful."

This balance can be achieved by the individual or by the couple. While all couples have to deal with issues related to the home-work conflict to some extent, "dual-career couples," where both mates have careers about which they care deeply, have unique strengths and vulnerabilities. Studies show that dual-career couples have a number of advantages over couples in which the husband works and the wife stays home. The most obvious advantage is a considerable financial edge gained by having two incomes. Dual-career couples also have stronger marital relationships; marital satisfaction and self-esteem are higher when both partners have careers. In several studies, women who work report greater self-esteem, effectiveness, well-being, and marital satisfaction than do unemployed women. Similarly, husbands of women who work full-time report happier marriages, have fewer infectious diseases, and are less prone to psychiatric impairment than husbands married to housewives. While the gains felt by the wives were more in terms of self-actualization, the gains felt by the husbands were more in terms of the egalitarian relationship. Several of the husbands whose wives started working after being housewives for many years discovered, sometimes to their own surprise, that not only were they—the husbands—skilled and competent in their new domestic responsibilities, but they actually enjoyed the extra time they were spending with the kids.[5]

Several studies have found that the careers of couples who share the same career, or the same field, benefit as well. A study of 86 sociologist couples who held appointments at the same academic departments found that the wives were more successful than women sociologists in general. They obtained higher degrees, more promotions, and continued with their careers longer.[6]

In another study of 200 psychologist couples it was found that when compared with a group of male and female psychologists who were not married to fellow professionals, the psychologist pairs produced more publications than their same-sex counterparts.[7] Similar findings were obtained in a study of dual-career lawyers. Moreover, it was found that the husbands of professional women were more likely to respect professional competence and achievement not only in their wives, but in women in general.[8]

Children (especially daughters) also benefit when both parents work. It was found, for example, that daughters of working mothers were more likely than daughters whose mothers stayed home to choose their mothers as role models and as the people they most admired. Adolescent daughters of working mothers were active and autonomous and admired their mothers but were not unusually tied to them. For daughters of all ages, having a working mother meant seeing the world as a less restrictive place.[9]

While dual-career couples have many advantages over traditional couples, they also have a higher divorce rate than traditional couples. Clearly, dual-career couples are pressured to make adaptations that are not required within more conventional marriages. The psychiatrists Carol and Theodore Nadelson say that dual-career couples are often faced with difficult choices:

> For example, the husband who is transferred to a new location may have to consider not only his wife's social adjustment and interests, his children's schooling and relationships with peers, but, to a greater extent, his wife's career possibilities. *She* may not be able to obtain a position equal to her present one, or her career advancement may, in fact, be jeopardized by a change in location. Wives share a complementary dilemma. The wife may be offered a potentially gratifying career opportunity, only to recognize that this shift might put added pressure on her family, especially if a location change may be required. She may decide to decline the offer, or she may seek another apparent solution: that one partner commute. This latter pattern has

become frequent in recent years. The costs of these changes may be significant enough to cause a rupture in the marital relationship.[10]

Dual-career couples may also be forced to reconsider their family roles (what is an appropriate activity for a man/husband/father or a woman/wife/mother) and to adapt emotionally to new roles and expectations. The Nadelsons cite competition, envy, and unrealized expectations as significant areas of conflict in dual-career couples.

In our own work we discovered that the main complaint of dual-career couples was lack of time. This was especially true when both mates had careers they valued, which demanded a lot of their time. When asked about stress in his marriage, one happily married man said:

> *Most* stressful is the inability to resolve the conflict between money and time. Making the kind of money I want to have obliterates the emotional connection that I want to have. But I don't want to give up the income of a good job. Yet, I am working too much for it to really make sense if I'm going to balance my life the way I believe I want to—and the way I believed it would be when we fell in love. . . . While there is no question in my mind about what I would choose if I had to make the choice between my work and my relationship with Elaine, luckily (or maybe unfortunately) I don't have to make a choice. So I end up giving the best part of my days to my work.

His wife's response reflects a similar sentiment:

> I love my work. It is, and has always been, a very important part of my life and of my definition of myself. Terry has not always been as happy in his work, so I am delighted that he enjoys and is successful in it now. Yet the time commitment both jobs require is the greatest strain on the relationship. It takes so much out of us that when we are together, in the evening or on weekends, we are totally wiped out. Even though I have complete confidence in our love for each other, I know from personal experience the accumulative effect such continuous stress can have on a relationship. I know that if we want the romance to remain in our relationship we have to be on guard and make sure it doesn't get lost.

Certain conflicts around issues of time management are inevitable when both mates are constantly negotiating the demands of an important career and the demands of an important relationship.

Time is one resource that cannot be recouped or expanded. No matter how energetic, clever, and skillful a couple is, they can never have more than twenty-four hours in a day.

One way to address issues such as time is for both mates to list their work and home demands side by side and for both of them together to examine each other's lists. Even when couples have been together for many years and claim to know each other intimately, this process can produce some unexpected surprises. A wife may discover that the demand to have dinner on the table by a certain time and the guilt feelings associated with going out for dinner with the family are values and judgments that she carries in her own head, perhaps because they were learned in childhood. She may discover that her husband views going out for dinner as a far more positive and exciting option and that he would love to do it more often.

A man may discover that being a superb provider, which he believed to be the most important responsibility of a husband, is not very important to his wife. For his wife, the times spent together as a family may be more important than the raise her husband might get if he spent extra time working after hours.

Even when a certain demand is recognized as having been real by both mates, after close scrutiny they may decide that, given their current priorities, it is no longer essential. In other cases they may decide that even if a demand was legitimate and reasonable in the past, it no longer is. Listing the home and work demands, examining them together, being willing to recognize self-imposed demands, and being open to negotiate all demands are the most important first steps in achieving a marriage-work balance.

Finding a balance between work and marriage enables people to get a sense of meaning from both, and provides twice the chance of finding some significant meaning as relying on either work or marriage alone.

Appendix 1

How Burned Out Are You?

Y OU can compute your burnout score by completing the questionnaire shown in Table A–1. You can use it for diagnosing how you feel about your work or for diagnosing how you feel about your life just today or in general.

Of the thousands who responded to this self-diagnosis instrument, none scored either 1 or 7. The reason is obvious. It is unlikely that anyone would be in a state of eternal euphoria implied by the score 1, and it is unlikely that someone who scored 7 would be able to cope with the world well enough to participate in a burnout workshop or a research project.

If your score is between 2 and 3 you are doing well. The only suggestion we make is that you go over your score sheet to be sure you have been honest in your responses. If your score is between 3 and 4, it would be wise for you to examine your work and life and evaluate your priorities and consider possible changes. If your score is higher than 4, you are experiencing burnout to the extent that it is mandatory that you do something about it. A score of higher than 5 indicates an acute state and a need for immediate help.

TABLE A–1
A Self-Diagnosis Instrument

You can compute your burnout score by completing the following question-naire.

How often do you have any of the following experiences? Please use the scale:

1	2	3	4	5	6	7
Never	Once in a great while	Rarely	Sometimes	Often	Usually	Always

_____ 1. Being tired.
_____ 2. Feeling depressed.
_____ 3. Having a good day.
_____ 4. Being physically exhausted.
_____ 5. Being emotionally exhausted.
_____ 6. Being happy.
_____ 7. Being "wiped out."
_____ 8. "Can't take it anymore."
_____ 9. Being unhappy.
_____ 10. Feeling run-down.
_____ 11. Feeling trapped.
_____ 12. Feeling worthless.
_____ 13. Being weary.
_____ 14. Being troubled.
_____ 15. Feeling disillusioned and resentful.
_____ 16. Being weak and susceptible to illness.
_____ 17. Feeling hopeless.
_____ 18. Feeling rejected.
_____ 19. Feeling optimistic.
_____ 20. Feeling energetic.
_____ 21. Feeling anxious.

Computation of score:

Add the values you wrote next to the following items:
1,2,4,5,7,8,9,10,11,12,13,14,15,16,17,18,21(A) _____.

Add the values you wrote next to the following items:
3,6,19,20(B) _____, subtract (B) from 32(C) _____.

Add A and C(D) _____.

Divide D by 21 _____. This is your burnout score.

Appendix 2

The Burnout Measure

T HE 21 items in Table A–1 represent the three components of burnout: physical exhaustion (e.g., feeling tired and run-down, having sleep problems, being weak and suscep-tible to illness), emotional exhaustion (e.g., feeling depressed, trapped, hopeless), and mental exhaustion (e.g., feeling worthless, disillusioned, and resentful).

Test-retest reliability of the measure was found to be .89 for a one-month interval, .76 for a two-month interval, and .66 for a four-month interval. Internal consistency was assessed by the alpha coef-ficients for most samples studied; the values of the alpha coeffi-cients ranged between .91 and .93. All correlations between the indi-vidual items and the composite score were statistically significant at the .001 level of significance in all the studies in which the measure was used. The overall mean value for all the samples studied (total-ling over 5,000 subjects) was 3.3. A factor analysis gave evidence that the measure assesses a single meaningful construct. Factor I, which accounted for 69 percent of the variance, had the highest loadings with feeling "I can't take it anymore," "depressed," and "wiped out."

Construct validity of the burnout measure was examined by correlational analysis with several other theoretically relevant measures; for example, burnout was found to be negatively correlated with self-ratings of satisfaction from work, from life, and from oneself. In one study involving 322 human service professionals, the following correlations between burnout and the three satisfaction measures were found: for satisfaction from work, $r = -.62$, $p < .001$; for satisfaction from life, $r = -.65$, $p < .001$; and for satisfaction from oneself, $r = -.62$, $p < .001$. In all cases the highly significant correlations indicated that the more burned out the professionals were, the less satisfied they were with their work, their lives, and themselves. The high, yet less than perfect correlation between burnout and satisfaction from work shows that the two are related but not identical.

Another consequence of burnout is job turnover. In a sample of 129 social service workers, burnout was significantly correlated with an intention to leave the job ($r = .58$, $p < .01$). In a sample of 130 human service professionals who responded to a twenty-item Hopelessness Questionnaire,[1] the correlation between hopelessness and burnout was .59 ($p < .001$). In a study of fourteen residential facilities for the developmentally disabled (done in collaboration with Steve Weinberg and Bill Garove) high-burnout facilities had significantly higher turnover rates than low-burnout facilities ($t(12) = 3.00$, $p = .01$). The mean turnover rate for the high-burnout facilities was 48.8 percent as compared with 17 percent for the low-burnout facilities. High-burnout facilities also had a significantly higher number of directors within the past five years ($t(12) = 3.23$, $p = .01$). Mean tenure for directors in the high-burnout facilities was one year and ten months, compared with four years and seven months in the low-burnout facilities.

Burnout is also related to physical health problems. In a sample of 181 telephone operators (studied in collaboration with Jacob Golan) burnout was significantly correlated with poor physical health ($r = .46$, $p < .001$). In a study of 298 police officers (done in collaboration with Mimi Silbert), burnout was correlated with such on-duty symptoms as headaches ($r = .32$, $p < .001$), loss of appetite ($r = .33$, $p < .001$), nervousness ($r = .38$, $p < .001$), backaches ($r = .20$, $p < .001$), and stomach aches ($r = .32$, $p < .001$). It was also significantly correlated with alcohol consumption ($r = .37$, $p < .002$).

In a study involving 118 elementary school teachers we found that self-diagnosis of burnout was significantly correlated with diagnosis by a close colleague ($r = .37$, $p < .001$). In this study, after diagnosing themselves, the teachers were asked to estimate the degree of burnout reported by one of their close colleagues. The significant correlation, in addition to demonstrating that one can recognize burnout in others, also served as an instrument validation.

The Burnout Measure's high face validity can be seen in the close correspondance between the items and the theoretical definition of burnout, as well as in respondents' positive reaction to it, as defining their own level of job burnout.

Notes

Preface

1. The study was done in collaboration with Dalia Etzion. The mean burnout score for 66 managers who simply filled out the burnout measure was 2.8. The mean burnout score for the 21 managers who were first told that "the most idealistic people burn out most" and then asked to fill out the questionnaire was 3.5. The difference is significant at p < .01.

Chapter 1. The Burnout Experience

1. A. D. Kanner, D. Kafry, and A. Pines, "Lack of Positive Conditions as a Source of Stress," *Journal of Human Stress* 4, no. 4 (1978): 33–39.
2. H. J. Freudenberger, "Burnout: Occupational Hazard of the Child Care Worker," *Child Care Quarterly* 6, no. 2 (Spring 1980): 5–16.
3. K. L. Armstrong, "How Can We Avoid Burnout?" *Child Abuse and Neglect: Issues on Innovation and Implementation*, DHEW Publication No. (OHOS) 78–30148,2 (1978): 230–238.
4. In our studies the correlations between burnout and sleep distur-

bances ranged from $r = .28$ ($p < .01$) to $r = -.20$ to $r = -.46$ ($p < .001$).

5. In a study involving 130 subjects who responded to a hopelessness questionnaire (A. T. Beck, A. Weissman, D. Lester, and L. Trenxler, "The Measurement of Pessimism: The Hopelessness Scale," *Journal of Consulting and Clinical Psychology* 42 [1974]: 861–865), the correlation between the combined burnout score and hopelessness was $r = .59$, $p < .001$.

6. In one of our studies of 33 men and 73 women it was found that for men the correlation between burnout and loneliness was $r = .40$; for women it was $r = .27$. Both are statistically significant at the .01 level.

7. We examined the correlation between burnout and satisfaction from self, from work, and from life in most of our samples. The correlation between burnout and satisfaction from work ranged from $-.24$ to $-.63$ (with an average correlation of $-.45$). The correlation between burnout and satisfaction from life ranged from $-.32$ to $-.70$ (with an average correlation of $-.51$). The correlation between burnout and satisfaction from self ranged from $-.32$ to $-.73$ (with an average correlation of $-.51$). All the correlations were statistically significant.

8. For example, M. C. Kelman, "Violence Without Moral Restraint: Reflections on the Dehumanization of Victims and Victimizers," *Journal of Social Issues* 29 (1973): 25–61; D. J. Vail, *Dehumanization and the Institutional Career* (Springfield, IL: Charles C. Thomas, 1966); A. Pines and T. Solomon, "Perception of Self as a Mediator of the Dehumanization Process," *Personality and Social Psychology Bulletin* 3, no. 2 (1977): 219–223; P. G. Zimbardo, "The Human Choice: Individuation, Reason and Order versus Deindividuation, Impulse and Chaos," in *Nebraska Symposium on Motivation: 1969*, ed. W. J. Arnold and D. Levine (Lincoln: University of Nebraska Press, 1970).

9. M. Buber, *I and Thou*, 2d ed. (New York: Scribner's, 1958).

10. In a sample of 129 social service workers the correlation between burnout and wanting to leave the job was .58 ($p < .01$). In another sample of 181 Israeli telephone operators the correlation between burnout and tardiness (the number of days a year in which employees were late for work) was .30 ($p < .001$). The study was done by J. Golan. "Attitudes, Personal Characteristics and Organizational Factors and Their Relationship to Absenteeism among Telephone Operators." Thesis for an M.Sc. degree in Management Sciences, submitted to the faculty of management, Tel-Aviv University, 1979. Correlations of burnout with new job searches ($r = .49$), extension of work breaks ($r = .47$), days absent ($r = -.52$), and days late ($r = .37$) were also reported by J. W. Jones in "The Staff Burnout Scale: A Validity Study" (paper presented at the 52nd annual meeting of the Midwestern Psychological Association, St. Louis, May 1–3, 1980).

11. H. J. Freudenberger, "The Staff Burnout Syndrome in Alternative Institutions," *Psychotherapy: Theory, Research and Practice*, Spring 1975: 73–82.
12. W. D. Gentry, S. B. Foster, and S. Fruehling, "Psychological Response to Situational Stress in Intensive Care Nursing," *Heart and Lung* 1 (1972): 793–796.
13. Freudenberger, "The Staff Burnout Syndrome."
14. Armstrong, "How Can We Avoid Burnout?"
15. J. W. Jones, "Staff Burnout and Employee Counterproductivity," in J. Jones (ed.) *The Burnout Syndrome* (Park Ridge, IL: London House Press, 1981), pp. 126–138.
16. A. H. Stanton and M. S. Schwarts, *The Mental Hospital: A Study of Institutional Participation in Psychiatric Illness and Treatment* (New York: Basic Books, 1954).
17. The correlation between self-assessment and assessment of burnout by colleagues for the two samples combined was $r = .37$ ($p < .001$).
18. J. P. Lysaught, *An Abstract for Action. National Commission for the Study of Nursing and Nursing Education* (New York: McGraw-Hill, 1970).
19. C. H. Kempe, "Child Protective Services: Where Have We Been? What Are We Now? And Where Are We Going?" *Child Abuse and Neglect: Issues on Innovation and Implementation*, DHEW Publication No. 78–30147, 5 (1978): 19–28.
20. I. Adizes, "Mismanagement Styles," *California Management Review* 19, no. 2 (1976): 5–30.
21. A. Camus, *The Myth of Sisyphus* (New York: Vintage Books, 1955).
22. Martin Lipp, M.D. has also described this process in his chapter on coping and occupational hazards of physicianhood in his book, *Respectful Treatment—The Human Side of Medical Care* (New York: Harper & Row, 1977), pp. 206–215.

Chapter 2. Two Paths:
Burnout Versus Peak Performance

1. E. Becker, *The Denial of Death* (New York: Free Press, 1973).
2. W. D. Harrison, "A Social Competence Model of Burnout," in B. Farber (ed.), *Stress and Burnout* (New York: Pergamon, 1983).
3. Lack of significance was found in several of our studies to be a major cause of hopelessness, depression, and burnout. For example, in a sample of 267 police officers and in a sample of 101 managers, the correlation between significance and burnout was $r = -.27$ ($p < .05$). The more sense of significance individuals get from their work, the less likely they are to burn out.

4. B. A. Farber, "The Process and Dimension of Burnout in Psychotherapists." Paper presented at the meeting of the American Psychological Association, Montreal, September 1980.

5. C. R. Rogers, *On Becoming a Person* (Boston: Houghton Mifflin, 1961).

6. A. Maslow, *Toward a Psychology of Being* (New York: Van Nostrand, 1962).

7. E. Locke, "The Nature and the Causes of Job Satisfaction," in M. D. Dunette (ed.), *Handbook of Industrial and Organizational Psychology* (Chicago: Rand McNally, 1976).

8. Harrison, "A Social Competence Model of Burnout."

9. In the sample, studied in collaboration with Steve Weinberg et al. in 1979, the correlation between burnout and self-actualization was $r = -.30$ ($p < .05$).

10. In several of our studies autonomy was found to be positively correlated with job satisfaction, and negatively correlated with burnout. That is to say, the more autonomy, the less burnout. For example, in a sample of 198 mental retardation workers, the correlation was $r = -.32$. In a sample of 52 Social Security Administration workers the correlation was $r = -.35$. (Both p values $< .05$.)

11. S. Terkel, *Working* (New York: Pantheon Books, 1974).

12. H. Drummond, "The Epidemic Nobody Tries to Treat," *Mother Jones*, September-October 1977, pp. 11–12.

13. A. V. Horwitz, "Sex-role Expectations, Power and Psychological Distress," *Sex Roles* 8 (1982): 607–623.

14. M. E. P. Seligman, *Helplessness: On Depression, Development and Death* (San Francisco: W. H. Freeman, 1975).

15. Martin Lipp, *The Human Side of Medical Care* (New York: Harper & Row, 1977), p. 559.

16. The only correlation found in the study of Social Security Administration workers was between pay and agency evaluation ($r = .26, p < .05$).

17. J. R. P. French, Jr. and R. D. Caplan, "Organizational Stress and Individual Strain," in A. J. Marrow (ed.), *The Failure of Success* (New York: AMACOM, 1972).

18. C. L. Cooper and J. Marshall, "Occupational Sources of Stress," *Journal of Occupational Psychology* 49 (1976): 11–28.

19. For example, Chris Argyris, *Integrating the Individual and the Organization* (New York: John Wiley, 1964) and C. L. Cooper, *Group Training for Organizational Development* (Basel, Switz.: S. Kager 1973).

20. M. Marx-Ferree, "The Confused American Housewife," *Psychology Today* 10, no. 4 (1976): 76–80.

21. In the study involving 76 mental health workers it was found that when work relationships were good, staff members were more likely to express positive attitudes toward the institution as a whole ($r = .49$),

to enjoy their work ($r = .38$), and to feel successful in it ($r = .31$). They also rated the institution more highly ($r = .41$), described their reasons for being in the mental health field as "self-fulfillment" ($r = .41$), had more "good days," and described the average schizophrenic patient in more positive terms. (All correlations in both studies are significant at $p < .001$.) See A. Pines and C. Maslach, "Characteristics of Staff Burnout in Mental Health Settings," *Hospital and Community Psychiatry* 29, no. 4 (1978): 233–237.

22. A. Pines, and A. D. Kanner, "Nurses' Burnout: Lack of Positive Conditions and Presence of Negative Conditions as Two Independent Sources of Stress," *Journal of Psychosocial Nursing* 8, no. 20 (1982): 30–35. See also A. D. Kanner, D. Kafry, and A. Pines, "Conspicuous in Its Absence: The Lack of Positive Conditions as a Source of Stress," *Journal of Human Stress* 4, no. 4 (1978): 33–39.

23. R. S. Lazarus, *Psychological Stress and Coping Process* (New York: McGraw-Hill, 1966).

24. Such variables as overload, conflicting demands, decision load, and guilt are examples of stresses for most people. For example, in the study involving 724 human service professionals, the correlation between burnout and overload was $r = .35$; burnout and conflicting demands was $r = .31$; decision load $r = .30$; and guilt $r = .42$ (all correlations are statistically significant).

Chapter 3. Burnout in Management

1. J. B. Rohrlich, *Work and Love* (New York: Crown Publishers, 1980).
2. D. Gowler and K. Legge (eds.), *Managerial Stress* (Epping, England: Grower Press, 1975).
3. W. E. Oates, *Confessions of a Workaholic* (Nashville: Abingdon Press, 1971).
4. W. Bridges, *The Seasons of Our Lives* (San Francisco: The Wayfarer Press, 1977).
5. M. Friedman, and R. H. Rosenman, *Type A Behavior and Your Heart* (Greenwich, CT: Fawcett Publications, 1974).
6. C. Cherniss, *Staff Burnout, Job Stress and the Human Services* (Beverly Hills, CA: Sage, 1980).
7. A. M. Garden, "Burnout: The Effect of Personality" (unpublished doctoral dissertation, Alfred P. Sloan School of Management, 1985). See also A. M. Garden, "Burnout: The Effect of Jungian Type," Alfred Sloan School of Management working paper WP 1588–84, 1984.
8. C. G. Jung, *Psychological Types*, Vol. 6 of *Collected Works*, Bollingen Series XX (Princeton: Princeton University Press, 1960).
9. A. Pines, "On Burnout and the Buffering Effects of Social Support,"

in B. A. Farber (ed.), *Stress and Burnout in the Human Professions* (Elmsford, NY: Pergamon Press, 1983).
10. S. G. Ginsburg, "The Problem of the Burned Out Executive," *Personnel Journal*, August, 1974.
11. H. J. Freudenberger, "Counseling and Dynamics: Treating the End-Stage Person," in W. S. Paine (ed.), *Job Stress and Burnout* (Beverly Hills, CA: Sage, 1982): pp. 175–185.
12. A. Antonovsky, *Health, Stress and Coping* (San Francisco: Jossey-Bass, 1979).
13. S. Kobasa and S. Maddi, "Personality and Constitution as Mediators in the Stress-Illness Relationship," *Journal of Health and Social Behavior* 22, (1981): 368–378.
14. Sixty-six American managers and 66 Israeli managers participated in the study. The mean burnout score was 3.4 for the American sample and 2.8 for the Israeli.
15. A. Pines, D. Kafrey, and D. Etzion, "Job Stress from a Cross Cultural Perspective," in K. Reid (ed.), *Burnout in the Helping Professions*. Unpublished manuscript (Kalamazoo: Western Michigan University Press, 1980); D. Etzion, A. Pines and D. Kafry, "Coping Strategies and the Experience of Tedium: A Cross-Cultural Comparison Between Israelies and Americans," *Journal of Psychology and Judaism* 1, no. 7 (1982): 30–41; and D. Etzion and A. Pines, "Sex and Culture in Burnout and Coping," *Journal of Cross Cultural Psychology* 17, no. 2 (1986): 191–209.
16. D. C. McClelland, *The Achieving Society* (New York: Van Nostrand, 1961).
17. For example, in a sample of 205 professionals, success was correlated with burnout $r = -.48$.
18. Friedman and Rosenman, *Type A Behavior*.
19. R. J. Burke, J. Shearer, and E. Deszoa, "Burnout Among Men and Women in Police Work." Unpublished manuscript (Toronto: York University, 1984).

Chapter 4. Burnout in the Helping Professions

1. H. I. Lief and R. C. Fox, "Training for 'Detached Concern' in Medical Students," in H. I. Lief, V. I. Lief, and N. R. Lief (eds.), *The Psychological Basis of Medical Practice* (New York: Harper & Row, 1963), p. 13.
2. D. D. Federman, "Can Compassion Survive? Pressures Imperil M.D.'s Conscience and Motivation," *Stanford Observer*, March 1976, p. 5. The article was adapted from Professor Federman's address to the Stanford School of Medicine, 1975.

3. D. Oken, "The Unknown Factor: The Doctor and How He Does His Doctoring," *Frontiers of Psychiatry,* June 15, 1978, p. 12.
4. "The 'Jungle' Today," in *Education,* Maclean's (Canada), March 8, 1976, p. 52.
5. A. M. Bloch, "Combat Neurosis in Inner City Schools." Paper presented at the 130th annual meeting of the American Psychiatric Association, May 4, 1977.
6. A. Kadushin, *Child Welfare Services* (New York: Macmillan, 1974).
7. For example, Jim Coins, then a clinical psychologist at the University of California in Berkeley, has shown that talking on the phone to depressed clients has a negative effect on the mood of the therapist.
8. Y. Feldman, H. Spotnitz, and L. Nagelberg, "One Aspect of Case Work Training through Supervisors," *Social Casework* 34 (April 1953): 153.
9. Kadushin, *Child Welfare Services.*
10. W. Regiatt, *The Occupational Culture of Policemen and Social Workers* (Washington, D. C.: American Psychological Association, 1970), p. 11.
11. Kadushin, *Child Welfare Services.*
12. M. Kramer, *Reality Shock* (St. Louis: Mosby, 1974).
13. J. M. M. Hill, "The Representation of Labor Turnover as a Social Form," in B. O. Pettman (ed.), *Labor Turnover and Retention* (New York: Wiley, 1975), pp. 73–93.
14. For example, A. E. Every and J. A. Authier, *Microcounseling* (Springfield, IL: Charles C. Thomas, 1978).
15. M. Lipp, *The Wounded Healer* (New York: Harper & Row, 1980).
16. Lief and Fox, "Training for 'Detached Concern.'"
17. D. Etzion, "Achieving Balance in a Consultation Setting," *Group and Organization Studies* 4, no. 3 (1979): 366–376.
18. B. Bettelheim, *A Home for the Heart* (New York: Bantam Books, 1974), p. 280.
19. J. Golan, "Attitudes, Personal Characteristics, and Organizational Factors and Their Relationships with Absenteeism among Telephone Operators." Thesis for M.Sc. degree in Management Sciences, Organizational Behavior, submitted to the Faculty of Management, Tel Aviv University, 1979; J. W. Jones, "The Staff Burnout Scale: A Validity Study." Paper presented at the 52nd annual meeting of the Midwestern Psychological Association, St. Louis, May 1–3, 1980.
20. A. Pines and C. Maslach, "Characteristics of Staff Burnout in Mental Health Settings," *Hospital and Community Psychiatry* 29, no. 4 (1978): 233–337.
21. Lief and Fox, "Training for 'Detached Concern.'"
22. M. Millman, *The Unkindest Cut: Life in the Backrooms of Medicine* (New York: Morrow, 1977).
23. Lief and Fox, "Training for 'Detached Concern.'"
24. Etzion, "Achieving Balance in a Consultation Setting."

25. E. E. Jones, D. E. Kanause, H. H. Kelley, R. E. Nisbett, S. Valins, and B. Weiner (eds.), *Attribution: Perceiving the Causes of Behavior* (Morristown, NJ: General Learning Press, 1972).
26. C. Maslach, "Burnout: The Loss of Human Caring," *Human Behavior* 5 (September 1976): 16–22.

Chapter 5. Burnout in Bureaucratic Organizations

1. M. Weber, *Economy and Society: An Outline of Interpretative Sociology*, ed. G. Roth and C. Witlich (New York: Bedminster Press, 1968), p. 1002.
2. D. Bacon, "Mess in Welfare—The Inside Story," *U.S. News and World Report,* February 20, 1978, pp. 21–24. The case study is based on this report. The other quotes in the case study are also from this source.
3. Ibid.
4. Ibid.
5. Ibid.
6. Ibid.
7. Alexis de Tocqueville, *Democracy in America* (Garden City, NY: Doubleday, 1969).
8. K. L. Armstrong, "How Can We Avoid Burnout?" *Child Abuse and Neglect: Issues in Innovation and Implementation,* DHEW Publication No. (OHDS) 78–30148, 2 (1978): 230–238.
9. In the study, which involved 52 employees of a large bureaucratic organization, their mean burnout was 3.6. In a study of 205 professionals the mean burnout scores for human service were 3.1, business 3.2, science 3.3, art 3.2.
10. The correlation between burnout and overall satisfaction from work was $r = -.58,$* with overall satisfaction from self $r = -.45,$* with overall satisfaction from life $r = -.44,$* with satisfaction from supervisors $r = -.32,$* with satisfaction from the department $r = -.26,$ with satisfaction from the public $r = -.22,$ with satisfaction from clients $r = -.53,$* with satisfaction from co-workers $r = -.17,$ with satisfaction from work $r = -.43,$* with mean satisfaction from various work activities $r = -.57,$* with wanting to leave the job $r = +.44$* (*indicates that the correlation is statistically significant at .01 level).
11. J. R. D. French and R. D. Kaplan, "Organizational Stress and Individual Strain," in A. J. Marrow (ed.), *The Failure of Success* (New York: AMACOM, 1973).
12. French and Kaplan, "Organizational Stress and Individual Strain."
13. J. G. Miller, in R. W. Waggoner and D. J. Carek (eds.), *Communication in Clinical Practice* (Boston: Little, Brown, 1964), pp. 201–224.
14. Both studies are quoted in Z. L. Lipowski, "Sensory and Information

Inputs Overload: Behavioral Effects," *Comprehensive Psychiatry* 16, no. 3 (1975): 199–221.

15. The study was conducted in collaboration with Steve Weinberg in the Management Training Program of the University of Alabama in Birmingham.

16. R. L. Kahn, "Job Burnout, Prevention and Remedies," *Public Welfare* (Spring 1978), pp. 61–63.

17. G. Kirkham, "From Professor to Patrolmen: A Fresh Perspective on the Police," *Journal of Police Science and Administration* 2, no. 2 (1977): 127–137.

18. The study is quoted by W. Kroes in *Society's Victim—The Policeman: An Analysis of Job Stress in Policing* (Springfield, IL: Charles C. Thomas, 1976), p. 27.

19. A. Pines and D. Kafry, *The Impact of a Burnout Workshop on Occupational Tedium,* Technical Report, Berkeley, CA, 1979.

20. The correlation between burnout and overload in this particular study was $r = .30, p < .05$.

21. The study of child-care workers is described in C. Maslach and A. Pines, "The Burnout Syndrome in Day Care Settings," *Child Care Quarterly,* 6, no. 2 (1977): 100–113. The study of mental health workers is described in A. Pines and C. Maslach, "Characteristics of Staff Burnout in Mental Health Settings," *Hospital and Community Psychiatry* 29, no. 4 (1978): 233–237.

22. N. Watson and J. Sterling, *Police and Their Opinions* (Gaithersburg, MD: International Association of Chiefs of Police, 1969).

23. In the study, involving 52 employees of a bureaucratic organization, the correlation between burnout and administrative hassles such as paper work, red tape, and communication problems was $r = .25. p < .05$.

24. M. E. Seligman, *Helplessness: On Depression Development and Death* (San Francisco: Freeman Press, 1979).

25. J. E. Singer and D. C. Glass, *Urban Stress* (New York: Academic Press, 1972).

26. E. J. Langer and J. Rodin, "The effects of choice and enhanced personal responsibility for the aged: A field experiment in an institutional setting," *Journal of Personality and Social Psychology* 34(1976): 191–198.

27. The study was done by L. Fidell and J. Prather at California State University, Northridge. It was reported by Carol Tavris in *Psychology Today* 10, no. 4 (1976): 78.

28. In a study of 52 employees of a bureaucratic organization the correlation between burnout and autonomy was $r = -.35$. In a study of 205 professionals (human service, business, service, art, etc.) the correlation was $r = -.28$. Both results are significant at .05 level.

29. Pines and Kafry, *Impact of a Burnout Workshop.*
30. In the study involving 205 professionals, the mean burnout for the "have to" respondents was $\bar{x} = 3.5.$, for the "want to" respondents $\bar{x} = 3.1$. The difference is statistically significant at $p < .0001$. In a study involving 84 students the means were $\bar{x} = 3.8$ for "have to" and $\bar{x} = 3.3$ for "want to," $p < .001$.
31. Kroes, *Society's Victim.*
32. Pines and Kafry, *Impact of a Burnout Workshop.*
33. In a study involving 205 professionals the following correlations with burnout were found: with rewards $r = -.33$, with appreciation $r = -.32$, with a sense of significance $r = -.21$, with a sense of success $r = -.24$, with physical health $r = -.39$, with satisfaction from pay $r = .01$.
34. R. Pruger, "The Good Bureaucrat," *Social Work* (July 1973): 26–32.
35. Ibid.
36. N. V. Rayner, M. W. Pratt, and S. Roses, "Aids Involvement in Decision Making and the Quality of Care in Institutional Settings," *American Journal of Mental Deficiency* 81, no. 6 (1977): 570–577.
37. Pruger, "The Good Bureaucrat."
38. Rayner, Pratt, and Roses, "Aids Involvement in Decision Making."
39. W. L. French and C. A. Bell, *Organizational Development: Behavioral Science Interventions for Organizational Improvement,* 2d ed. (Englewood Cliffs, NJ: Prentice-Hall, 1978).

Chapter 6. Burnout in Women

1. R. D. Arvey and R. H. Gross, "Satisfaction Levels and Correlates of Satisfaction in the Homemaker Job," *Journal of Vocational Behavior* 10 (1977): 13–24.
2. Ibid.
3. M. Marx Ferree, "The Confused American Housewife," *Psychology Today* 10, no. 4 (1976): 76–80.
4. Ibid., p. 76.
5. Ibid.
6. Jessie Bernard, a research scholar at the Department of Sociology, Pennsylvania State University, is the author of *The Future of Marriage, The Future of Motherhood,* and several other books on sex roles, marriage, and the family.
7. A. Oakley, *The Sociology of Housework* (New York: Pantheon, 1975).
8. Arvey and Gross, "Satisfaction Levels."
9. Reported by Carol Tavris in "Women's Work Isn't Always the Answer," *Psychology Today* 10, no. 4 (1976): 78.
10. Among our various research samples we had a group of 32 homemakers. We also worked with homemakers in our burnout workshops.

11. Oakley, *Sociology of Housework.*
12. The study was done in collaboration with Joy Stapp and Trudy Solomon and was described in detail in the following publications: A. Pines, "The Influence of Goals on People's Perceptions of a Competent Woman," *Sex Roles* 5, no. 1 (1979): 71–76.
13. For a detailed description of the study, see A. Pines and D. Kafry, "The Experience of Life Tedium in Three Generations of Professional Women," *Sex Roles,* 7, no. 2 (1981), 117–134.
14. For a detailed description of the study, see A. Pines and D. Kafry, "Tedium in the Life and Work of Professional Women as Compared with Men," *Sex Roles,* 7, no. 10 (1981), 963–977.
15. M. Hennig and A. Jardim, *The Managerial Woman* (New York: Doubleday, 1976).
16. The correlation between burnout and self-actualization for men was $r = -.18$, for women $r = -.29$. Only for women was the correlation statistically significant ($p < .05$). The correlation between burnout and self-expression for men was $r = -.01$, for women $r = -.42$. Only for women was the correlation statistically significant ($p < .05$). The correlation between burnout and personal relations was $r = -.42$ for women and $r = -.21$ for men.
17. D. Etzion, "Burning Out in Management: A Comparison of Women and Men in Matched Organizational Positions." Paper presented at the Second International Interdisciplinary Congress on Women, Croningen, Holland, April 17–19, 1984.
18. See Note 16.
19. See Note 12.
20. R. J. Schiffler, "Demographic and Social Factors in Women's Work," in S. H. Osipow (ed.), *Emerging Women Career Analysis and Outlook* (Columbus, OH: Charles E. Merrill, 1975).
21. R. Rapoport and R. N. Rapoport, "Further Considerations on the Dual Career Family," *Human Relations* 24 (1971): 519–533.
22. We investigated the conflict between life and work as a burnout correlate in eight of our samples. The correlations ranged from .24 and .38 and all were statistically significant.
23. Tavris, "Women's Work."
24. Oakley, *Sociology of Housework.*
25. Ibid.
26. S. H. Osipow, "Concepts in Considering Women's Careers," in Osipow (ed.), *Emerging Women.*
27. The work has been described in detail in the following publications: A. Pines, "Burnout and Life Tedium in Three Generations of Professional Women "(paper presented at the American Psychological Association Convention, San Francisco, California, August 26–30, 1977); Pines and Kafry, "The Experience of Life Tedium"; Pines and Kafry, "Tedium in the Life and Work of Professional Women."

28. C. L. Cooper, and J. Marshal, "Occupational Sources of Stress: A Review of the Literature Relating to Coronary Heart Disease and Mental Ill Health," *Journal of Occupational Psychology* 49 (1976): 11–28.
29. R. L. Kahn, D. M. Wolfe, R. P. Quinn, J. D. Snoek, and R. A. Rosenthal, *Organizational Stress* (New York: Wiley, 1964).
30. D. T. Hall, "Pressures from Work, Self and Home in Life Stages of Married Women," *Journal of Vocational Behavior* 6 (1975): 121–132.
31. In the study involving 424 women, cited earlier in the chapter, the correlation between burnout and life/work conflict was $r = .34, p < .001$.
32. The correlation between burnout and distractions at work was $r = .36$, burnout and distractions at home $r = .35$; both are significant at the .001 level.
33. Hall,"Pressures from Work, Self and Home."
34. The study involved 563 subjects and was done in collaboration with Steve Weinberg and the Management Training Program at the University of Alabama. The correlation between life/work overlap in terms of stresses and burnout was $r = 42, p < .01$.

Chapter 7. Intrapersonal Coping Strategies

1. M. Friedman and R. Rosenman, *Type A Behavior and Your Heart* (Greenwich, CT: Fawcett Publications, 1974).
1a. Friedman and Rosenman (1974), p. 209.
2. S. Kobasa and S. Maddi, "Personality and Constitution as Mediators in the Stress-Illness Relationship," *Journal of Health and Social Behavior* 22 (1981): 365–378.
3. S. R. Maddi, "The Existential Neurosis," *Journal of Abnormal Psychology* 72 (1967): 311–325.
4. R. Walton, in his article "Alienation and Innovation in the Work Place," in J. O'Toole (ed.), *Work and the Quality of Life* (Cambridge, MA: MIT Press, 1974), pp. 227–245, writes about innovative management techniques where autonomous work groups were given collective responsibility for the large segments of the production process so that jobs were enriched and employees had more variety, autonomy, and a sense of significance.
5. M. Csikszentmikalyi, *Beyond Boredom and Anxiety: The Experience of Play in Work and Games* (San Francisco: Jossey-Bass, 1975).
6. N. Krogius, *Psychology in Chess* (Albertson, NY: RHM Press, 1976).
7. V. E. Frankl, *The Doctor and the Soul* (New York: Bantam Books, 1967), p. 35.
8. A study involving 29 professionals indicated that frequency of reporting complete concentration, feeling of harmony with the environment,

control of self-demand for action were negatively correlated with burnout.

9. For example, in a study involving 205 professionals, variety in life was correlated with burnout $r = -.23, p < .01$; for 84 students the correlation was $r = -.44, p < .001$.
10. E. Duffy, *Activation and Behavior* (New York: Wiley, 1962).
11. J. P. Zubeck, *Sensory Deprivation: Fifteen Years of Research* (New York: Appleton-Century-Crofts, 1969).
12. Christopher Burney, *Solitary Confinement* (New York: Coward-McCann, 1952).
13. Duffy, *Activation and Behavior*.
14. Reported by Manson Syndicate in the *San Francisco Chronicle*, May 9, 1979.
15. B. Russell, *The Conquest of Happiness* (New York: Liveright, 1930).
16. A. Monat and R. S. Lazarus, *Stress and Coping* (New York, Columbia University Press, 1977).
17. D. Kafry and A. Pines, "Coping Strategies and the Experience of Tedium." Paper presented at the American Psychological Association Convention, Toronto, August, 1978.
18. R. S. Lazarus, "Psychological Stress and Coping in Adaptation to Illness," *International Journal of Psychiatry in Medicine* 5 (1974): 321–332.
19. Kafry and Pines, "Coping Strategies."
20. Ibid.
21. Dov Eden, "Toward an Analysis of Stress Situation and Response Effectiveness," private communication, Tel Aviv University, Israel.
22. The correlation between burnout and physical health in different studies ranged between $-.20$ and $-.46$, all correlations statistically significant.
23. P. G. Zimbardo, *Shyness: What It Is, What to Do about It* (Reading, MA: Addison-Wesley, 1977).

Chapter 8. Social Support Systems

1. K. Lewin, *Resolving Social Conflicts. Selected Papers on Group Dynamics* (New York: Humpe and Brothers, 1945), pp. 94, 95.
2. Ibid.
3. M. Pilisuk and S. Hillier Parks, "Networks of Social Support: A Review." Unpublished manuscript, University of California–Davis, 1980.
4. S. Cobb, "Social Support as a Moderator of Life Stress," *Psychosomatic Medicine* 5, no. 38: 300–314.
5. G. Caplan, *Support Systems and Community Mental Health* (New York: Behavioral Publications, 1974).
6. A. Pines, "The Buffering Effects of Social Support," in B. A. Farber

(ed.), *Stress and Burnout in the Human Service Professions* (Elmsford, NY: Pergamon Press, 1983), pp. 155–174.

7. The correlation between burnout and various social support systems was as follows: family $r = -.18$, work $r = -.22$, friends $r = -.23$, co-workers $r = -.25$, acquaintances $r = -.17$. (All p values are equal to or smaller than .001.)

8. The correlation between unconditional support and burnout was $r = -.21, p < .001$.

9. The correlation between the frequency of being lonely and burnout was $r = .47$, and family relations $r = -.23$, and work relations $r = -.26$, and relations with friends $r = -.32$, and relations with co-workers $r = -.26$, and relations with acquaintances $r = -.28$, and unconditional support $r = -.33$. (All p values are equal to or smaller than .001.)

10. C. L. Cooper and J. Marshall, "Occupational Sources of Stress: A Review of the Literature Relating to Coronary Heart Disease and Mental Health," *Journal of Occupational Psychology* 49 (1976): 11–28.

11. M. Marx Ferree, "The Confused American Housewife," *Psychology Today* 10, no. 4 (April 1976): 76–80.

12. H. J. Freudenberger, "The Staff Burnout Syndrome," *Alternative Institutions Psychotherapy: Theory Research and Practice* 12, no. 1 (1975): 72–72.

13. See for example, C. Maslach and A. Pines, "Burnout: The Loss of Human Caring," in A. Pines and C. Maslach (eds.), *Experiencing Social Psychology* (New York: Random House, 1979), pp. 245–252.

14. A. Pines and C. Maslach, "Characteristics of Staff Burnout in Mental Health Settings," *Hospital and Community Psychiatry* 4, no. 29 (1978): 233–237.

15. Maslach and Pines, "Burnout."

16. N. R. F. Maier, *Problem Solving Behavior vs. Frustration Behavior, Psychology in Industrial Organizations* (Boston: Houghton Mifflin, 1973).

17. C. Cherniss, "Social Support Networks," in K. Reid (ed.), *Burnout in the Helping Professions.* Unpublished manuscript (Kalamazoo: Western Michigan University, 1980).

18. From the motion picture *Burnout*, MTI Teleprograms Inc., 4825 North Scott Street, Schiller Park, IL.

19. A. Pines and D. Kafry, "Tedium in the Life and Work of Professional Women as Compared with Men," *Sex Roles*, 7, no. 10 (1981): 963–977.

20. D. Kafry and A. Pines, "Coping Strategies and the Experience of Tedium." Paper presented at the Annual Meeting of the American Psychological Association, Toronto, August 1978.

21. E. E. Jones and R. E. Nisbet, "The Actor and the Observer: Divergent Perceptions of the Causes of Behavior," in E. E. Jones et al. (eds.),

Attribution: Perceiving the Causes of Behavior (Morristown, NJ: General Learning Press, 1971), pp. 79–94.

22. M. Snyder, E. D. Tanke, and E. Berscheid, "Social Perception and Interpersonal Behavior: On the Self-Fulfilling Nature of Social Stereotypes," *Journal of Personality and Social Psychology* 35 (1977): 656–666.

Chapter 9. Organizational Coping Strategies

1. The study was done in collaboration with Steve Weinberg and the Management Training Program at the University of Alabama. Mean burnout scores ranged from $\bar{x} = 2.9$ to $\bar{x} = 3.4$, $p < .0004$.
2. E. Eldar, "Burnout in Hospital Nurses and Its Association with Objective Measures of Department Characteristics." Thesis for M.Sc. degree in Management Sciences, Organizational Behavior, submitted to the faculty of Management, Tel Aviv University, Israel. One of the goals of the study was to provide a detailed observational analysis that will explain these different patterns.
3. C. Maslach and A. Pines, "The Burnout Syndrome in the Day Care Setting," *Child Care Quarterly* 6, no. 2 (Summer 1977): 100–113.
4. A detailed description of this case is presented in A. Pines and C. Maslach, "Combatting Staff Burnout in a Day Care Center: A Case Study," *Child Care Quarterly* 9, no. 1 (1980): 5–16.
5. Maslach and Pines, "Burnout Syndrome."
6. A. Pines and C. Maslach, "Characteristics of Staff Burnout in Mental Health Settings," *Hospital and Community Psychiatry* 29, no. 4 (1978) 233–237.
7. For example, Mitzi Duxbury, professor of nursing at the University of Minnestoa, has documented the relationship between burnout and turnover in perinatal units all over the United States. John W. Jones, a psychologist at De Paul University in Chicago, found that burnout was significantly correlated with measures of job turnover, absenteeism, tardiness, discipline, and alcohol use.
8. In a study involving 205 professionals, the correlation between burnout and the availability of time out was $r = -.18$, $p < .05$. For 85 students the correlation was $r = -.35$, $p < .05$.
9. Maslach and Pines, "Burnout Syndrome."
10. Pines and Maslach, "Characteristics of Staff Burnout."
11. Ibid.; Maslach and Pines, "Burnout Syndrome."
12. Ibid.
13. H. J. Freudenberger, "The Staff Burnout Syndrome in Alternative Institutions," *Psychotherapy: Therapy Research and Practice* 12, no. 2 (Spring 1975): 73–82.
14. Pines and Maslach, "Characteristics of Staff Burnout."

15. A. Pines and D. Kafry, "Occupational Tedium in a Social Service Organization" (Research report, Berkeley, Calif. 1979). The mean burnout for dealing with problem cases was 5.1, for providing information to the public 3.1, for examining evidence 3.1, for providing technical guidance 2.7, for clerical tasks 2.2.
16. A. M. Block, "Combat Neurosis in Inner City Schools." Paper presented at the 130th Annual Meeting of the American Psychiatric Association. May 1977.
17. E. Walster and E. Aronson "The Effect of Expectancy of Task Duration on the Experience of Fatigue," *Journal of Experimental Social Psychology* 3 (1967): 41–46.
18. Maslach and Pines, "Burnout Sydrome"; Pines and Maslach, "Characteristics of Staff Burnout."
19. For example, R. Kahn, "Job Burnout, Prevention and Remedies," *Public Welfare*, Spring 1978, pp. 61–63.
20. Personal communication, Mitzi Duxbury, School of Nursing, University of Minnesota. R. Van Der Merwe and S. Miller, "The Measurement of Turnover," in B. O. Pettman (ed.), *Labor Turnover and Retention* (New York: Wiley, 1975), pp. 3–30.
21. For example, in a study by D. Kafry and A. Pines, "The Experience of Tedium in Life Work," *Human Relations* 33, no. 7 (1980): 477–503, involving 205 professionals, the correlation between burnout and environmental pressures at work was $r = .27, p < .001$, while that between burnout and comfortable physical environment was $r = -.29, p < .001$.
22. A. Mehrabian, *Public Spaces and Private Places* (New York: Basic Books, 1976).
23. For example, in the study involving 205 professionals, both the correlation between burnout and bureaucratic interference and the correlation between burnout and administrative hassles were $r = .20, p < .05$.
24. R. E. Walton, "Alienation and Innovation in the Work Place," in J. O'Toole (ed.), *Work and the Quality of Life* (Cambridge, MA: MIT Press, 1974), pp. 227–245.
25. In the study involving 205 professionals, the correlation between burnout and adequate rewards at work was $r = -.33, p < .001$.
26. F. Herzberg, *Work and the Nature of Man* (Cleveland: World Publishing, 1966).

Chapter 10. Burnout Workshops

1. Organizational settings in which workshops were held included: management seminars, child-care centers, elementary schools, junior high schools, high schools, community colleges, university extension pro-

grams, special education schools, a school for the blind, a language school, departments of public health and welfare, departments of health, social service agencies, vocational service units, community mental health centers, home health and counseling centers, departments of rehabilitation, departments of human resources, departments of social services, Social Security offices, psychiatric clinics in and out of hospitals, a state hospital, veterans administration hospitals, community hospitals, medical centers, emergency units, dialysis units, departments of nursing, psychiatry departments, a prison, probation departments, management training programs, a career planning and placement center, the army, and others.

Professions that participated in the workshops were corporate executives and managers at all levels, psychiatrists, psychologists, counselors, physicians, nurses, dentists, dental hygienists, dental assistants, dialysis workers, perinatal social workers, occupational therapists, physical therapists, social workers, welfare workers, child welfare attendants, mental retardation workers, community mental health workers, alcoholism workers, child abuse workers, prison personnel, probation officers, child-care workers, teachers, college professors, career planning and placement counselors, student personnel administrators, labor management administrators, Social Security supervisors and staff, vocational service workers, special education teachers and counselors, superintendents of mental retardation facilities, business managers, lawyers, policemen, organizational development experts, priests, nuns, and army psychologists.

2. Unsolicited feedback of participants immediately following the workshops, both written and verbal, has been consistently very positive. We have made numerous attempts to evaluate this feedback more systematically. In one department of public health and welfare, for example, 132 participants responded to the department's own training activity evaluation. The overall ratings of the workshop were: 80 participants rated it "excellent," 41 rated it "very good," 11 rated it "good," 0 rated it "poor," and 0 rated it "very poor."

In another department of social service in the Midwest six months after a workshop, we asked participants to rate its effectiveness for defining the problems of burnout and for combating it. Thirty participants responded to this postworkshop questionnaire. All respondents rated the workshop very highly on both effectiveness questions: the average response to both questions was "very good." Two years after this workshop a second burnout workshop was conducted with the same participants. Informal feedback from participants indicated that support systems that were established as a result of the first workshop were still functioning and effectively combating burnout two years later.

3. The evaluation study of this workshop used a nonequivalent control group design. This design involves an experimental group and a control group. Both groups are given a pretest and posttest. The control group and the experimental group do not have preexperimental sampling equivalence, rather, the groups constitute naturally assembled collectives, as similar as availability permits yet not so similar that one can dispense with the pretest. The assignment of the experimental manipulation—in this case, the burnout workshop—to one group or the other is assumed to be random and under the experimenter's control (D.T. Campbell and J. C. Stanley, *Experimental and Quasi Experimental Designs for Research* [Chicago: Rand-McNally, 1973], pp. 47–50).

   A total of 53 social service employees from two different offices participated in the study. The two offices were chosen because they were considered similar in location, size, clients, and performance. Twenty-three employees (3 men and 20 women) participated from the "experimental" office and 30 employees (10 men and 20 women) participated from the "control" office.

   All the employees in the experimental group participated in a one-day burnout workshop. A questionnaire was administered to all employees. It included the 21-item Burnout Measure (Appendix 1) plus a description of work features, attitudinal variables, satisfaction, and stress from work activities. Employees in the experimental and control groups filled out the questionnaire three times: (1) pretest: one week before the workshop to establish a base line; (2) short-term posttest: one week after the workshop; (3) long-term posttest: six months after the workshop. In addition, a short feedback questionnaire was administered to the experimental group immediately after the workshop.

4. One week before the workshop, the questionnaire was administered to all employees to establish base line. One week after the workshop, employees in both the experimental group and control group were again given the questionnaire. This questionnaire was given for the second time to assess the short-term impact of the workshop.

   Preexperimental responses to the questionnaire were compared to postexperimental responses, with the assumption that those changes that occurred only in the experimental group were the result of the burnout workshop. Only 15 employees out of the 23 who participated in the workshop completed both the pre- and postquestionnaire. Subject loss is especially serious with such small samples as ours and it raises questions about the validity and the generalizability of the data.

   Results for the employees who completed the questionnaire twice show that burnout in the experimental group decreased slightly ($p < .10$) and satisfaction from co-workers went up significantly ($p < .01$). Employees in the experimental group were also more satisfied with their supervisors, their contact with the public, and their clients after the workshop. Employees in the control group, who did not participate in the workshop, did not show this consistent and positive attitude change.

5. Six months after the burnout workshop the experimental group and the control group were given the second posttest. The questionnaire was given for the third time to assess the long-term impact of the workshop. Preworkshop responses to the questionnaire and short-term posttest responses were compared to the long-term postworkshop responses, with the assumption that those changes that occurred only in the experimental group were the result of the burnout workshop. The changes that were in evidence in the second posttest were assumed to indicate the long-term effects of the workshop.

Due to the high attrition rate of participants in the study, a comparison of the pretest and the two posttests is not scientifically sound. Only 8 experimental-group employees of the 23 in the workshop completed all three questionnaires, and only 14 of the 30 control-group employees did so. Such small samples make any sophisticated statistical analysis meaningless and raise serious doubts about the validity and generalizability of the data.

The major impact of the workshop was on the social aspects of the job, and some of that impact, though weakened, remained after six months.

Chapter 11. The Spillover of Burnout from Work to Marriage

1. A. H. Cantril and C. W. Roll, Jr., *Hopes and Fears of the American People* (New York: Universe Books, 1971).
2. The three studies, in which the stresses in work and at home were compared, were presented in D. Kafry and A. Pines, "The Experience of Tedium in Life and Work," *Human Relations* 33, no. 7 (1980): 477–503.
3. In the second of the three studies, for example, the average correlation between overall work satisfaction and burnout was $r = -.38$ as compared to an average of $r = -.52$ for life satisfaction.
4. A. Pines, *Keeping the Spark Alive: Preventing Burnout in Love and Marriage* (New York: St. Martin's Press, 1988).
5. A review of these studies, in which dual career couples were compared to couples in which the wife didn't work, is included in F. Pepitone-Rockwell (ed.), *Dual-Career Couples* (Beverly Hills, CA: Sage, 1980).
6. T. W. Martin, K. J. Berry, and R. B. Jacobon, "The Impact of Dual-Career Marriages on Female Professional Careers." Presented at the

annual meeting of the National Council on Family Relations, Salt Lake City, August 1975.

7. R. Bryson, J. Bryson, M. Licht, and B. Licht, "The Professional Pair: Husband and Wife Psychologists," *American Psychologist* (1976): 10–16.

8. C. F. Epstein, "Law Partners and Marital Partners: Strains and Solutions in the Dual Career Family Enterprise," *Human Relations* 24: (1971): 549–563.

9. F. I. Nye and L. W. Hoffman (eds.), *The Employed Mother in America* (Chicago: Rand McNally, 1963).

10. C. C. Nadelson and T. Nadelson. "Dual-Career Marriages: Benefits and Costs." In Pepitone-Rockwell. *Dual Career Couples,* p.95.

Appendix 2. The Burnout Measure

1. A. T. Beck, A. Weissman, D. Lester, and L. Trexler, "The Measurement of Pessimism: The Hopelessness Scale," *Journal of Consulting and Clinical Psychology,* 42 (1974): 861–865.

Selected Bibliography

Chapters in Books

Maslach, C., and Pines, A. "Burnout, the Loss of Human Caring." In A. Pines and C. Maslach (eds.), *Experiencing Social Psychology*. New York: Random House, 1979, 1984.

Pines, A. "Marriage Burnout from Women's Perspective." In C. Tavris (ed.), *Everywoman's Emotional Well-Being*. New York: Doubleday Books, 1986.

Pines, A. "Who's to Blame for Helper's Burnout?" In C. D. Scott (ed.), *Heal Thy Self; The Health of Health Professionals*. New York: Brunner-Mazel, 1986.

Pines, A. "The Burnout Measure." In J. Jones (ed.), *Police Burnout*. Park Ridge, IL:: London House Press, 1985.

Pines, A., and Silbert, M. "Police Officer's Burnout." In J. Jones (ed.), *Police Burnout*. Park Ridge, IL: London House Press, 1985.

Pines, A., and Kafry, D. "Occupational Tedium in the Social Services." In M. A. Williamson (ed.), *Introduction to Applied Psychology*. Richmond, British Columbia: Open Learning Institute, 1983.

Pines, A. "Changing Organizations: Is a Work Environment without Burnout an Impossible Goal?" In W. S. Paine (ed.), *Job Stress and Burnout*. Beverly Hills, CA: Sage, 1982.

Pines, A., and Kanner, A. "Nurses' Burnout: Lack of Positive Conditions and Pres-

244 Selected Bibliography

ence of Negative Conditions as Two Independent Sources of Stress." In E. A. McConnell (ed.), *Burnout in the Nursing Profession.* St. Louis: Mosby, 1982.

Pines, A., and Maslach, C. "Characteristics of Staff Burnout in Mental Health Settings." In A. Briggs and A. Agrin (eds.), *Crossroads: A Reader for Psychosocial Therapy.* Rockville, MD: The American Occupational Therapy Association, 1982.

Pines, A. "Helper's Motivation and the Burnout Syndrome." In T. A. Wills (ed.), *Basic Processes in Helping Relationships.* New York: Academic Press, 1981.

Pines, A., and Kafry, D. "Coping with Burnout." In J. Jones (ed.), *The Burnout Syndrome.* Park Ridge, IL: London House Press, 1981.

Pines, A., Kafry, D., and Etzion, D. "Job Stress from a Cross Cultural Perspective." In K. Reid (ed.), *Burnout and the Helping Professions.* Kalamazoo: Michigan University Press, 1980.

Articles in Scientific Journals

Etzion, D., and Pines, A. "Sex and Culture as Factors Explaining Burnout and Coping among Human Service Professionals: A Social Psychological Perspective." *Journal of Cross Cultural Psychology* 17, no. 2 (1986): 191–209.

Etzion, D., Kafry, D., and Pines, A. "Tedium among Managers: A Cross Cultural American-Israeli Comparison." *Journal of Psychology and Judaism* 1, no. 7 (1982): 30–41.

Kafry, D., and Pines, A. "Life and Work Tedium." *Human Relations* 33, no. 7 (1980): 477–503.

Pines, A. "Marriage Burnout: A New Conceptual Framework for Working with Couples." *Psychotherapy in Private Practice* 5, no. 2 (1987): 31–44.

Pines, A. "Marriage Burnout: A New Conceptual Framework." *Marriage and Divorce Today* 11, no. 7 (September 1985): 1.

Pines, A., and Aronson, E. "The Antecedents, Correlates and Consequences of Sexual Jealousy." *Journal of Personality* 51, no. 1 (1983): 108–136.

Pines, A., and Aronson, E. "Combatting Burnout." *Children and Youth Services Review* 5 (1983): 263–275.

Pines, A. "Burnout: A Current Problem in Pediatrics." *Current Problems in Pediatrics,* May 1981.

Pines, A., and Aronson, E. "Polyfidelity: An Alternative Lifestyle Without Sexual Jealousy." In G. Clanton (ed.), "Jealousy," *Alternative Lifestyles,* 4, no. 3 (1981): 373–392.

Pines, A., and Kafry, D. "The Experience of Life Tedium in Three Generations of Professional Women." *Sex Roles* 7, no. 2 (1981): 117–134.

Pines, A., and Kafry, D. "Tedium in College." *College Student Personnel Abstracts,* 1980.

Pines, A., and Maslach, C. "Combating Staff Burnout in a Child Care Center: A Case Study." *Child Care Quarterly* 9, no. 1 (1980): 5–16.

Pines, A. "Tedium in the Work of Infection Control Practitioners." *Asepsis* 1, no. 5 (1980): 1–2.

Pines, A. "The Influence of Goals on People's Perceptions of a Competent Woman." *Sex Roles* 5, no. 1 (1979): 71–76.

Pines, A., and Kafry, D., and Etzion, D. "Burnout: An Occupational Danger." *Shurot* (Hebrew), April 1979, pp. 12–15.

Pines, A., and Solomon, T. "The Social Psychological Double Bind of the Competent Woman." *Research in Education*, February 1979.

Pines, A., and Kafry, D. "Occupational Tedium in Social Service Professionals." *Social Work* 23, no. 6 (1978): 499–507.

Pines, A., and Maslach, C. "Burnout in Mental Health Professionals." *Child Abuse and Neglect: Issues on Innovation and Implementation* 2 (1977): 239–245.

Stapp, J., and Pines, A. "Who Likes Competent Women?" *Human Behavior* 5, no. 11 (1976): 59–60.

Papers Presented at Conferences

Aronson, E., and Pines, A. "Sexual Jealousy." Western Psychological Association, Honolulu, May 1980.

Kranner, A., Kafry, D., and Pines, A. "Stress Results from the Absence of Positive Experience as Well." Western Psychological Association, Honolulu, May 1980.

Pines, A. "Marriage Burnout: A Theoretical Model and Some Research Findings." The International Congress of Applied Psychology, Jerusalem, Israel, July 1986.

Pines, A. "A New Social-Psychological Approach for Work with Couples." International Congress of Family Therapy, Jerusalem, Israel, June 1986.

Pines, A. "Marriage Burnout from Women's Perspective." The Association for Women in Psychology, Oakland, CA, March 1986.

Pines, A. "Sex Differences in Marriage Burnout." American Psychological Association, Los Angeles, August 1985.

Pines, A. "Marriage Burnout: A New Conceptual Framework for Working with Couples." American Psychological Association, Los Angeles, August 1985.

Pines, A. "On Men, Women, and Marriage Burnout." Association for Humanistic Psychology 25th Anniversary Conference, San Francisco, March 1985.

Pines, A. "Burnout in Marriage and Other Long Term Relationships." American Psychological Association, Anaheim, CA, August 1983.

Pines, A. "Burnout in Marriage." Fourth International Congress of Family Therapy, Tel-Aviv, Israel, July 1983.

Pines, A. "The Organizational Implications of Defining Burnout as a Social Problem." American Psychological Association, Washington, DC, August 1982.

Pines, A., and Etzion, D. "Burnout and Coping with Its Antecedents: A Cross Cultural/Sexual Comparison (Women × Men × Israelis × Americans),"

International Interdisciplinary Congress on Women, Haifa, Israel, December 1981.

Pines, A. "The Burnout Measure." First National Conference on Burnout, Philadelphia, November 1981.

Pines, A., and Aronson, E. "Polyfidelity: A Lifestyle Without Jealousy?" American Psychological Association, Los Angeles, August 1981.

Pines, A., and Aronson, E. "Burnout: From Tedium to Personal Growth." American Psychological Association, Montreal, September 1980.

Pines, A., and Kafry, D. "Tedium in College." Western Psychological Association, Honolulu, May 1980.

Pines, A., Kafry, D., and Etzion, D. "A Cross Cultural Comparison Between Israelis and Americans in the Experience of Tedium and Ways of Coping with It." Western Psychological Association, San Diego, April 1979.

Pines, A. "Characteristics of Burnout in Human Service Workers." Twenty-first Annual Clinical Conference, Asilomar, CA, June 1978.

Pines, A., and Solomon, T. "The Double-Bind of Professional Women." Western Psychological Association, San Francisco, April 1978.

Pines, A. "How to Develop 'Detached Concern' and Prevent Burnout." American Association of Mental Deficiency, San Antonio, TX, October 1977.

Pines, A. "Burnout and Life Tedium in Three Generations of Professional Women." American Psychological Association, San Francisco, August 1977.

Pines, A. "Emotional Involvement of Helping Persons—Where Do You Draw the Line?" Annual Convention on Child Abuse and Neglect, Houston, TX, April 1977.

Pines, A., and Solomon, T. "Perception of Self as Mediator of the Dehumanization Process." American Psychological Association, Washington, DC, September 1976.

Stapp, J., and Pines, A. "Career or Family? The Influence of Goals on Liking for a Competent Woman." Western Psychological Association, Los Angeles, CA April 1976.

Movie

Burnout. MTI Teleprograms, A Division of Simon & Schuster, Deerfield, IL. Pines, A., technical advisor, and co-author (with Aronson, E.) of accompanying manual entitled Burnout.

Index

how to cope with them,
128–130
work stress, 118–121
Work
attitudes to, sex-role differences
in, 122, 126
dissatisfaction with, 16
environment: *see* Environment
expectations of, 34–35
features, as correlates of burnout, 203
in home, 152
preoccupation with, 78
sense of "cosmic significance"
from, 66
sense of meaning from, 9–11,
15–16, 45, 59–61, 83, 97, 213

separating outside life from, 86,
128–129, 152
Workaholism, 66–67, 83, 152
Work and Love (Rohrlich), 60
Work conditions, improving, 195–
196
Work hours, limiting number of
stressful, 190–192
Working (Terkel), 37
Working women's work stress,
118–121
Work relations, 38, 171–176,
226*n*.21
Workshops: *see* Burnout workshops
Wounded Healer, The (Lipp), 88
Wrong career, case study of, 21–22